ΑΩ

The Names of God
(A Non-exhaustive Look at an Inexhaustible Subject)

By Dudley M. Harris

© 2016 Kurios Publishing

This book is dedicated to my wife, Martha, for her constant encouragement and care for me.

Thank you Ed Chinn for your encouragement as well. You are a blessing in my life.

A special thanks to Dr. David Keyser for his publishing expertise and helpful insight.

To all who faithfully read these chapters as they were published on my blog, KuriosReflections.blogspot.com, I am grateful for your comments. Thanks for the support.

Cover concept and design by Nicolas Harris.

Cover images credits [i]

Preface

Most of my life has been spent in worship ministry. Leading others into the presence of our Lord is not something I take lightly. I became aware of the need to expand my vocabulary of worship in order to more clearly communicate my heart to God and to more effectively help others connect with their Creator.

The list of names used in this book is the result of that search for an expanded vocabulary for worship. I asked the worship team members to come up with names by which they communicate with God, or have heard used as references to Him.

Since starting this project I have found more names that are not part of this list. I decided to omit them at this time, but perhaps it will become a Volume II project. In the meantime, I hope this resource helps you commune with the Lord in ways you never imagined. As you learn more of God's nature and character you will find it easier to open yourself up to Him and express your heart with words that express more fully your love and desire for Him.

There are not enough entries in this volume to use it as a daily devotional. However, there are plenty to keep you occupied for several years as you plumb the depths of these names even more fully than I have in these pages.

Just as the gospel writer declared of Jesus, there is no way to ever print enough volumes to fully describe our God. That should not keep us from trying!

What others have said about this book:

"This book is teeming with life! Dudley Harris gives us meaningful and inspiring spiritual and scriptural insight of both well-known and not-so-common names of God. From Abba and Avenger to Worthy and Yahweh, this is a book that helps us get to know the triune God better and, with the knowing, to love Him even more!
Dudley's down-to-earth stories make the lofty concepts come alive to the reader. He draws from his years of experience as a worship pastor and a son of the Father to lovingly craft this offering. Whether you take a name a day, or read through the whole book in one sitting, these are writings that you will want to return to again and again."
- **David Baroni** worship songwriter, artist and author

"I once read, 'The Hebrew Sages say that naming a baby is a most profound spiritual moment. Naming a baby is a statement of their character, specialness and path in life. At the end of life a good name is all we have left.' It seems that the Hebrews put more intentional thought into the meaning of the name of their child than we do. Their name was descriptive and even defined 'who they were'. Dudley has grasped this truth and expressed it well as he has gleaned the Scriptures and shared with us the Names of God! As each name is revealed and a small description given we can experience the true character of our Lord. Much of the time in life we focus on "what He does" but Dudley has shown us 'Who He is'. May this help us say like Paul, 'that I may know Him...' Enjoy the journey as finite man explores the infinite Lord!"
- **Jimmy Hayes** pastor

"God's characteristics and personality are immeasurably deep. God has revealed different facets of His depths to different biblical characters through His unique and immensely deep name. When you gather all of these names together you get to see the beginning of God in His fullness. Dudley Harris has made a great stride in gathering God's various names together to help us see God for who He truly is, the Great I Am. You will be blessed by taking advantage of Dudley's extensive research through the Scriptures and His heart for the knowledge and truth of God." - **Bobby Gourley** Senior Pastor, Christ Chapel

Index

	Page
Abba	13
Above All	15
Adonai (Our Master)	19
Almighty God	23
Alpha and Omega	25
Always Awake	27
Ancient of Days	29
Anointed One	31
Avenger	33
Awesome God	35
Blessed	37
Bread of Life	39
Bridegroom	41
Bright Morning Star	43
Calmer of Storms	45
Captain of the Hosts	47
Clothed With Honor	49
Clothed With Majesty	51
Clothed With Strength	53
Cloud by Day	55
Comforter	57
Compassionate	59
Conqueror of Our Enemies	61
Consolation	63
Consuming Fire	65
Counselor	67
Covenant Keeper	69
Covered With Light	71
Creator	73
Crown of Glory	75

Defense	79
Deliverer	81
Dew	83
Director of My Path	85
Disciplinarian	87
Doer of Wonders	89
Dwelling Place	91
El Elyon (The most High God)	93
El Olam (Everlasting God)	95
El Shaddai (God Almighty)	97
Emmanuel	99
Eternal God	101
Everlasting Arms	103
Everlasting Strength	105
Everlasting to Everlasting	107
Excellent in Wisdom (Working)	109
Faithful	111
Father	113
Father of Glory/Lights/Spirits	117
Father of the Fatherless	121
Feeder of the Hungry	123
Fire by Night	125
First and Last	127
Forgiving	129
Fortress	131
Friend That Sticks Closer Than a Brother	133
Gentle	137
Gift Giver	141
Giver of Good Things	143
Glorious	145
Glorious Lord	147
Glory	149

God of Gods	153
God With Us	155
Good	157
Good Shepherd	159
Gracious	161
Great	163
Guide	165
Habitation	169
Healer	171
Healer of Broken Hearts	173
Helper	175
Helper of the Fatherless	177
Hiding Place	179
High Tower	181
Holy	183
Holy One	185
Holy Spirit	187
Husband	191
Husbandman (Gardener)	193
I Am	195
In All	197
Infinite Understanding	199
Jealous	201
Jehovah (The Self-Existent One; I AM)	203
Jehovah-Elohim (The Lord God)	205
Jehovah-Jireh (The Lord Will Provide)	207
Jehovah-M'kaddesh (The Lord Who Sanctifies)	209
Jehovah-Nissi (The Lord Our Banner)	211
Jehovah-Rapha (The Lord Who Heals)	213
Jehovah-Rohi (The Lord My Shepherd)	217
Jehovah-Sabaoth (Lord of Hosts)	219

Jehovah-Shalom (The Lord Our Peace)	221
Jehovah-Shammah (The Lord Is Present)	223
Jehovah-Tsidkenu (The Lord Our Righteousness)	227
Jesus	229
Judge	231
Judge of the Widows	233
Just	235
Keeper	239
King of All the Earth	241
King of Glory	245
Lamb That Was Slain	247
Lawgiver	249
Lifter of My Head	251
Light	253
Light of the World	255
Lily of the Valley	257
Living Water	259
Longsuffering	261
Lord	263
Lord God Omnipotent	265
Lord of Hosts	267
Lord of Lords	269
Lord of the Sabbath	271
Lord on High	273
Love	275
Lover of My Soul	279
Lovingkindness	283
Majesty	285
Maker of Heaven & Earth	287
Man of War	291
Master	293

Merciful	295
Messiah	297
Mighty	299
Mighty and Terrible	301
Mighty in Wisdom	303
Miracle Worker	305
Most High	307
Near	309
Never Changing	311
Never Weary	313
Omnipresent	315
One Who Hides Himself	317
One Who Sanctifies	319
Our Strength	321
Peacemaker	323
Physician	325
Potter	329
Powerful	333
Prince of Peace	337
Promise Keeper	339
Provider	341
Ready to Forgive	345
Reconciler	349
Redeemer	351
Refiner	353
Refuge	355
Refuge from the Storm	359
Repairer of the Breach	361
Rescuer	363
Revenger	365
Righteous	369

Rock	371
Rock of My Refuge	377
Rock of My Salvation	379
Rose of Sharon	381
Ruler	383
Salvation	387
Satisfier of Desires	391
Satisfier of the Longing Soul	395
Savior	399
Shade on Our/My Right Hand	401
Shadow from the Heat	403
Shepherd	405
Shield	407
Slow to Anger	409
Son of God	413
Song	417
Soon Coming King	419
Strength to the Needy	421
Strength to the Poor	423
Strong	425
Sustainer	427
Teacher	429
The Amen	431
The Christ	435
The Door	437
The Head of the Body	439
The Life	441
The Resurrection	445
The Risen Lord	449
The True Vine	451
The Truth	453
The Way	457
Through All	459

Trust	463
Truthful	467
Upright	471
Walks on Wings of the Wind	475
Wisdom	477
Worthy	481
Yahweh	485

… but the people who know their God shall be strong, and carry out great exploits.

Daniel 11:32b (NKJV)

Abba

There's no better place to start than with the beginning. The word "abba" is Greek and means "father." It is derived from the Hebrew word "ab", which also means "father." Humanly speaking, mankind traces their roots to Adam – the first man, created by God. But man's cry throughout scripture is for the true *Abba*, God Himself.

Dr. Eddie Lawrence, in his book "Breath of God", describes this word in much more detail. In Genesis, after God had fashioned man out of the "dust of the earth", He breathed into man the breath of life. Genesis 2:7 (ESV) "then the LORD God formed the man of dust from the ground and breathed into his nostrils the breath of life, and the man became a living creature." Dr. Lawrence describes the "sound" that breath makes when exhaled. It very closely resembles the pronunciation of the Hebrew word "ab." God actually gave to man, through Adam, His fatherly presence. The life-flow of mankind comes from *Abba* and is perpetuated through the generations of man.

To know God as *Abba* is to acknowledge that He is the beginning of all things, the origin of life itself, and the sustainer of life. The very breath we breathe is from *Abba*, God. Try something today. Become aware, even if for a moment or two, that every minute of every day air is flowing in and out of your body. With each inflow of oxygen into our lungs, an outflow (exhalation) follows. Can you see the close resemblance to the word "exaltation"? With each conscious exhaling of air let us release an exaltation to *Abba*, our Father. Realize today that God is closer to us than the air we breathe.

Above All

In Ephesians 4 the Apostle Paul is writing to the Church to help us understand that we are One Body. "You were all called to travel on the same road and in the same direction, so stay together, both outwardly and inwardly. You have one Master, one faith, one baptism, one God and Father of all, who rules over all, works through all, and is present in all. Everything you are and think and do is permeated with Oneness." (Ephesians 4:4-6 The Message)

The phrase "rules over all" is the same phrase the King James Bible states as "above all." The phrase is straightforward to understand. The word "all" means just that: all! It means nothing is omitted. There are no exceptions. All.

To say something is "above all" means there is nothing else above it. It also implies that this covers every category. Power? God is all-powerful. Knowledge? God is all-knowing. Love? God is Love! Longest? God is everlasting. Regardless of the aspect of our existence God is *above all*.

This brings great comfort to those who have trusted their lives into God's hands. If we struggle God helps us rise above the circumstances; He is *above all*. When accusers come and wag their finger in our face God helps us understand His truth concerning us; God is *above all*. When we seem to lose our way God can bring us back to the path He has for us; God is *above all*.

Several years ago Lenny LeBlanc and Paul Baloche wrote the song *Above All*. Lenny shared the story of the writing session that produced the song. The verses came pretty quickly but they struggled with the chorus.

> Above all powers, above all kings
> Above all nature and all created things
> Above all wisdom and all the ways of man
> You were here before the world began
>
> Above all kingdoms, above all thrones
> Above all wonders the world has ever known
> Above all wealth and treasures of the earth
> There's no way to measure what You're worth[ii]

They kept trying to take the chorus of the song to a higher level, really build the music, and proclaim things like "Wonderful, Awesome, Magnificent, Almighty." However, each attempt just seemed futile and hollow. They broke for lunch. Lenny and some others went out but Paul stayed behind. When Lenny and the others returned they were amazed at what Paul had written. Instead of trying to go higher he went a totally different direction.

> Crucified, laid behind a stone
> You lived to die, rejected and alone
> Like a rose, trampled on the ground
> You took the fall and thought of me
> Above all[iii]

I can see why the song became so popular. It vividly illustrates how God, who is Above All, chose to send His precious Son to die in our place. He knew there was no one else capable of becoming the perfect sacrifice required to free man from sin's grasp.

When Abraham received the promise of a son God gave him a picture of his future. "Your offspring will be like the sands on the seashore." Abraham struggled with "seeing" the vision God had described. Later God comes to Abraham again to give another picture of the future He had planned for Abraham. "Your offspring will be like the stars in the sky. Can you count them?" Once Abraham started *looking up* he was able to receive the promise from God.

God is *Above All*! Get your head out of the sand and cast your eyes toward the sky. Your God is *Above All* and wants to bring you up to His level.

Adonai

This name of God is intriguing. It only appears by itself one time in scripture. However, it appears many other times represented by the letters YHWH, typically pronounced Yahweh. When you see the word LORD used in all capital letters it is the name *Adonai*.

This name of God is considered divine. Israel would not even speak the name in order to give it reverence. In Exodus 6:3 God states, "I appeared to Abraham, to Isaac, and to Jacob, as God Almighty, but by my name the LORD (*Adonai*) I did not make myself known to them."

God chose to withhold an aspect of His nature until this exchange with Moses. God knew that Israel would need an intimate connection with their Creator in order to trust Him as they were led from slavery to a new life in Canaan, the Promised Land.

It reminds me of names that spouses will give to one another. When they become "one" in marriage the bond between them is unique. Many times they call each other by names that only they know. These names are never used in public. They are reserved only for their intimate relationship.

LORD, or *Adonai*, was a name that God revealed to Israel to give them intimate insight into His character and nature. He would be their LORD. David declared, "The LORD is my Shepherd…" and "O LORD, our Lord, how excellent is thy name …"

Later in the book of Exodus Moses and God have this exchange:

Exodus 33:15-19 (ESV) And he said to him, "If your presence will not go with me, do not bring us up from here. For how shall it be known that I have found favor in your sight, I and your people? Is it not in your going with us, so that we are distinct, I and your people, from every other people on the face of the earth?"

And the LORD said to Moses, "This very thing that you have spoken I will do, for you have found favor in my sight, and I know you by name." Moses said, "Please show me your glory." And he said, "I will make all my goodness pass before you and will proclaim before you my name 'The LORD.' And I will be gracious to whom I will be gracious, and will show mercy on whom I will show mercy.

God showed Moses, and through him, Israel, all of God's goodness and proclaimed His name, *Adonai*, before them. God was saying to them, "I AM Sovereign. I AM LORD." A sovereign is a supreme leader. In a monarchy it is the king! God is saying that in His kingdom He is the King.

Here is one last thought on this. In the Book of the Revelation of Jesus Christ (Revelations) one of the churches to which letters were written is Pergamos. The word "Pergamos" comes from a root word that means, "castle or tower." That sounds like a place where a king would dwell. One of the promises made to this church was this: Revelation 2:17 (ESV) He who has an ear, let him hear what the Spirit says to the churches. To the one who conquers I will give some of the hidden manna, and I will give him a white stone, with a new name written on the stone that no one knows except the one who receives it.'

Isn't that something? Not only does God have a name reserved for us (*Adonai*), He also has given us a name that He will reveal to us that no one else knows. He loves us so much!

Almighty God

One approach to studying words or phrases in the Bible is to use "the law of first reference." The first time something is mentioned gives us important information about why that particular word or phrase is used. Such is the case with today's Name of God: *Almighty God*. This is the English interpretation for the Hebrew phrase El Shaddai.

The story of Abraham is filled with firsts when it comes to God-man relationships. Paul later records in Romans that Abraham was the "father of us all" because he chose to believe God, who against hope believed in hope, that he might become a father. Through much of the story of the interaction between God and Abraham, the writer of the account (believed to be Moses) indicated that God presented himself to Abraham as LORD (Yahweh, or Adonai as we learned yesterday).

However, after Abraham took measures of his own to fulfill God's promise to him (Ishmael) God presented Himself by a new name: *Almighty God*. Abraham needed assurance that God was able to work out the plan that had been given him from the start. God planned for Abraham to have a son through his wife, Sarah, and through that son God would bless all nations.

Almighty God tells us that there is nothing too difficult for Him. If you feel confined to a prison cell with walls 10 feet thick, *Almighty God* is able. If you are barren and cannot conceive, *Almighty God* is able. If you have hopes and dreams that have eluded you for years, *Almighty God* is able. If you are seeking for a place to belong but instead have wandered for what seems like an eternity, *Almighty God* is able.

If necessary, take on the posture of Abraham. He, against hope, believed in hope. He did not consider the facts that he was now impotent and Sarah was well beyond childbearing years to be impossible for God to still fulfill His promise. Abraham did not consider the fact that he had wandered throughout the Middle East looking for a "place that God would show him", only to find himself "there" when he believed the promise of God.

You may be well acquainted with God as Adonai, our intimate Sovereign. You may know Him as a father, Abba. Today allow Him to be *Almighty God* in your life. Only when Abraham ended his pursuit of trying to accomplish God's will in his life, *Almighty God* stepped in and changed everything … forever.

Alpha and Omega

One of the last names attributed to God in scripture is found in the last book of the Bible. Revelation 21:6 refers to God as *Alpha and Omega*. These two words represent the first and last letters in the Greek alphabet. It would be the equivalent of saying that God is the A to Z.

> Revelation 21:6 (ESV) And he said to me, "It is done! I am the Alpha and the Omega, the beginning and the end. To the thirsty I will give from the spring of the water of life without payment.

It is done! Those are great words to hear when engaged in any project. In this case, God was "revealing Himself", showing John the full revelation of the plan to redeem mankind. God summed it up by stating "I am the beginning and the end." Many businesses use A-Z to describe their services, indicating they can do it all. This is hardly a fair comparison, but God IS able to do it all.

He created our world and placed us in it. He gave us the very air we breathe. He has called us to live the life He provided for us; a life full of joy and peace, love and fulfillment. He has called us to be sons and daughters.

Another aspect of being *Alpha and Omega* is it contains every other expression within it. All words are created by using the letters A-Z. You can assemble a unique combination of letters to create, or coin, a new word yet all of the letters are still just A-Z. That gives us insight into more of the character of God. All things that exist, past, present, or future, are simply representations of God; or more precisely, the attributes of God. Alpha and Omega does not define God. However, God IS the *Alpha and Omega*, and therefore defines everything else.

Learning a new language is difficult. It is said that to become fluent in a language one must move from "mentally translating" everything to actually "thinking" in the new language. I believe it is the desire of God for us to move from "mentally translating" who He is to actually "thinking" like He thinks. Let us become so familiar with God's ways and His thoughts toward us until we can say it like Paul did in Acts.

Acts 17:27-28 (ESV) "... that they should seek God, and perhaps feel their way toward him and find him. Yet he is actually not far from each one of us, for "'In him we live and move and have our being'; "'For we are indeed his offspring.'"

Anything you may be facing today only exists because God is ... He was before all things and He will be after all things. If you can spell it then God has dominion over it! Let's rejoice in knowing the *Alpha and Omega*.

Always Awake

Psalm 121:4 (ESV) Behold, he who keeps Israel will neither slumber nor sleep. He is eternal. He is everlasting. He is God.

We can take comfort in knowing that the God in whom we have placed our trust will never be unavailable when we are in need. He will never be distracted and let us fall into trouble. "Slumber" implies tiredness. God is all-powerful. He never grows weary or gets distracted.

1 Kings records the story of Elijah and the confrontation with the prophets of Baal. Look at the exchange between them.

1 Kings 18:25-27 (NKJV) Now Elijah said to the prophets of Baal, "Choose one bull for yourselves and prepare it first, for you are many; and call on the name of your god, but put no fire under it." So they took the bull which was given them, and they prepared it, and called on the name of Baal from morning even till noon, saying, "O Baal, hear us!" But there was no voice; no one answered. Then they leaped about the altar which they had made.

And so it was, at noon, that Elijah mocked them and said, "Cry aloud, for he is a god; either he is meditating, or he is busy, or he is on a journey, or perhaps he is sleeping and must be awakened."

Elijah knew that his God would never sleep or slumber. His God is *Always Awake*. Can you imagine calling on God and not getting a response? We have the confidence of knowing that God is *Always Awake*.

Ancient of Days

The word "ancient" in scripture does not mean just "old." It has the connotation of beyond time; eternal. The name *Ancient of Days* ascribed to God by Daniel speaks to God existing outside of time. He is beyond time. According to Genesis 1 God created time. He is timeless.

The Hebrew word translated "ancient" used in Daniel 7 means venerable: "accorded a great deal of respect, especially because of age, wisdom, or character." By referring to God as *Ancient of Days*, Daniel was giving God great honor, placing him above all others. In this setting, Daniel is describing a vision where there were multiple thrones. The *Ancient of Days* stood out. He was easily distinguished from the others based on the description Daniel gives. He is to be revered.

Our God reigns; forever! He reigned before time. He reigns now. He will reign in the future. He will reign after time ends. He is ancient, not old. God is no relic. He is not a fragile antique. He is as much God now as He has ever been. His power does not diminish with time. You can trust a God like that.

Anointed One

When looking at the Names of God this list from which I am drawing from includes names for all three members of the Godhead: Father, Son, and Holy Spirit. Today's name is one attributed to the Son. During the life of Jesus one of the most pivotal moments came when He entered the temple and read from the book of Isaiah.

Here is the account as recorded by Luke.

> Luke 4:18-21 (ESV) "The Spirit of the Lord is upon me, because he has anointed me to proclaim good news to the poor. He has sent me to proclaim liberty to the captives and recovering of sight to the blind, to set at liberty those who are oppressed, to proclaim the year of the Lord's favor." And he rolled up the scroll and gave it back to the attendant and sat down. And the eyes of all in the synagogue were fixed on him. And he began to say to them, "Today this Scripture has been fulfilled in your hearing."

Here is the passage from Isaiah.

> Isaiah 61:1-3 (ESV) The Spirit of the Lord GOD is upon me, because the LORD has anointed me to bring good news to the poor; he has sent me to bind up the brokenhearted, to proclaim liberty to the captives, and the opening of the prison to those who are bound; to proclaim the year of the LORD's favor, and the day of vengeance of our God; to comfort all who mourn; to grant to those who mourn in Zion— to give them a beautiful headdress instead of ashes, the oil of gladness instead of

mourning, the garment of praise instead of a faint spirit; that they may be called oaks of righteousness, the planting of the LORD, that he may be glorified.

The *Anointed One* being referenced in this passage is not just any preacher. It's not just any prophet or teacher. This was THE *Anointed One*. The word used for anointed is interpreted "Messiah." When Jesus stood and read this passage, then followed it by saying, "This scripture was fulfilled in your hearing", He was proclaiming Himself to be the *Anointed One*, the Messiah.

Jesus left heaven to become a man, to live as a man, fulfill all righteousness, and become the propitiation for our sin. He was able to accomplish this because God anointed Him, filling Him with the Holy Spirit. Jesus was, and is, the *Anointed One*.

He is worthy of our worship. He will always lead us to the Father. Thank you, *Anointed One* of God, for your sacrifice.

Avenger

Psalm 94:1 (ESV)
O Lord, God of vengeance,
  O God of vengeance, shine forth!

Romans 12:19 (ESV) Beloved, never avenge yourselves, but leave it to the wrath of God, for it is written, "Vengeance is mine, I will repay, says the Lord."

1 Thessalonians 4:6-7 (ESV) that no one transgress and wrong his brother in this matter, because the Lord is an *avenger* in all these things, as we told you beforehand and solemnly warned you. For God has not called us for impurity, but in holiness.

The meaning of avenge in Hebrew is different than in Greek. In Hebrew it carries the attitude of revenge; getting even when wronged. The New Testament meaning, and the one attributed to God as Avenger, means one who carries out justice.

There is a major difference between these two. David, in the Old Testament, wrote what is known as imprecatory psalms. These are prayers where David asked God to serve as the Avenger and deal with the enemies of David and Israel.

In the New Testament, Jesus took a different approach. He commanded us to pray for our enemies, but not as David did. Jesus said to bless those that curse you and despitefully use you.

The basic difference is Law vs. Grace. Under the law we want revenge. Living by the law brings our human instinct out because it is such a burden to try to live right. We struggle and strain to live by the law. Then, when we see others violate the laws that we keep, we want swift vengeance to be carried out on them. We want someone to punish them for the very thing that we ourselves struggle to obey.

Grace knows that none of us can keep the law. Therefore, we show mercy for those that violate it. Revenge is not ours, but the Lords. He is the only one capable of carrying out true justice because He is the only one that fulfilled every dot on the i and crossed every t. The truly amazing thing is that He does not even exact judgment on sinners. So, yes, God is the *Avenger*. However, He chooses to deal with those that violate His law with kindness and mercy in order to draw them to a place of repentance.

Just to be complete on the subject, there will be a time of judgment when an accounting for sin will be met. However, those who respond to the drawing of the Lord by the Holy Spirit and receive forgiveness for transgressing the law of God will be spared the justice that they once deserved. Thank you, Lord!

Awesome God

Deuteronomy 7:21 (ESV) You shall not be in dread of them, for the LORD your God is in your midst, a great and awesome God.

The King James Bible does not use the English word "awesome" when translating the Hebrew word "yare." Most modern translations do. In the KJV it uses words like fearful, terrible, dreadful, etc. These words, in our current vernacular, have negative connotations. So modern translators have chosen awesome.

At the root of it, the word means to revere; hence, to "be in awe." God is truly awe-some. When our human minds begin to imagine our God it takes us to images that words cannot justly describe.

Upon describing the recent ice storm this week my friend Neal Wright used a phrase that is not common these days. He said, "The view of the ice on tree limbs was heartbreaking." That word today is seen as negative, as in severe grief or disappointment. However, the origin of the word is more like "producing an intense emotional reaction or response <heartbreaking beauty>."

I believe both are accurate. It just depends on the perspective one takes during the experience. For one who has lived their life in a pursuit of knowing God, to discover His will and understand His character, to finally see Him will be an awesome experience. They will fall on their face in reverence and worship Him as Creator, Father ... God.

On the other hand, one who lives their life is disbelief that there is a creator, or worse yet, flaunts their disbelief in the face of God, will also have an encounter with Him. It will be "yare" for them: fearful, dreadful, and terrible.

Let us live our lives in reverence of the *Awesome God* so we will not have to fear the "terrible day of the Lord."

Blessed

> Psalm 144:1 (ESV) *Blessed* be the LORD, my rock, who trains my hands for war, and my fingers for battle;

This name for God is really up to us to bestow upon Him. It one of the few things we actually get to do for God. The "bless" in this verse is "barak": to kneel; by implication to bless God (as an act of adoration). When we kneel before our God it blesses Him, and we get blessed in the process.

> Luke 1:68 (ESV) "*Blessed* be the Lord God of Israel, for he has visited and redeemed his people

The New Testament word for "bless" is "eulogeo": to speak well of, i.e. (religiously) to bless (thank or invoke a benediction upon, prosper). When we utter praises unto our God He is *Blessed*.

How humbling is it to think that we have the ability to make our God *Blessed*. Let's focus our attention on that today. Let's spend time adoring our Creator, speaking well of Him and all He has done, is doing, and will do, for us. He is truly worthy of our blessing.

Bread of Life

John 6:31-35 (ESV) Our fathers ate the manna in the wilderness; as it is written, 'He gave them bread from heaven to eat.'" Jesus then said to them, "Truly, truly, I say to you, it was not Moses who gave you the bread from heaven, but my Father gives you the true bread from heaven. For the bread of God is he who comes down from heaven and gives life to the world."

They said to him, "Sir, give us this bread always." Jesus said to them, "I am the *bread of life*; whoever comes to me shall not hunger, and whoever believes in me shall never thirst.

The name *Bread of Life* is clearly a name used in reference to Jesus. In the passage cited above, Jesus is making it clear that the manna provided to their forefathers in the wilderness was not given by Moses. It came from their Creator, God. Without it they would have starved in the wilderness. In like fashion, Jesus has been sent as "manna" for our souls, the *Bread of Life,* to keep us from perishing.

In the Garden of Eden, Adam was told that because of sin he would die. This was the beginning of physical and spiritual death. Through the second Adam, Jesus, provision was made for a way to escape the second (spiritual) death. Once we partake of the *Bread of Life* (Jesus) we would never hunger (spiritually) again.

Bread was, and is, a staple in the Middle Eastern diet. It was part of every meal served in that day. Remember the 40 days Jesus spent in the wilderness? Satan tempted Jesus when He was hungry to turn the stones into bread. The enemy was using the very reason Jesus came to cause Him to stumble. Jesus came to feed the spiritually hungry and provide that for which they truly hungered – the *Bread of Life*.

Today let us purpose to partake of the REAL manna provided by our Creator God – the *Bread of Life*.

Bridegroom

Revelation 19:9 (ESV) And the angel said to me, "Write this: Blessed are those who are invited to the marriage supper of the Lamb." And he said to me, "These are the true words of God."

There cannot be a *Bridegroom* without a Bride. This name of God is one attributed to Jesus. He left heaven to give His life to purchase for Himself a Bride. He came to build His Church. Just as a bride hopes and dreams of meeting a man that will complete her, that will love her unconditionally, that will protect her, and provide for her, so we as part of the Church (the Bride) long for a *Bridegroom*. Once we find Him everything changes.

The Song of Solomon is filled with phrases that describe the love between a bride and her bridegroom. This book is a prophetic look at the relationship between the Church and her *Bridegroom*, Jesus.

Our worship is nothing more that our hearts crying out to our *Bridegroom*. Take time today to tell the Lord what He means to you. Declare your love for Him then demonstrate it by showing that love to others. That is the way others learn that they, too, have a Bridegroom that has given His life for them.

There will be a celebration in heaven when the *Bridegroom* (Jesus) will finally be with His Bride (the Church). Help fill the table by inviting others to join with us at that celebration.

Bright Morning Star

One of the last names attributed to God in scripture is *Bright Morning Star*. It refers to Jesus because of the comment made to John toward the end of the Book of the Revelation of Jesus Christ.

Revelation 22:16 (ESV) "I, Jesus, have sent my angel to testify to you about these things for the churches. I am the root and the descendant of David, the *bright morning star*."

There is a saying that states "It's always darkest before the dawn." Jesus is the *Bright Morning Star* that illuminates even the darkest hour. "Even if we walk through the valley of the shadow of death…" He is with us. The Bible tells us that in heaven there is no need of the sun because Jesus is there, the *Bright Morning Star*. (Revelation 22:5)

One of my favorite song phrases comes from the group 2nd Chapter of Acts. I can't recall the song title, but the phrase said, "Lookin' at the sun don't bother me now, 'cause there's a brighter Light within me somehow." When you have the *Bright Morning Star* on the inside of you, the light of the sun pales in comparison.

With each new day, God meets us with new mercies and grace, and provides light for our path – the *Bright Morning Star* – to guide us into the plans and purposes that are prepared for us. Walk with Him!

Calmer of Storms

Two places in scripture give us the name *Calmer of Storms*. Psalm 107:29 (ESV) He made the storm be still, and the waves of the sea were hushed. This is a prophetic view of the life of Christ. Then in the New Testament: Mark 4:39 (ESV) And he awoke and rebuked the wind and said to the sea, "Peace! Be still!" And the wind ceased, and there was a great calm.

The people were amazed at Jesus, saying, "Even the winds and seas obey Him." It certainly makes sense that the One who created the earth and all that is in it would have dominion over it. Jesus is still in the business of calming storms. When someone cries out for help He is there to speak peace into the situation.

In both passages it speaks of people travelling to a destination. Along the way a storm comes to keep them from reaching their destination. The storm is sent to destroy them and keep them from their destiny. Fortunately, the travellers knew the source of their help. They called out to the *Calmer of Storms* and He brought peace to the situation and allowed them to continue on to their destination.

The *Calmer of Storms* is the same God that is Always Awake. He is Above All. Call out to Him now and let Him bring His calming presence to your life and then guide you into the fullness of your destiny.

Captain of the Hosts

Joshua 5:13-15 (ESV) When Joshua was by Jericho, he lifted up his eyes and looked, and behold, a man was standing before him with his drawn sword in his hand. And Joshua went to him and said to him, "Are you for us, or for our adversaries?" And he said, "No; but I am the commander of the army of the LORD. Now I have come." And Joshua fell on his face to the earth and worshiped and said to him, "What does my lord say to his servant?" And the commander of the LORD's army said to Joshua, "Take off your sandals from your feet, for the place where you are standing is holy." And Joshua did so.

This is believed to be a pre-incarnate visit from Christ. The main reason for that interpretation is in verse 15. When an angel appears, and men fall down to worship them, the angel commands them to get up because they are not God. The response given by the "man" is quite the opposite. The same words are used here that God spoke to Moses at the burning bush. This is holy ground.

Notice, also, that the word "LORD" in verse 14 is all capitals. This means it is the Hebrew word for God, Yahweh. So the "man" standing before Joshua was the *Captain of the Hosts* of Yahweh – Jesus. It is so fitting that, as the people of God prepared for their first major battle in the Promised Land, God came personally to encourage Joshua just as He had done with Moses.

I love Joshua's first response. He sees Jesus, the *Captain of the Hosts*, and immediately asks, "Are you for us, or them?" Joshua knew that the side the "man" chose was going to win. I am intrigued by the Lord's response. He said, "No."

We are constantly praying, "Lord, help me to …" Or, "Lord, make them …" Jesus did not claim to "take sides" in the matter at hand. He simply stated, "I am here." Jesus came to establish His Kingdom in that moment. The only response Joshua had was to worship.

Oh, that we could get the revelation of this! Instead of trying to make God out to be on our side, that we would, instead, worship Him and allow Him to establish His Kingdom in our presence. The *Captain of the Hosts* came to Joshua. He will also come to you. One of my favorite verses in scripture is 2 Chronicles 16:9a (ESV) , "For the eyes of the LORD run to and fro throughout the whole earth, to give strong support to those whose heart is blameless toward him."

My prayer is that this day you will welcome the *Captain of the Hosts* of the LORD into your situation and let Him establish His Kingdom in your life.

Clothed with Honor

Psalm 104:1 (KJV) Bless the LORD, O my soul. O LORD my God, thou art very great; thou art clothed with honour and majesty.

The word "honor" is the Hebrew word "hode." It means grandeur (i.e. an imposing form and appearance).

The English Standard Version says it this way: Psalm 104:1 (ESV) Bless the LORD, O my soul! O LORD my God, you are very great! You are clothed with splendor and majesty,

The honor we show the Lord is different than the honor we show toward one another. We should not look on other men or women as being "very great" to the point of worshipping them. The "honor" used toward one another is that of respect. Respect goes both directions in society. Honor in the human sense does not just flow up toward the top of the hierarchy. It should be a mutual treatment of our fellows, up and down. Actually, true honor has to begin at the top of any organization; church, business, family, etc.

The name of God we look at today depicts an honor that is reserved for God, and God alone. He is *Clothed with Honor*. When we see the Lord for who He is we will be in awe. Scripture tells us that no man can see the face of God and live (Exodus 33:20). I believe that is why John gives us this promise: 1 John 3:2 (ESV) Beloved, we are God's children now, and what we will be has not yet appeared; but we know that when he appears we shall be like him, because we shall see him as he is.

On earth we are mere reflections of the true One *Clothed with Honor* (splendor and majesty), but when we finally behold Him we will be transformed by the experience, just as Jesus was on the Mount of Transfiguration. That day is coming. Until then, we worship and show "honor" to the Lord, and we show love and respect to our fellow man. This is the order of the Lord.

Clothed with Majesty

Psalm 93:1 (ESV) The LORD reigns; he is robed in majesty; the LORD is robed; he has put on strength as his belt. Yes, the world is established; it shall never be moved.

The Hebrew word for majesty is "geut" (pronounced gay-ooth'). It means "excellent things, lifting up, majesty." To be *Clothed with Majesty* implies that it is part of your make-up. You cannot separate the attribute from the One being described. This is certainly the case with God. As has been mentioned before in these posts, the reference to LORD means it is the Hebrew word Yahweh. This word was not even spoken by those reading the texts.

One reason for such reverence to be shown was because of the majesty of God. In a very small way it is like seeing the Grand Canyon for the first time, or other "Wonders of our World". There are no words to immediately describe what you see. It takes time to allow your mind to respond to the stimulus. When we see the LORD's creation we understand that He is *Clothed with Majesty*.

The Hebrew word for clothed is "labash" (pronounced law-bash'). It means, "properly wrap around." When you combine the two words you understand that this "majesty" is not accidental. It is not in any way unintentional. To me, this further illustrates that *Clothed with Majesty* is more than a descriptive phrase. It speaks to the very nature of God, rather than how He appears. It also means to me that He is always this way, not just when you catch Him on a good day.

So, take in the beauty of the world around you. Be in awe. Let it take your breath away. Then, consider that this is just a mere reflection of the true beauty of the One *Clothed with Majesty*. Let's worship Him!

Clothed with Strength

Psalm 93:1 (ESV) The LORD reigns; he is robed in majesty; the LORD is robed; he has put on strength as his belt. Yes, the world is established; it shall never be moved.

The origin of words is a curious study. Today's *Name of God* contains the Hebrew word "oz." I can easily see how this might have been the inspiration for the fictional character called "The Wizard of Oz."

The word is interpreted as strength. Its root word is "azaz", which means, "to be stout." Most effective running backs in football have a low center of gravity. They are usually described as "stout" because of the relatively wide build.

When considering this attribute as it relates to God, it gives the understanding that He is immovable, not easily affected by storms that blow or rains that beat down. As we have said before, this is not just a description of God. It is part of His make up. He is strength. The word for "clothed" gives us this image. He is wrapped in strength.

Later is this verse an illusion is made describing the effect God has on the earth. Because God is *Clothed with Strength* "the world is established; it shall never move." Just as the earth can support the weight of mighty buildings, and does not crumble under their foundations, so is our God. He is one upon whom we can build a life that cannot be shaken.

If you have never placed your trust in this God that is *Clothed with Strength* then let today be the day. Begin building the rest of your life on a foundation that cannot be destroyed.

Cloud by Day

Exodus 13:21-22 (ESV) And the LORD went before them by day in a pillar of cloud to lead them along the way, and by night in a pillar of fire to give them light, that they might travel by day and by night. The pillar of cloud by day and the pillar of fire by night did not depart from before the people.

After bringing Israel out of Egypt, Moses led them to the mountain of God where they spoke at the burning bush. God instructed Moses, "Go bring my people back to this mountain so they can worship Me." God promised Israel that He would never leave them. He would lead them as a *Cloud by Day*, and Fire by Night.

The *Cloud by Day* not only gave them direction for their journey through the wilderness, leading them to the promised land, but also provided shade from the blazing sun. If anyone ever doubted the presence of God they needed only to look for the *Cloud by Day* that was constantly with them. It brought comfort and assurance that God had a plan.

Occasionally the *Cloud by Day* would be stationary. When this happened the people would set up camp and remain there until the *Cloud by Day* would move. This continued for 40 years. When the Cloud moved they moved. When the Cloud stopped they stopped. Obedience to the leading of the Lord will ensure His presence in our lives.

In the Old Testament the presence of God was externally experienced because the Holy Spirit had not yet been sent to dwell in man. This happened on the Day of

Pentecost. The Holy Spirit was sent by Jesus, as promised, to dwell in man and be the same comfort, guide, assurance, etc., that the external presence of the *Cloud by Day* had been for Israel. We no longer follow external manifestations because we have the Inward Witness, the Holy Spirit.

Let us learn to follow Him just as Israel followed the *Cloud by Day* and was eventually led into the promise that God had given them.

Comforter

> Isaiah 66:13 (ESV) As one whom his mother comforts, so I will comfort you; you shall be comforted in Jerusalem.

One of the most welcomed attributes of God is that of *Comforter*. Man is in constant search of comfort. Most inventions were born out of man's need for comfort, ease, productivity, etc. Most drug and alcohol abuse begins from a need for comfort: body, mind, or spirit.

The reality of man's deepest desires, however, is the search for the *Comforter*. Only God can provide the comfort man needs. This is made very evident by Jesus. One of the last things Jesus told his followers was this, "I'm going away, but I will send another *Comforter*, the Holy Spirit, and He will abide with you forever!"

The followers of Jesus had experienced the *Comforter* in a personal way. That is why they were so distraught at His departure, but the promise made by Jesus was certainly good news to their ears. The promise of "another *Comforter*" was enough motivation for them to wait for weeks in the upper room in expectation of the fulfillment of that promise.

The good news for us is that the *Comforter* is still here. He abides in the Believer. When you are born again the Spirit of God comes in you and makes you "alive again." One of the benefits of the Spirit's presence in your life is to "guide you into all peace." That is some kind of *Comforter*. No longer do we have to strive for external peace, but we can live off of the internal presence of the *Comforter*.

Invite Him in today!

Compassionate

> Lamentations 3:22 (NKJV) Through the LORD'S mercies we are not consumed, Because His compassions fail not.

Today's name is another that not only is used as a reference to God, but also speaks to His nature. Just as God "is" love, God is also *Compassionate*. God's compassions "fail not."

Compassion is a completely selfless emotion. It is showing concern for others. It is a desire that things be better for someone else other than you. Because God does not have a need His only concern is for others.

> Psalm 145:8 (NKJV) The LORD is gracious and full of compassion, Slow to anger and great in mercy.

He is full of compassion. His compassions fail not. He wants you to be at peace. He wants you to be at rest. He wants you to be healed. He wants you to be free from anything that would cause you pain or grief. He is *Compassionate*.

Jesus was God in flesh. Matthew made this observation.

> Matthew 9:36 (ESV) When he saw the crowds, he had compassion for them, because they were harassed and helpless, like sheep without a shepherd.

Compassion motivated Jesus to demonstrate God's love. That same compassion should be the same thing that prompts Christians to show God's love to others. God's love never makes demands of people in order to qualify. Compassion is not conditional. Let us see others and allow compassion to move us to demonstrate God's love to them.

Conqueror of Our Enemies

Psalm 108:13 (ESV) With God we shall do valiantly; it is he who will tread down our foes.

We sing this name often. It is declared over circumstances of all kinds; anything seen as opposing us, keeping us from our hearts desires. However, the key to the truth found in the name *Conqueror of Our Enemies* is found in the word "our." When looking at the verse cited the emphasis is found in the first two words: with God.

"With God" has many implications. If I am with God, I am in agreement with His plan, His purpose, and His pursuit. He is God. I am with Him. The only reason I do valiantly is because He does valiantly. I'm with Him. That's what Paul meant when he said, "We are more than conquerors." (Romans 8:37)

The psalmist then goes on to say, "… tread down our foes." The only reason it would be my foe is because it is a foe to God. My foe is conquered because of God.

It is easy for us to assume who is our foe and who is not. I really don't think that should be our concern. Our focus should remain on whether we are "with God" or not. If we are with Him then the foe is irrelevant. This foe will be tread down by the *Conqueror of Our Enemies*.

Today, let us set our eyes on God, find out what He is doing, and make sure that we are with Him. We will never have to face an enemy alone.

Consolation

Romans 15:5 (KJV) Now the God of patience and consolation grant you to be likeminded one toward another according to Christ Jesus:

Another name for God that speaks to His nature is *Consolation*. The Greek word used here is "paraklesis." It comes from the root word "paraklete," which means advocate or helper. In Christianity, the term "paraclete" most commonly refers to the Holy Spirit.

A literal interpretation of the word is: alongside, together, with. When the Holy Spirit came to abide in us He came to be, as Jesus described Him, another Helper. *Consolation* means: comfort received by a person after a loss or disappointment. Accepting Christ means also accepting the trials and tribulation that comes from denying yourself. Jesus said, "In this world you will have tribulation, but be of good cheer; I have overcome the world." Trials come but the Holy Spirit is there to console us.

This is very different than showing pity, or in any way enabling us. The purpose in God, our *Consolation*, is to provide us with comfort to help us heal. He then directs us into the truth concerning the disappointment or loss so we can see how God wants to help us live beyond the trials that attempt to steal joy and peace from us. *Consolation* provides a balm for our wounds and peace for our soul.

Allow the complete work of the Holy Spirit to operate in your life. Receive the *Consolation* provided for you through Jesus. The Helper is with you.

Consuming Fire

Deuteronomy 4:24 (ESV) For the LORD your God is a consuming fire, a jealous God.

Fire is a force that has two very distinct traits. It can destroy most anything if given time and intensity. We saw that with the World Trade Center buildings on 9/11. However, when used with controlled purpose, fire can purify metal ores, cook meals, warm our homes, and provide necessary light.

The same is true for the word "consuming." It can mean to utterly destroy beyond recognition, or it can mean to totally overwhelm and saturate.

When using the name *Consuming Fire* when speaking of God I believe all of the above meanings can be applied. We see clearly in the Old Testament where God totally annihilated nations that rose up to oppose His purposes. By His hand cities were destroyed. Because of sin, men and women were brought down. These are all results of the wrath of God. He is a *Consuming Fire*.

When we take a look in the New Testament we see this attribute of God applied again, but this time it has a different purpose. Paul speaks of testing our works by fire. That which is of the flesh – wood, hay, and stubble – will be burned, destroyed; that which is of the Spirit – gold, silver, and precious stones – will be purified, and remain. This is evidence of the grace of God. He is a *Consuming Fire*.

You cannot escape the presence of God. You cannot escape the judgment of God. You cannot escape the

Consuming Fire. So the question becomes, "Why would we even try to escape Him?" If we, instead, would run to the *Consuming Fire* and allow Him to purify us by burning away all that is not of Him, we do not have to fear being consumed (utterly destroyed) by Him in judgment.

The Hebrew boys that were thrown into the furnace passed through the fire without being singed or having even the scent of smoke on their clothing. The ropes that had them bound, however, were burned from them without leaving a trace of their presence on them. This is the *Consuming Fire* that loves us beyond our comprehension. This is the God that wants us to be totally restored exactly the way He created us: perfectly whole – spirit, soul, and body.

Allow the *Consuming Fire* to do His work of redemption in you today.

Counselor

> Isaiah 28:29 (ESV) This also comes from the LORD of hosts; he is wonderful in counsel and excellent in wisdom.

I am married to one of the most amazing counselors. She can listen for hours on end to others as they share their problems or concerns. She has such compassion that it motivates her to work with others to find the root of the issue, bring the truth of God concerning the situation, and see them totally delivered and set free from the bondage caused by the lies the enemy has introduced into their life.

She is an example of what the *Counselor*, the Holy Spirit, wants to do in our lives.

The meaning of the word used for *Counselor* means, "to give advice, plan, or show prudence." It is from a root word that means, "to advise, to deliberate, or resolve."

Part of the nature that God placed inside man is a free will. The *Counselor* comes to us to give information (advice) on what we should do as we face decisions in life. He has a plan for us if we will only submit our will to His. The scripture He has given is full of wisdom that, when applied to our life, will result in prudent decisions.

The *Counselor* is a primary work of the Holy Spirit, but remember that this same Holy Spirit has gifts that He has given to the Church to empower Her to live free from the bondage that the curse of sin introduced to mankind. We need to learn to live in freedom, but know that the

Counselor is ever-ready to give us advice when needed, reveal His plan for us, and resolve any issue that might present itself.

    Let's learn to hear the voice of the *Counselor* and follow His advise completely.

Covenant Keeper

Psalm 89:34 (ESV) I will not violate my covenant or alter the word that went forth from my lips.

One of the traits bemoaned as passed from the current generation is the ability to keep ones word. Our forefathers made deals with a handshake. Their word was their bond.

Our God is still that way. His word will never pass away. He is a *Covenant Keeper*. Since the creation God has made covenant with mankind. Man would fail; God remained faithful.

In the Garden of Eden God made a covenant with mankind that took over 4000 years to bring to pass. He promised to crush the head of the enemy through the seed of a woman. Jesus was the seed that fulfilled the promise made by God, the *Covenant Keeper*. Jesus came to earth through Mary, born of a virgin. He lived a sinless life, fulfilling the law completely, becoming the perfect sacrificial lamb. He died on the cross, was raised from the dead, ascended to heaven, and was seated at the right hand of God the Father.

Jesus now intercedes for us to help us live the life to which we are called: to be like Jesus. God fulfilled His covenant to redeem mankind. He made a new covenant by promising the Holy Spirit to come and fill the believer, empowering them to be witnesses in the earth of the love of God. That covenant was fulfilled at Pentecost. The Holy Spirit is still with us.

The *Covenant Keeper* has promised that Christians would spend eternity with Him. He will keep that covenant as well. Trust your life to the *Covenant Keeper* by receiving the redemption provided through Christ.

Covered with Light

Psalm 104:1-2 (ESV) Bless the LORD, O my soul! O LORD my God, you are very great! You are clothed with splendor and majesty, covering yourself with light as with a garment, stretching out the heavens like a tent.

Light has an amazing effect on everything: It reveals, cleanses, warms, dries, nourishes, comforts. When afraid, light brings peace. When lost or misguided, light brings rescue. It is no wonder that the first act of creation was God saying, "Let there be light!"

It is said of heaven that there will be no need for a sun in heaven because Jesus IS the light. God is Covered with Light. Jesus is the "covering" of God; that part of God became flesh and dwelt among us, and we beheld His glory.

A consistent character attribute of God is that He has always desired for mankind to be like Him. At creation, the Godhead conferred and said, "Let us make man in Our image." That is still God's desire for mankind, only now it is more specific: to be conformed to the image of His Son, Jesus.

Years ago I heard an evangelist by the name of T. L. Osborn say, "Don't read the Bible to find out what happened to others. Read it to find out what God wants to do in you. Don't read the story of Mary, the mother of Jesus, and be happy for Mary. Read it and realize that YOU are also highly favored, and that YOU also are to be used of God to bring forth miracles in the earth."

When we understand the true nature of God we begin to realize that anything we learn of His character and nature, He desires for us to be the same way. Our Covered with Light God wants us covered with light. He wants us to shine in our world and become a beacon of hope to humanity. He wants us to radiate the love of God, just as Jesus did when He walked on earth. Pure light is called "white" light. It has every color spectrum in it making is appear white. When any of the colors are tainted or filtered, the light becomes tainted and begins to reflect the change in color.

Let us examine our hearts today to see if there is anything that is keeping all the spectrums of light from shining through so that the light we emit will be the pure light of God. It will have an effect on the world around you.

Creator

I'm addressing the names in this series in alphabetical sequence. However, if I were taking them in order of relevance, this probably would have been one of the first. It is by this name that mankind had its first encounter with Almighty God: *Creator*.

> Genesis 1:1 In the beginning God created the heavens and the earth.

It is beyond comprehension that a created being could presume to understand the one that created it. That is exactly what mankind attempts when they examine God, to figure Him out, to understand His ways, and in any way try to describe Him based on their own intellect. The following illustration is one that I came up with several years ago that clearly shows how ludicrous this notion of "explaining" the Creator really is.

Imagine you are a gold fish in a glass fish bowl. In an attempt to make sense of your world you begin to observe your surroundings. Obviously, the entire world is made up of water. There are objects outside of the space you can access, but since you cannot contact them you develop theories as to their origin and nature. Food appears every day. You don't know where is comes from, or if the supply will ever come to an end.

Occasionally one of the "creatures" outside of the glass dome that seems to have you contained scoops you out of your normal habitat and place you in a temporary basin. After a short time you are returned to your native environment that seems to be cleaner than when you left. That pattern repeats itself over and over until you die. You cannot expand your world. You cannot in any way affect the creatures outside of your world. Life is mundane and useless.

It is impossible to be objective when you are part of the system being analyzed. The only way for us to truly understand the *Creator* is to get information from the outside. We have been given revelation into the character and nature of God so that we can understand Him and know Him. He wants us to know Him. He wants us know He loves us and has made a way for us to live full of joy and peace. He made a way for us to overcome the enemy by trusting in His grace.

Our *Creator* wants us to become a reflection of Him. He created us in His image. He has given us His Spirit to empower us to live the life to which He has called us. That same Spirit teaches us by revelation about the *Creator* so we can more effectively show our world the truth about Him. The reality is the *Creator* wants us to know Him and has taken great measures to write His word on paper so we can read it and study it, but His ultimate desire is for His words to be written on our heart.

Crown of Glory

Isaiah 28:5-6 (ESV) In that day the LORD of hosts will be a crown of glory, and a diadem of beauty, to the remnant of his people, and a spirit of justice to him who sits in judgment, and strength to those who turn back the battle at the gate.

A crown is something that is bestowed upon another. It represents a posture of ruling over a certain domain. The Royal Family of Britain wears the crown of rule over Great Britain. Miss America wears the crown signifying her reign over the field of candidates, and becomes the representative of the organization for the following year.

In God's Kingdom the crown is worn by Jesus Christ. He is the *Crown of Glory*.

The Bible has a recurring theme regarding the People of God. It speaks often of "the remnant." Regardless of what occurs there are always some, a remnant, that remain faithful to the call of God. This verse from Isaiah gives a promise to "the remnant" that God would be their *Crown of Glory*.

One of my favorite anthems from my youth was a song called "The Church Triumphant", written by Bill and Gloria Gaither. My favorite group from that era, Truth, used to sing it. Their director, Roger Breland, would speak these lines in the middle of the song. I once had them memorized.

God Has Always Had A People!

Many a foolish conquer made the mistake of thinking that because he had forced the Church of Jesus Christ out of site, that he had stilled its voice and snuffed out its life.

But God Has Always Had A People!

The powerful current of a rushing river is not diminished because it is forced to flow underground. The purest water is the stream that bursts crystal clear into the sunlight after it has fought it's way through solid rock.

There have been charlatans who like Simon the magician, sought to barter on the open market that power which cannot be bought or sold.

But God Has Always Had A People: Men who could not be bought and women who were beyond purchase.

Yes, God Has Always Had A People!

There have been times of affluence and prosperity when the Church's message was nearly diluted into oblivion by those who sought to make it socially attractive, neatly organized, and financially profitable. It has been gold plated, draped in purple and encrusted with jewels. It has been misrepresented, ridiculed, blotted, and scorned.

These followers of Jesus Christ have been according to the whim of the times elevated as sacred leaders and martyred as heretics. Yet through it all, there marches on that powerful army of the meek, God's chosen people that can't be bought, flattered, murdered, or stilled. On through the ages they march.

The Church, God's Church Triumphant, is Alive and Well!

Now listen child of God. It's alive!

Discouraged pastor it's His Church and it's alive!

Lonely Missionary, sow your seeds with confidence!

It's alive my broken hearted friend!

Old saint, you're not alone and forgotten, the Church is alive!

Busy mother, cast your cares on Jesus!

It's alive young student; you're not alone in serving the Lord!

Faithful father, there's rest in the Lord! The Church is alive!

Cynical skeptic you haven't killed God with your noisy unbelief.

He's Alive!

So, Family of God, raise you hands and praise the Lord, for the Church, God's Church Triumphant, Is Alive and Well![iv]

One day this thing we call life will come to an end. Either we will die or Jesus will return. Either way, Christians have a promise from God that involves the *Crown of Glory*. First of all, we have the presence of God with us in the form of the Holy Spirit that abides in the believer. The Holy Spirit guides us into a life of God's presence, or glory. The plan of God is for us to move into an ever-increasing experience of the glory of God.

Secondly, when we do see our Lord face to face, either through death or the second-coming, we will have the *Crown of Glory* Himself: Jesus.

1 Peter 5:4 (ESV) And when the chief Shepherd appears, you will receive the unfading crown of glory.

Let us purpose to remain faithful. If we do we will receive the *Crown of Glory*.

Defense

> Psalm 94:22 (NKJV) But the LORD has been my defense, And my God the rock of my refuge.

Safety is one of the basic human needs. Everyone wants and needs to feel safe. Many mental psychoses originate from fear. It certainly follows that God would come to us as a place of refuge; *Defense*. The Hebrew word used for this name of God is "misgawb." It means a high, inaccessible place; refuge. It comes from a root word that means safe, strong.

One of the most important aspects of salvation is often overlooked. To me, salvation is the process of becoming identified with Christ. We are identified with Him in several ways: in His death, burial, resurrection, ascension, and seating at the right had of God. The death, burial, and resurrection are referred to often. However, the fact that Jesus ascended and was seated at the right hand of God completed the plan that God set in motion to fully reconcile man back to Himself.

Without the understanding of our position at the right hand of God we can never operate in the full power and authority given us by God through redemption.

> Ephesians 1:21 (ESV) far above all rule and authority and power and dominion, and above every name that is named, not only in this age but also in the one to come.

That is the place where we live with our *Defense*. Even while we live our life on earth our heart and mind are in a high, inaccessible place with God. As we learn to live from that place of our authority in Christ we will enjoy more fully the life given to us by God. Take refuge in a safe, strong place; God, our *Defense*.

Deliverer

Psalm 91:3 (ESV) For he will deliver you from the snare of the fowler and from the deadly pestilence.

It is no accident that scripture refers to the tactics of satan as a scheme: a clever and often dishonest plan to do or get something. The snare is used to trap prey. This verse refers specifically to a fowler, or one who hunts birds.

It also mentions deadly pestilence. The root Hebrew word for pestilence means "to systematically speak destructive words in order to subdue."

Both of these are just examples of situations from which God will *Deliverer* you.

"Deliver" means: to snatch away. Perhaps you've heard the expression "snatch victory from the jaws of defeat." That is exactly what the psalmist is declaring to us. Just when the enemy thinks a trap has been set for us the *Deliverer* comes to our rescue. When the enemy (the accuser of the brethren) brings accusations toward you the *Deliverer* will come to bring truth and silence the "pestilence" trying to take you down.

I love the faith shown by the psalmist when he said, "For he will deliver you …" There is no doubt. God, our *Deliverer*, stands ready to rescue you from every scheme the enemy brings.

God has a better life in mind that to constantly being "snatched" from traps. He sent the Holy Spirit to live in us. One of the blessings of the Spirit's presence in our life is to bring light to our path, direct our steps, and speak to us the will of God in every circumstance. It is good to know the *Deliverer* is able to keep us from becoming captive to the enemy's devices, but a better life is to live above the fray, in the peace God has provided by His Spirit.

Dew

Hosea 14:5 I will be like the dew to Israel; he shall blossom like the lily; he shall take root like the trees of Lebanon;

When you live in an arid climate any moisture is a blessing. Israel, for the most part, used to be desert. The main source of fresh water is the Sea of Galilee, and Jordan River that flows from it. In modern-day Israel, thanks to massive feats of engineering, the country has fresh water. This has not always been the case.

In Hosea's day Israel was still primarily a desert land. Rainfall was scarce, mostly in the winter. *Dew* was always a welcomed sight because it would water the ground, and the crops that might be present. God promised to be like the *Dew*. He would bring refreshing during the dry seasons.

In addition to the benefit of water, the word used for "dew" comes from a Hebrew that means to strew or cover. God is declaring over Israel that He will be a covering to him. That leads to the remaining part of the verse: "he shall blossom like the lily; he shall take root like the trees of Lebanon." God is like the *Dew*.

Thinking of dew reminded me of Psalm 133. I studied this psalm recently and was drawn to the phrases "dew of Hermon" and "dew on the mountains of Zion" in Psalm 133:3.

The root word for Hermon is "devoted or sacred." The water that falls on Hermon, including *Dew*, runs down and supplies the Sea of Galilee, the primary water source for Israel. Psalm 133 speaks of the anointing, comparing it to the anointing. The *Dew* seems to be the primary source of "anointing" for Israel.

The types and shadows here are very evident. God says He will be like the Dew (covering). His anointing will "cover" from the top of the head to the hem of the garment; in other words, completely. The anointing of God comes without any effort on our part. It moistens the dry places and is new every morning.

Let the *Dew* cover you today with His grace and power that will allow you to live in peace and freedom.

Director of My Path

Proverbs 3:6 (ESV) In all your ways acknowledge him, and he will make straight (direct) your paths.

There are many ways to look at this particular name of God. The first thing to note is that there are multiple paths. I do not think this says that God will dictate every move that we make. He created us with a will and gave us the ability to make choices.

This proverb is conditional. It begins with the stipulation of us acknowledging God in all of our ways. To acknowledge God is to admit our need for Him, the *Director*, in every aspect of our life. We are to seek His guidance every moment of every day. Relationships, vocation, finances, etc. are all to be under God's direction.

The promise is made, then, that when we choose to acknowledge the *Director*'s influence in our life He promises to make our paths straight. This is comforting in the sense that a straight path is easier to navigate. A path that is straight does not require as much effort to navigate.

Another way to view God's role as *Director* is in the sense of a stage production. There is a script that everyone is to follow. The roles are defined by the author of the story. The scenery is constructed, wardrobe selected, and interpretation of the story's presentation are all left to the discretion of the *Director*.

For the Christian, our role is given by the directive to "be like Christ." Every other aspect of our life is simply a detail that is laid before us as choices to be made. That is why we need the influence of the *Director* in our life. There is a way in every choice we make that will take us on a straight path, leading us closer to the goal of being Christ-like. We must heed the voice of the *Director* as He gives us cues that will result in the best "performance" available for our life.

When you realize that we have an audience of One, the *Director* Himself, it makes our "performance" of life so much easier. Let's choose today to take the stage, embrace our role, and give our *Director* the performance of a lifetime.

Disciplinarian

Psalm 89:32 (ESV) then I will punish their transgression with the rod and their iniquity with stripes,

Unfortunately, this name for God is one of the most well-known; even before that of Him being Love, Creator, Advocate, Comforter, etc. For many, the only view of God they have is that of *Disciplinarian*. It is unfortunate that some never get beyond seeing Him as an angry God with a big stick just waiting on them to mess up.

Everything God does in our life is for our good and is motivated by His unending love. He desires every person to become a son or daughter; fully restored in their relationship with Him through Jesus. God's plan for us is to become Christ-like in every aspect of our life.

Part of any relationship involving training will include discipline. The very term used for Christians is that of a disciple. The role of a disciple is to conform their will to that of the teacher. In Jesus' day, when someone wanted to be identified with a teacher or master, they would submit themselves to be baptized by the teacher. This was a public declaration that the one being baptized has surrendered their will to that of the teacher. The same is true for the Christian.

When we enter into covenant with God we identify with Christ in every way: His death, burial, resurrection, ascension, and seating at the right hand of God. By dying to our self-will we take on His will for our life: to be conformed into the image of His Son, Jesus. We conform to His love for others, His passion to redeem the lost ones, His focus to do the will of the Father, and His sacrificial giving of Himself.

Most of the confusion regarding God's discipline is in the methods He employs to bring discipline to His children. Some think that sickness, disease, and calamity are sent by God to teach us or correct us in some way. Jesus was very clear in His teaching regarding the Father. He told us, "In this world you will have tribulation." Then added, "But be of good cheer; I have overcome the world." *

Like any good Father, the *Disciplinarian* uses words to bring correction to the believer. When we disobey the commands of our God we step outside of the covering He has provided for us. By living in His will for us we enjoy the grace extended toward us when we submitted our lives to Him. By sending His word to us, printed in scripture or a word spoken to us in due season, the *Disciplinarian* brings correction to get us back where we need to be. Failure to heed the voice of God will lead to more time spent outside of His covering, exposing us to more of the enemy's attacks.

Let us be aware of that Still Small Voice of the Holy Spirit and also be quick to respond completely to the instructions of the *Disciplinarian* so we can enjoy the close fellowship that God desires for us.

---

* There is much more to be said here but it is outside the scope of this particular study.

Doer of Wonders

> Psalm 77:14 (ESV) You are the God who works wonders; you have made known your might among the peoples.

The psalmist, in an attempt to separate Jehovah from others that might be referred to as "god", declared, "You are the God who works wonders." Most deities are known by some wonder that man has seen. The planets, for instance, once discovered were assumed to be gods. It caused man to "wonder" so therefore it must be a "god."

The primary difference in Jehovah and these other "gods" is clear; Jehovah is the *Doer of Wonders*, not the result of a wonder. Jehovah actually created the wonders that give these other "gods" their names. He hung the sun, moon, and stars. He called light into existence. Everything is upheld by His word.

The really amazing part of this is Jehovah is still the *Doer of Wonders*. He chooses to involve Himself with His creation, to help those who choose to follow Him. When the Creator of man interacts with His creation, it appears to man as a wonder.

Let us never loose the awe and respect due the *Doer of Wonders*. He is worthy of our praise. His wonders will never cease.

Dwelling Place

Psalm 90:1 (ESV) Lord, you have been our dwelling place in all generations.

The Hebrew word for "dwelling place" means *abode*. For men it would be their house; for animals, their lair. But in this instance God is our *Dwelling Place*. It's where we feel at home, and the location irrelevant.

In the Old Testament people would erect altars, or monuments, to mark the location where they encountered God. Because God did not dwell in them as He does in us today in the Holy Spirit mankind was limited to brief, or even chance, encounters with God. Once they had an encounter they were prone to go back and visit those places in order to relive the moment when they knew God's presence.

God's presence is man's strongest desire. When we become a Christian and have our first encounter with His presence He comes and makes His home in us by the Holy Spirit. Our spirit is recreated and becomes His habitation. In so doing, we no longer have to look for Him. He is always with us. We no longer have to yearn for His presence. He is always with us.

God is our *Dwelling Place*. We are also His dwelling place! Let us learn to be aware of his presence in our lives at all times. He is never far away. He is closer than the air we breathe.

El Elyon
(The Lord Most High)

Genesis 14:17-18 (ESV) After his return from the defeat of Chedorlaomer and the kings who were with him, the king of Sodom went out to meet him at the Valley of Shaveh (that is, the King's Valley). And Melchizedek king of Salem brought out bread and wine. (He was priest of God Most High.)

The Law of First Reference is a device used by Bible scholars to interpret the meaning of words found in scripture. This name for God, *El Elyon*, means *Most High God*. It was first used in telling the story of Abram when he went to war with five kings to recapture Lot, Lot's possessions, and the people of Lot's household.

Some of the other kings that were previously defeated by the five kings came to bless Abram for redeeming their possessions as well. Melchizedek, king of Salem, was one of them. The reference to *El Elyon* comes when stating that Melchizedek was a priest of the *Most High God*.

It is believed by most scholars that Melchizedek was a pre-incarnate visitation of Christ. Hebrews 6 speaks of Melchizedek being a forerunner of Christ; that Melchizedek was priest forever.

El Elyon means "elevation, lofty; by implication, supreme." In order for Melchizedek to have an eternal priesthood it must be in service to Jehovah God, the Creator, the *Most High God*. There is none above Him. He is the origin of all things. Everything flows from Him and returns back to Him. Our God is not just the first of many; He is the One and Only.

>Psalm 57:2 (ESV) I cry out to God Most High, to God who fulfills his purpose for me.

The psalmist is seeking justice. He states, "I will appeal to the highest court possible." El Elyon would be the equivalent to the U. S. Supreme Court, legally speaking. Their decision is final. The *Most High God* has final say in our life. As the psalmist declared, "He will fulfill His purpose for us." Regardless of what accusation the enemy can bring to us there is always a higher court to which we can appeal: the *Most High God*. No one can overrule Him.

In the same way, our High Priest, Jesus Christ, has made a way for us to enter into the presence of God. He opened the holy of holies by tearing down the curtain that separated man from their Creator. We now have access to come before our Maker, the *Most High God*, and fellowship with Him as friend with Friend.

If you are a Christian then you have been identified with Christ in His death, burial, resurrection, ascension, and seating at the right hand of the *Most High God*. Let us learn to live from this elevation, "far above all principality, power, might, and dominion, and every name that is named, not only in this world, but also in that which is to come." (Ephesians 4:10)

El Olam
(The Most High God)

> Genesis 21:33 (ESV) Abraham planted a tamarisk tree in Beersheba and called there on the name of the LORD, the Everlasting God.

Just as we saw when we considered God's name, Ancient of Days, we found the meaning did not mean "old" as we might consider as age. This name for God, *El Olam*, or Everlasting God, does not mean old. It mean timeless.

The Hebrew word olam has in its meaning the idea of horizons. When you are near the ocean or on a high mountain you can see a long way, but your sight is limited by the curvature of the earth. Things seem to just fade away, or reach a "vanishing point." That is olam. You know there's more beyond what you can see, but it is not visible to our eye. Things beyond the horizon are "concealed"; another aspect of olam.

Because God is an Everlasting God it means He has been there when it happened and will be there when it happens. He has always been; He will always be. He is the Everlasting God. Even when you are not conscious of Him, He is still God. "Out of mind" is another meaning of olam.

For the scientifically minded, He is on a continuum. Time does not apply to Him. As we saw earlier, the Ancient of Days, also known as the Everlasting God, created time. The Creator is always greater than the creation. Time only exists so that our finite minds can function. We are placed in time at birth; we leave time at death. We come from an eternal Creator; as Christians, we are received back by the Everlasting God to be with Him forever.

In that sense, we are also eternal, or everlasting, because we were made in His image. What we do when we are on "pause" while here on earth will determine whether we are received back into His presence. Let us pursue knowing this Everlasting God so we can spend eternity with Him.

El Olam, the Everlasting God, is on the horizon of your life. Pursue Him. He is not "concealed" from you; He is hidden FOR you. Seek and you will find; knock and it will be opened. He wants you to know Him. Why else would He have given us so many names to understand Him? He loves you that much!

El Shaddai (God Almighty)

Exodus 6:3 (ESV) I appeared to Abraham, to Isaac, and to Jacob, as God Almighty, but by my name the LORD I did not make myself known to them.

This name was dealt with previously (see The Names of God – Almighty God). However, there is more that can be added here.

When you look at the name *El Shaddai* it may seem a bit poetic. A song by Michael W. Smith, sung by Amy Grant, made this name a relative household word. It sounds so pretty when sung by her melodic voice. The reality is this name is nothing like the song.

The Hebrew word "shadday" is taken from the root word "shadad." It means: "burly, powerful, impregnable (unable to be penetrated), to ravage."

That hardly sounds poetic. It flies in the face of the typical effeminate image that most attribute to God. Yes, God is love. He is kind. He is gracious. He is creative. He is also strong, and deliberate, and powerful, and absolute.

When you commit your life to *El Shaddai* you can rest assured that you are in good hands. Paul said it best in 2 Timothy 1:12b (ESV) But I am not ashamed, for I know whom I have believed, and I am convinced that he is able to guard until that Day what has been entrusted to me.

We will see later in this series that God is a Strong Tower, a Safe Refuge, and He is *El Shaddai, God Almighty*. Let us see God in every facet through which He has revealed Himself. You cannot pick and choose the characteristics that you prefer and ignore the rest. Sometimes it is hard to see God certain ways because of prior experience. If you were abused by a parent or other male figure it can be difficult to see God as "burly."

You must realize that He is also the Lifter of Our Head, a Friend, and Loving Father. He would never do anything to harm you or cause you hurt.

Embrace Him in every aspect and allow Him to conform you to His image, which is His greatest desire for your life. It takes a God that is powerful and impregnable to keep us in the middle of storms that come, to guide us through the Valley of Death, and bring us into eternal life. Let Him be *El Shaddai*.

Emmanuel

Isaiah 8:8 (ESV) ... and it will sweep on into Judah, it will overflow and pass on, reaching even to the neck, and its outspread wings will fill the breadth of your land, O Immanuel."

Matthew 1:23 (ESV) "Behold, the virgin shall conceive and bear a son, and they shall call his name Emmanuel"

The different spellings of this name come from the origin being reference. *Immanuel* is from Hebrew; the Greek spelling is *Emmanuel*. The latter is the most common in our vernacular. Regardless of the origin the meaning is the same: *God with us*.

To me, this is one of the most comforting names of God in scripture. It is easy, as humans, to stare into the starlit sky, or cast your eye over the vast horizon from atop a tall mountain, or listen to the numbing roar of the ocean at the beach, and not see the awesome power of our Creator. It is nice to know we serve an all-powerful Sovereign that rules the universe.

However, when we face unbearable turmoil, or bend from the weight of cares that seem to overwhelm us, or hear bad news that shakes the very foundations of our existence, it is just as comforting, if not more so, to know that *God is with us*; *Emmanuel*! When you know God is with you it makes unbearable a bit more tolerable. The weight of cares is lighter because He cares for you; *God is with us*. Bad news is less destructive because you know the He already knew, and has a plan to move you beyond this moment; *God is with us*.

The incarnation of Christ is perhaps the most hope-filled promise ever given to mankind. When they learned that God was not just somewhere out there. He came and dwelt among us, and we beheld His glory, that of the only begotten Son of God – *Emmanuel*. He showed us that life as a human on planet earth does mean something. We can live in fellowship with our Creator to accomplish His purpose for us. *God is with us.*

As a matter of fact, He is with us when we are not aware of His presence. Even if we try to escape His presence we cannot, because *God is with us*. He will never leave us or forsake us. Allow this truth to become part of your conscious thinking. Brother Lawrence encouraged this in his book "The Practice of the Presence of God (The Best Rule of a Holy Life)". Even in the mundane things in life we must realize that God is with us. When this becomes a way of life it makes it easier to allow God to help us through the "big" things that seem to make us shipwreck.

Emmanuel, God with us. Every day. Every moment. Right now. So regardless of what you are facing know that God is there, and He is able to get you beyond the current circumstances. He loves you … and He is here.

Eternal God

Deuteronomy 33:27 (ESV) The eternal God is your dwelling place, and underneath are the everlasting arms. And he thrust out the enemy before you and said, 'Destroy.'

The Hebrew word for "eternal" means "front, the fore part." To say God is *Eternal God* means He is always before us. When we arrive at a place *Eternal God* has already been there, leading, preparing, making our path straight. He is the *Director of our Paths*, as we saw in a previous post.

Another translation for this Hebrew word means "East." This is interesting when you look at this in light of what God told Moses in Exodus 33:23. Moses asked God to show him His glory. God replied, "I'll pass before you and show you My back parts." The Hebrew word for "back parts" means "hinder parts, that which is behind, His past, or West." So when you combine these two glimpses of God you see quickly that He is *Eternal God*.

You cannot measure East to West because it is infinite. It is interesting that God gives us the assurance that when He redeems us, "as far as the east is from the west, so far does he remove our transgressions from us." [Psalm 103:12 (ESV)] This is very reassuring. Once you are in Christ, you cannot go anywhere "in God' and find a place where God will judge you for your sin. He is *Eternal God*.

I once sang with a group called Windborne. We had an eclectic repertoire; a blend of Southern Gospel and Contemporary Christian. One of the songs we used is called

"What Sins Are You Talkin' About?" The second verse says:

> When my flesh becomes weak
> It's then I can speak
> To the Savior Who's with me each day,
> "Oh, Father, forgive me, hear my plea,"
> And He washes my sin away;
> Each time that I bow to give Him thanks
> For removing my guilt and shame,
> He cannot recall what I'm talkin' about,
> For His answer is always the same.
>
> Chorus:
> "What sins are you talkin' about,
> I don't remember them anymore;
> From the Book of Life they've all been torn out,
> I don't remember them anymore."[v]

I realize the exegesis on that is not 100% accurate, but it illustrates how far God removes us from our sin. He, the *Eternal God*, is the only one that could find them. And He has promised that He would not!

Take this name of God, *Eternal God*, and begin to see yourself "in Him". He is before you, He is behind you, and there is nowhere else for anything to be!

Everlasting Arms

Deuteronomy 33:27 (ESV) The eternal God is your dwelling place, and underneath are the everlasting arms. And he thrust out the enemy before you and said, 'Destroy.'

Psalm 136:12 (ESV) with a strong hand and an outstretched arm, for his steadfast love endures forever;

Isaiah 51:9 (ESV) Awake, awake, put on strength, O arm of the LORD; awake, as in days of old, the generations of long ago. Was it not you who cut Rahab in pieces, who pierced the dragon?

Isaiah 63:12 (ESV) who caused his glorious arm to go at the right hand of Moses, who divided the waters before them to make for himself an everlasting name,

The two Hebrew words that make up this name of God, *Everlasting Arms*, occur four times in scripture. Each time the meaning is the same. God is always (everlasting) present, even when you do not see Him, to undergird you with His strength (arms).

The "everlasting" aspect has been considered several times in previous blog entries. The Hebrew word is olam. It does not mean old, but instead means perpetual. Just as we saw in the previous post, *Eternal God*, He is always before us and always behind us. There is nowhere we can go that He is not already there.

This word "everlasting" is included many times when speaking of covenant between God and man. When the *Everlasting Arms* enters into covenant with us He will keep His end of the covenant. Nothing that man can do will keep the *Everlasting Arms* from fulfilling His promises to us. Nothing the enemy can do will keep the *Everlasting Arms* from fulfilling His promises. Just as we saw in the post regarding El Shaddai, God is not a wimpy god, but strong and mighty. His arms are capable of holding you, to keep you safe through any trial or storm.

The reason for this study of The Names of God stem from Daniel 11:32b (NKJV), "… but the people who know their God shall be strong, and carry out great exploits."

When we serve a powerful God, He enables us, through His power, to do great things for His Kingdom. Please understand that God does not define "great" the same as we do. His definition is "the last shall be first, and the first shall be last." It takes the power of God to be a servant. I highly recommend the book, *God of the Mundane*, by Matthew B. Redmond, for more on this topic. Get a copy on Amazon.Com.[vi]

We can rest assured in our faith, knowing that the *Everlasting Arms* are ever-ready to help us. Rest in Him today.

Everlasting Strength

> Isaiah 26:4 (ESV) Trust in the LORD forever, for the LORD GOD is an everlasting rock.

If you have been keeping up with this blog you know that we've covered the word "everlasting" several times. The only thing I'll add here is the Hebrew word "olam" includes in its meaning "concealed, hidden." When you couple that with the Hebrew word for strength, "sur", you begin to see another attribute of God revealed through this name, *Everlasting Strength*.

"Sur" means "a cliff, rock, or boulder; a refuge." It is a safe place to either ride out a storm or find protection from an enemy. The added element from "olam" implies it is a concealed, or hidden place. Isaiah 45:15 (ESV) Truly, you are a God who hides himself, O God of Israel, the Savior.

Everlasting Strength is not available to everyone. It is a place reserved for the people of God. Proverbs 8:17 (ESV) I love those who love me, and those who seek me diligently find me. Those who love God will be in pursuit of Him, and He has assured us that when we seek Him diligently we will find Him!

> Jeremiah 29:13 (ESV) You will seek me and find me, when you seek me with all your heart. Not only is diligent pursuit necessary, but also whole-hearted pursuit expected from those who love God.

The good news for the New Testament believer is that the Holy Spirit has been sent to abide in us. One of the Spirit's purposes is to guide us into all truth – Jesus.

Another purpose of the Spirit's presence in our life is to bring peace – a secure place. This is the *Everlasting Strength* revealed in this name of God. The enemy cannot defeat us when we are at peace with God. Storms cannot separate us from God when we are resting in *Everlasting Strength*.

So, let us determine first of all to love the Lord with all of our heart, soul, mind, and strength. Then, let's pursue God diligently and whole-heartedly, with the Holy Spirit empowering us and leading us, we will find the place of *Everlasting Strength*; the secret place of God's presence. Jesus is how we gain access to this place. It all starts by surrendering our life to the Life Giver – Jesus. With Him comes everything else that we have discussed up to this point; and also all that we have yet to discover as we delve further into the Names of God.

Everlasting to Everlasting

Psalm 106:48 (ESV) Blessed be the LORD, the God of Israel, from everlasting to everlasting! And let all the people say, "Amen!" Praise the LORD!

About 20 years ago a poem was written that became very popular. The poem was called "The Dash", by Linda Ellis. It was inspired by considering a part of a persons eulogy, the birth and death dates. Between those dates there is typically a dash to signify from birth TO death. The dash represents our life; the time between being born and dying.

This image of the dash represents, better than any metaphor I know, that man is finite in terms of his life on earth. Because we live in a finite world inside a finite body it is difficult to imagine infinity. We can define it in mathematical terms, through physics, and even psychology, but we really cannot understand it.

Even after all of the Names of God that we have dealt with up this point, today's name is just icing on the cake: when we consider that God is *Everlasting to Everlasting*. This explicitly describes the neverendingness of God. He has eternally been and He will eternally be. He has no beginning and He has no ending. God has no dash!

Our entire existence is contained within Him. There has never been a time that we have been outside of God. It is true that we do not have a relationship with Him before we encountered His love through Jesus, by the Holy Spirit. But we have never been outside of Him. There has never been a time that we existed, but not God. He is everlasting to everlasting.

One meaning of the word "olam", the Hebrew word for everlasting, is "horizon." Sometimes we say in human terms "as far as the eye can see", implying forever, but it is only the "forever" that we can envision. Our human existence is based on DNA. The chain of DNA, long though it may be, is finite. When cells replicate, part of the original cell's DNA chain goes with the new cell. Cells replicate thousands of times in our human life and eventually the DNA chain gets shortened, causing a mutation of the genes (commonly called aging) which leads to our eventual death. Man is finite.

Because God is *Everlasting to Everlasting*, He is from eternal to eternal. He is from infinite to infinite. He has no beginning and now ending. He always was and always will be … God.

Excellent in Wisdom (Working)

Isaiah 28:29 (ESV) This also comes from the LORD of hosts; he is wonderful in counsel and excellent in wisdom.

This name, or attribute, of God is interesting. In scripture there are many different Hebrew and Greek words that are translated into some form of the word "excellent." All of them are certainly applicable to God. This particular one is intriguing.

The context in this verse is the prophet recalling the skill observed in farming and reaping various crops. There is great skill necessary to raise a crop. The One who is *Excellent in Wisdom* is given credit for teaching the farmer. The chapter ends with vs. 29, "He is wonderful in counsel and excellent in wisdom." The word used for excellent in this verse is the Hebrew word "gadal." In simple terms is means to twist. However, its root word gives a little more insight into its meaning.

In this combination of words, *Excellent in Wisdom*, it gives the image of spinning a thread, or twisting a cord. When applied to this context it shows us that God is able to direct us through the intricate details needed to complete various tasks. Our human minds may not be able to comprehend the complexity, but with God's help He shows us the proper path to take.

While working as a Software Consultant in Atlanta part of my job was to resolve customer issues with our programs. On one occasion I was totally stumped on what to do to help correct a problem. During my morning commute I prayed and asked the Lord to help resolve the issue. In an instant the phrase "depletion indicator" came to mind. I did not recall having ever heard of that before.

After arriving at the office I went to one of the more seasoned consultants and inquired of him about the "depletion indicator." He described its purpose for me as I listened with amazement. By simply changing the Depletion Indicator from "N" to "Y" it corrected the customer's issue. I could have spent many hours tracing through thousands of lines of computer code looking for this. Instead, *Excellent in Wisdom* showed me the answer.

Regardless of your circumstance God knows the way from where you are to where you need to be. We need to draw from the right source to get the answers we need. Scripture tells us there is safety in a multitude of counselors. However, don't forget to ask the one Counselor that has all wisdom about all things, *Excellent in Wisdom*.

Faithful

> Lamentations 3:22-23 (ESV) The steadfast love of the LORD never ceases; his mercies never come to an end; they are new every morning; great is your faithfulness.

Of all the names for God that we have considered thus far I believe this one to be the top of the list. God is *Faithful*.

One of the first ways God revealed Himself to our world was through His words. Genesis 1 gives us the story of creation by telling us "God said ..." His words framed our world and everything in it. (Hebrews 11:3)

When God came to earth as the Son of Man, He appeared as The Word. (John 1) Our world is still here because of the word of Faithful God. Hebrews 1:3 (ESV) He is the radiance of the glory of God and the exact imprint of his nature, and he upholds the universe by the word of his power. After making purification for sins, he sat down at the right hand of the Majesty on high,

So, why all the talk about the word? I thought we were looking at God being *Faithful*. Here's why. As we just saw, the word of God is vital to our existence. It is how everything came to be, and it is how everything still remains. Without the *Faithful* one keeping His word we would perish. Malachi 3:6 (ESV) "For I the LORD do not change; therefore you, O children of Jacob, are not consumed.

If God ever changed His mind creation would perish. We have assurance from *Faithful* Himself that it will never happen. Hebrews 13:8 tells us that He is the same yesterday, today, and forever.

All other attributes of God are accentuated by this one. When you consider that God is love, it means so much more to realize that He will always love, because He is faithful. When you hear of God's mercy, knowing He is faithful allows you to rest assured His mercy does indeed endure forever. God's power gives us peace because we know He will always be powerful. He never rests or grows weary.

Faithful God is worthy of our worship. We can commit our life to Him without reserve because He is *Faithful*. Trust Him today.

Father

> Isaiah 63:16 (ESV) For you are our Father, though Abraham does not know us, and Israel does not acknowledge us; you, O LORD, are our Father, our Redeemer from of old is your name.

One of the greatest privileges I have in life is to be called a father. It is one of the highest callings for a man. The most prevalent image that God models for us is that of *Father*.

Consequently, one of the greatest areas of spiritual warfare waged by the enemy is against fatherhood. The media belittles the role of men in general, but especially fathers. One of the most destructive schemes of the enemy is divorce. Statistics show that the majority of divorces occur when the oldest child of a couple reaches the age of puberty. Just when a child is looking for identity and destiny, their foundation, their parents, are suddenly divided, causing them to become shipwrecked.

One of the most important roles fathers have in the life of their children is in the area of blessing. Again, because of ignorance or apathy, the blessing a father gives to a child has been practically eliminated from the Western culture. Instead of receiving a blessing from the very one they are seeking approval, they instead receive abuse or neglect at worst, or being ignored. This is not the way *Father* modeled for us.

Look at scripture. You will find specific times of blessing that God desires a person to receive in their lifetime. *Father* later implemented them in the Law of Moses to be sure that every Hebrew received a blessing.

First of all, after birth a child was brought before the priest to be blessed. The parents, and possibly others, would speak blessings over the child and commit it into the hands of *Father*.

Then at puberty each child would have a ceremony. For the male child it was a bar mitzvah; for the female, a bat mitzvah. These Hebrew phrases mean Son (bar) of the Covenant and Daughter (bat) of the Covenant. These ceremonies would be as big as a wedding. Much time and effort went into planning the event. All of the family and friends would gather. Gifts were given. The highlight of the night would be when the child was placed in a chair, then raised up high by other family members. They would march the child around the room like a king or queen being carried about. The whole time the father of the child walked before them proclaiming loudly, "This is my beloved son/daughter in whom I am well pleased!"

How could any child come away from that experience without feeling special? Other things would change after the bar/bat mitzvah. Their clothing would change. They were no longer considered children, but instead treated as a man or woman.

The next time of blessing would come when the child married. They would again come before the priest for a blessing and the wedding pronouncement. Parents would speak blessings over the new couple, pledging to assist them in any way needed. It would launch them into a union that was sealed by *Father* Himself.

Our *Father* intended for the elderly to be blessed; to be cared for and to be shown honor. This is also an area that the Western culture has practically eliminated from its view of society.

To know that our *Father* wants us to blessed exposes the deep love for which He loves us. He does not want to simply muddle through life and pay homage to the "great god in the sky." He wants us to know His heart and to follow His ways. His ways are intended for our greatest good. Without that understanding it is very difficult to give ourselves to Him fully.

Meditate on some of the Names of God that have been considered up to this point. Let us get to know our *Father* to point that we can trust Him fully and follow Him completely. Then we will know life.

Father of Glory/Lights/Spirits

James 1:17 (ESV) Every good gift and every perfect gift is from above, coming down from the Father of lights with whom there is no variation or shadow due to change.

Ephesians 1:17 (ESV) that the God of our Lord Jesus Christ, the Father of glory, may give you the Spirit of wisdom and of revelation in the knowledge of him,

Hebrews 12:9 (ESV) Besides this, we have had earthly fathers who disciplined us and we respected them. Shall we not much more be subject to the Father of spirits and live?

The same Greek word is used in all three of these; pater, which simply means, "father." There is another theme among these three verses that give is a picture of what is being communicated in this name of God: Father of Lights/Glory/Spirits. Each verse speaks of things that Father gives: 1) every good and perfect gift, 2) the Spirit of wisdom and revelation in the knowledge of Him, and 3) discipline. A good father not only communicates material blessings to their children, they also communicate wisdom for life, discipline to help live a full life, but most importantly lead them into a relationship with Jesus Christ. Father of Lights/Glory/Spirits is no exception. Actually, He is the model for all fathers to follow.

Let's look at the three different words coupled with the title of Pater, or Father, used in these verses to convey the heart of our God. The first is "lights." The Greek word translated "lights" in James 1:17 is "phos", which means, "to shine, make manifest, especially by rays." We saw in a previous post that all things are upheld by the Word of God. The things we see are actually made of things that we cannot see. Our God, the Father of Lights, makes the "manifest" in our life. Through our faith we have the evidence of things not seen (Hebrews 12:1). God breaks through the "stuff" around us to bring His good and perfect gifts when we are in need, when we cry out to Him in faith.

The second word used in conjunction with Father is the word "glory", which comes from the Greek word "doxa." The primary interpretation of the word is "glory", but we see more when we consider the root word "dokeo", which means, "to think, to seem truthfully, be accounted, of good reputation." This certainly speaks of our Father of Glory. The greatest gift God has ever given is His Son, Jesus Christ. Then after His ascension to heaven, Jesus sent us "another" gift; one just like Himself – the Holy Spirit. This Spirit is with us now to lead us into all truth concerning Christ, and to "reveal" the heart of the Father of Glory to us daily.

The last of these words to be coupled with Father is the Greek word "pneuma", which means, "a current of air, breath, or breeze." When we looked at the name of God, Abba, we talked about God breathing life into Adam. He actually "blew" His Spirit into Adam, and Adam became a living soul. In this light God is the Father of Spirits. He created your spirit. You received life directly from Him.

Another way to look at this attribute of God is in the area of correction, as Hebrews 12:9 tells us. God's primary means of correcting His children is by His Word. It comes to us like a gust of wind, the Wind of the Spirit, to lift us out of any muck or mire that tries to keep us neutralized, and fills our sails to carry us back on course when we may stray. Fresh air always revitalizes us when we are in a stagnate place. It blows away the dust and cobwebs or habits and traditions that may hinder our creativity.

You may have never considered your Heavenly Father in these ways. We need to allow our minds to see beyond the stereotypes that have bound our thinking about our Father and begin to see Him as Father of Lights, Father of Glory, and Father of Spirits.

Father of the Fatherless

Psalm 68:5 (ESV) Father of the fatherless and protector of widows is God in his holy habitation.

Nothing brings more human concern that orphans and widows. The thought of being alone drives people to want to help. Western society has evolved into a "caring" society in-name-only for the most part. We are quick to give money to a cause when the real need is human involvement. Money can only go so far to meet the needs of an orphan. A warm hug or conversation, really, just time, can fulfill a child's needs more than just money.

Our God is the *Father of the Fatherless*. As we saw in the last post, God is *Father of Spirits*, meaning He breathes life into every person, giving "birth" to your spirit by His Spirit. So, spiritually speaking, God is the Father of us all! Even if your earthly, or biological, father is not in your life you still have a Father. Whether your father is an absentee father or deceased you still have a Father, the *Father of the Fatherless*, to care for you.

Many people have a difficult time relating to God as a father because of the relationship they had with their earthly, or biological, father. I understand that. But if you could see how much the *Father of the Fatherless* loves you it would revolutionize your life. To know the love of THE Father gives you the confidence to embrace the destiny to which He has called you; to have the security in Him to step out in faith, knowing, and experience His best for you.

The Greek word used for "fatherless" is "yatom", which means "be lonely, or bereaved." So whether your father is absent (leaving you lonely) or deceased (leaving you bereaved) God is present, and always will be. It is from Him and through Him that you find your purpose in life. He is the One that has called you to be part of His kingdom. Even if your father is alive and present in your life, *Father of the Fatherless* still wants to be Father to you.

Let us learn to hear the voice of the Father and be quick to follow His direction for us. He will lead us into the fullness of the life He has prepared for us.

Feeder of the Hungry

> Psalm 146:5-8 (ESV) Blessed is he whose help is the God of Jacob, whose hope is in the LORD his God, who made heaven and earth, the sea, and all that is in them, who keeps faith forever; who executes justice for the oppressed, who gives food to the hungry. The LORD sets the prisoners free; the LORD opens the eyes of the blind. The LORD lifts up those who are bowed down; the LORD loves the righteous.

Another attribute, or name, of God is *Feeder of the Hungry*. The words used in reference verse are pretty simple. They mean the Lord "feeds the hungry." There are multiple implications to this. The first, and most obvious, is God provides food for our bodies. He created an environment that produces food for us to eat. Today's farmers are working as agents of the Lord to feed our world. If you know one please thank them today.

Secondly, the *Feeder of the Hungry* is always ready to bring spiritual nutrition to those that seek it. Jesus assured us of this: "Ask and you will receive, seek and you will find, knock and it will be opened." This reflects a desire, or hunger, in the one asking, seeking, and knocking. God always responds to hunger.

I know some will raise the question, "What about the starving people of the world? Why doesn't God do something for them?" First of all, we do not know what is in the hearts of those that are starving. People in India starve to death while cows walk around them eating the very food that could save them. Corrupt governments and greedy strong men hoard food and other supplies for money and allow their own countrymen to die of starvation. There are some in the USA that starve to death because of pride and self-will.

This brief blog post is not intended to be a comprehensive treatment of each topic. Suffice it to say that because of sin in the earth bad things happen. Sometimes they happen to very undeserving people. But, that does not change the character and nature of our God. He has provided a way of escape through Jesus Christ. Faith in Him opens avenues of provision and inspiration from Heaven itself. Trust the *Feeder of the Hungry* to come and meet you at your point of hunger. Let Him satisfy you with bread for food, and the Bread of Heaven, Jesus.

Fire by Night

Exodus 13:21 (ESV) And the LORD went before them by day in a pillar of cloud to lead them along the way, and by night in a pillar of fire to give them light, that they might travel by day and by night.

When Israel left Egypt they were going because they were told to leave. Egypt was the only life they knew. They had been there for their whole life. It's all they knew. They didn't know this God of Moses. Even after seeing the miracles of the plagues and being delivered from Pharaoh's army at the Red Sea they were confused and frustrated by their brief experience in the wilderness. God came to meet with Moses. There He made covenant with Moses and the people of Israel. He vowed to provide for them and protect them. God vowed to lead them into a land He prepared for them.

One of the ways God would lead them was as a Cloud by Day and a pillar of *Fire by Night*. The most important aspect of this, I believe, is *Fire by Night*. When you are in an unfamiliar place the night came become a terror. Surrounded by darkness, with only the word of Moses to go on, they were headed for a land they had never seen. The people of Israel needed some assurance.

A column of fire was always visible to them. When times of doubt would enter, or terror would attempt to seize their minds, the people of Israel would simply open the tent flap and see that God was present with them.

Fire by Night would lead them as they journeyed at night. He was a clear beacon for them to follow. An added benefit was heat in the middle of a cold wilderness. Day after day and night after night the faithfulness of God was demonstrated before them. The people came to trust *Fire by Night*. They could rest when it was time to rest with the assurance God was with them. They could trust His direction when it came time to move.

The Hebrew word for night is an interesting word. Although it is translated "night, midnight, or season", the word actually means "a twist." The word is "layla", pronounced "lah'-yil." When used in this context it means to "twist away from the light."

Here's what I get from this. God is ready to meet you where you are. Jesus came as "the light of the world." When you "twist away" from Jesus, *Fire by Night* is there to meet you in your "night season." Even in what scripture refers to as "the dark night of the soul", it cannot get too dark for *Fire by Night* to illuminate.

Instead of resisting the Light try looking into it. *Fire by Night* will expose anything that is keeping us from full relationship with Father. Let Him work to restore us into the image of the Son, Jesus Christ.

Cloud by Day was dealt with in a previous post. Read it to get the whole picture of this verse.

First and Last

> Isaiah 41:4 (ESV) Who has performed and done this, calling the generations from the beginning? I, the LORD, the first, and with the last; I am he.

This may be one of the most encouraging names of God that we have seen in this study. Isaiah declares that God is *First and Last*. He was in the Garden of Eden with the first generation that began with Adam and Eve. He has been with every generation since that time. He will be with the last generation as well. Nothing has happened without His knowledge. Therefore, He knows exactly what you face and exactly what you need to do.

Even though this name is very similar to Alpha and Omega, there are differences. Alpha and Omega speaks more to eternity past and eternity future. God always has been (Alpha) and will always be (Omega). *First and Last* speaks more to our human experience. God is not just God "out there", but He is "here" as well. He was with our forefathers. He will be with our children, and our children's children; all the way to the last generation. That gives us such freedom to release our children into His care, knowing He will never leave them or forsake them.

The last phrase in this verse is another name for God that we will study later. I want to mention it here. I AM is a name that occurs multiple places in scripture. It is really just the present-tense form of *First and Last*. When you look at any point in history you find the LORD; He is I AM! That is how bad memories can be healed. When you revisit the injurious thoughts that plague you, look around in that moment and find the LORD. He is there. Not only is

He with the first and last generation, He is with you from your first breath and will be with you until your last.

Any experience in your life was lived in the presence of *First and Last*. He was there, and will be there. Thank the LORD today for His presence in your life. Walk confidently into your future knowing *First and Last* is there.

Forgiving

Numbers 14:18 (ESV) 'The LORD is slow to anger and abounding in steadfast love, forgiving iniquity and transgression, but he will by no means clear the guilty, visiting the iniquity of the fathers on the children, to the third and the fourth generation.'

Another name or attribute of God is *Forgiving*. As this verse indicates, God is slow to anger. When seeing the human condition, the fallen nature acquired through Adam's sin, God sees us through eyes of love. His desire is to restore us to right relationship like the LORD had with Adam before the fall.

Even while the serpent was still in the Garden of Eden after deceiving Eve, God, the *Forgiver*, announced a plan to redeem mankind. God said there would be One that would come and crush the head of the serpent. That One is Jesus. The Forgiver sent His only Son to pay the price for the redemption of mankind. Jesus shed His blood, the blood required to atone for sin, and made a way for us to once again have fellowship with our Creator.

Forgiving is the very nature of God. Motivated by His steadfast love *Forgiving* removes iniquity and transgression from us when we receive the salvation provided through Jesus. We see in this verse that God will not clear the guilty. This emphasizes the reality that when Forgiving forgives sin we are no longer guilty. He removes sin from us, washed clean by the blood of Christ, and now seen as blameless by God Himself.

One other observation from this verse reveals another aspect of God's nature that will be dealt with in more detail later. Why would *Forgiving* "visit the iniquity" on future generations? I believe this shows the mercy of God. Generational sin continues until one generation finally gets the revelation of forgiveness through Jesus. God's forgiving nature, driven by love, is longsuffering to the point that He "visits" the sin to future generations in hopes that they will receive His way of escape.

Forgiving is looking for ways to remove your sin. He wants you free so that you can be restored to fellowship with God. The Hebrew word "necah" used for the word "forgiving" means "to lift." This makes perfect sense. By forgiving our sin, *Forgiving* "lifts" the condemnation that comes from sin so that we can live free. Receive His forgiveness today.

Fortress

Psalm 91:2 (ESV) I will say to the LORD, "My refuge and my fortress, my God, in whom I trust."

One of the most solemn places in Israel is Masada. It is a fortress built on a hill that was virtually impenetrable. A small band of Israelites held off an entire army for months. When it appeared certain the fortress would be sieged the Israelites chose suicide over being taken as prisoners.

Israel still takes new recruits in the armed forces to Masada to show them that Israel will never surrender. It is quite a sobering moment for the recruit, from what has been told.

The name Masada comes from the same Hebrew word interpreted "fortress" in Psalm 91:2. We have a God in whom we can trust. He is a *Fortress*. Unlike Masada, God is beyond being conquered. *Fortress* is a safe place for us. God covers us there with His mighty hand. Nothing can separate us from Him.

One of the most important aspects of Masada is its location on top of a huge rock. We are also fortified by *Fortress* on the Rock, Jesus Christ. When we place our trust in Him, God establishes a foundation in our life that is unmovable, unshakable, and eternal.

Take time to read Psalm 91 in its entirety. It will encourage you and build faith in *Fortress*.

There is one other aspect of this word that is used for "fortress." It is also interpreted as "net, or snare" in other places in scripture. When speaking of the LORD it is a good context. It speaks to when God, *Fortress*, comes to us to "catch us away" from certain situations in order to bring us to safety. So, regardless of whether you are "pursuing" God to get into His fortress, be aware that He is watching over us, prepared to "net" us to safety.

Whether a fortified structure or a safety net, *Fortress* stands ready to bring us to the safety of His presence and keep us there as long as is needed. Let us learn to live with our God as *Fortress*.

Friend That Sticks Closer Than a Brother

Proverbs 18:24 (ESV) A man of many companions may come to ruin, but there is a friend who sticks closer than a brother.

A true friend is a rare find. We can hope to have at least one in our lifetime. I've had several. I'm a blessed man.

I grew up with brothers; three of them. Brothers are by nature close, even when they fight like cats and dogs. However, when a brother is attacked by someone outside the family they come together as a single force to defeat the invader. That is the nature of brotherhood.

To imagine that there is one "closer than a brother" says much about the nature of that relationship. I believe this is speaking of Jesus Christ. The reason is this: brothers band together because they are born into the same family. Their allegiance is only as strong as their commitment to the family. A friend, however, is there by choice. The commitment of a friend is an act of will, not simply birth.

An example of this is David, King of Israel. In a study of his life you see relatives of David attempt to steal from him, usurp his authority, and even try to kill him. David had a friend. His name was Jonathan. His commitment to Jonathan was so strong that even after Jonathan died David sought out a relative of Jonathan's in order to show kindness to him.

Jesus Christ, a *Friend That Sticks Closer Than a Brother*, comes to us and offers redemption from sin and offers a way back to fellowship with Father. He does this out of love. He offers His hand to us as a friend. John 15:13 (ESV) Greater love has no one than this; that someone lay down his life for his friends. Jesus laid down His life so that we could be given life. That is a friend indeed.

I want to be a better friend. I want to be someone that is willing to lay my life down for others. I want to be a friend that others would want to have in their lives. The only way this is possible is to let the love of Jesus be evident in my life. I pray this day that the *Friend That Sticks Closer Than a Brother* teaches me how to be a friend.

Abraham was a man that God could use. Abraham was willing to be the beginning point in the plan of redemption. Through Abraham, God brought His Promise, the Messiah, into the earth. Now, because of one man's faith we can all be restored into right relationship with God.

> James 2:23 (ESV) and the Scripture was fulfilled that says, "Abraham believed God, and it was counted to him as righteousness"—and he was called a friend of God.

Abraham was not just a servant of The Almighty. He became God's friend. Imagine if this was your legacy, or mine: "I am a friend of God." That realization, if we were able to grasp it, would transform how we view our God. Some of us struggle with the idea of being God's friend because we don't know how to be a friend. We can all start where Jesus did; serve others, lay your life down for others, and you will be found friendly. Everyone wanted to be around Jesus. He did not condemn. He did not require certain behavior from you for Him to be in your presence. He simply showed love and kindness. He spoke the truth, in love. He showed others the Father's heart.

Our challenge this day is to start seeing God as a *Friend That Sticks Closer Than a Brother*. The rest will follow as we learn to let Him live through us.

Gentle

> Isaiah 40:11 (ESV) He will tend his flock like a shepherd; he will gather the lambs in his arms; he will carry them in his bosom, and gently lead those that are with young.

Can you imagine a robot the size of the Empire State Building trying to swab a newborn baby's ear? For many, this is how they view God. He is Almighty. He is Omnipotent. He is … Even Isaiah begins his description of God this way. Isaiah 40:10 (ESV) Behold, the Lord GOD comes with might, and his arm rules for him; behold, his reward is with him, and his recompense before him.

All of these things are true about God. But, it is just as true what Isaiah shares in the next verse. "… and gently lead those that are with young." God is *Gentle*. Scripture often portrays God as a Shepherd. Sheep require a lot of care. They are relatively helpless creatures. This passage describes how God, *Gentle*, cares for us, His flock. The little ones He carries; the pregnant ones He gently leads. This is quite a contrast to Creator of the Universe.

How can the God that fills all of space and time: 1) be aware that an ewe is pregnant, 2) be able to lead them with the tender care they need? The answer is simple: He is *Gentle*. Some of the least obvious, but the most powerful, covenant language is "loving-kindness and tender mercies." Yes, God is able to create the world with His word. Yes, God is able to split the earth and consume Korah and all of those with him, including their houses and possessions. Yes, God can split the Red Sea and deliver Israel from Egypt; then destroy the Egyptian army in the same sea. But,

God is also full of loving-kindness and tender mercy for those who will walk in covenant with Him.

Genesis tells us that when God made man and placed him in the Garden of Eden, God formed man in His likeness. The Godhead agreed they would make man in Their image. Later in the Genesis account of creation God saw that man was alone and realized it was not good. It says God took "a rib" from Adam. This is a poor translation. The Hebrew word "sela" is better translated "a side." I believe that Adam was created both male and female in one body. When "the side" was removed from Adam to create Eve, God removed the female part of "mankind" and created woman.

Keep in mind that Adam, the original male/female version of Adam, was created in God's image. This tells us that God has within Him both male and female tendencies. God knows how to be merciful, He knows how to be tender; He is *Gentle*. This gives all of us reason to take heart. God does not deal with us as a "man." He does not deal with us as a "woman." He deals with us from a place of confidence (like a shepherd; he will gather the lambs in his arms), but also from a place of gentleness (he will carry them in his bosom, and gently lead those that are with young).

Draw near to *Gentle* today and find a place of safety where we can share our heart without holding anything from Him. Matthew quoted Isaiah when he wrote, "Matthew 12:20 (ESV) a bruised reed he will not break, and a smoldering wick he will not quench, ..." A bruised reed is very fragile; He will not break it. Your emotions can become fragile, but *Gentle* will always respond in a loving, caring way. A smoldering wick cannot produce a bright light. It needs to be trimmed in order to burn efficiently.

Instead of snuffing it out, or quenching it, *Gentle* takes time to cut away the crusty part of the wick that cannot soak up the fuel and burn effectively. God trims us so that we burn brightly, emanating His love for the world to see.

When we understand this attribute of our God it gives us confidence that He will work in our lives to accomplish His purpose in us. We can trust a God like this. He is *Gentle*.

Gift Giver

James 1:17 (ESV) Every good gift and every perfect gift is from above, coming down from the Father of lights with whom there is no variation or shadow due to change.

God is a *Gift Giver*. One of the first verses of scripture learned by children is John 3:16: "For God so loved the world that He gave His only begotten Son; that whosoever believeth in Him shall be saved." God loves and He gives. This is His nature. It is not something He does, it is who He is.

James gives us more insight into *Gift Giver*. "Every good gift and every perfect gift is from above." That's a pretty bold statement. The two adjectives used to describe the gifts given by the *Gift Giver* paint a clear picture of what God wants to bring into our life. Good (Greek word "agathos") is anything that is of "benefit" to us. Perfect (Greek word "teleios") means "complete." *Gift Giver* desires to bring elements into our life that will be a blessing and help us grow into the image of His Son, Jesus.

James goes on to assure us that God is always a *Gift Giver*; "with whom there is no variation or shadow due to change." God always has been, and always will be, a *Gift Giver*. It has always been His nature, and will always be, to bless and nurture. It is not something He does, it is Who He is.

Gift Giver's motivation is not simply to give us everything we want. His focus is on that which is beneficial and completing. The whole concept of grace is based on giving. Some define grace as "unmerited favor." I have adopted a definition I heard from Jason Peebles. It says, "Grace is the desire and ability to do God's will." God gives us the desire to pursue Him. 1 John 4:19 (ESV) We love because he first loved us. He placed love in our hearts so we would have the capacity to love Him. Ephesians 4:7 (ESV) But grace was given to each one of us according to the measure of Christ's gift.

So you see, *Gift Giver* was at work even before you knew He was there. He was giving to you before you even knew you had received a gift. He placed within you the capacity to love and the ability to respond to that love. His desire for us is to be blessed. He wants to have everything necessary to accomplish His plans and purposes in our life. Our responsibility is to simply receive the gifts given. The Greek word used for "gift" in James 1:17 is "dosis." It means, "a giving." This implies it is a one sided transaction: a giving. In order for it to become a gift there must be a receiving.

Let us pursue the *Gift Giver* to learn how to receive from Him. It begins with trust – faith – that every gift from Him is for our good.

Giver of Good Things

> Matthew 7:11 (ESV) If you then, who are evil, know how to give good gifts to your children, how much more will your Father who is in heaven give good things to those who ask him!

Everyone likes presents. Many times it's not the size or the cost of the gift that matters. It is the idea that someone thought about you, and took time to get you a gift. I remember coming home from trips and giving my children gifts, usually something small. They were always so excited to know that I had been thinking of them while I was away.

God is a Giver of Good Things. How blessed we are to have a Father that loves us so much that He wants to bring good things into our lives.

It is in the nature of a father to give their children whatever they need. This is much more true of our Heavenly Father. Luke 11:11 (ESV) "What father among you, if his son asks for a fish, will instead of a fish give him a serpent;" Our Father is the Giver of Good Gifts.

> Psalm 103:2-5 (ESV) Bless the LORD, O my soul, and forget not all his benefits, who forgives all your iniquity, who heals all your diseases, who redeems your life from the pit, who crowns you with steadfast love and mercy, who satisfies you with good so that your youth is renewed like the eagle's.

It is the desire of our Father to bless His children. His desire is to bless us with every good thing. Psalm 84:11 (ESV) "For the LORD God is a sun and shield; the LORD bestows favor and honor. No good thing does he withhold from those who walk uprightly." When we are in covenant with God we walk in the benefits of His blessing. His blessing in our life is good and perfect.

Learn to walk with the Giver of Good Things and receive from Him.

Glorious

> Psalm 76:4 (ESV) Glorious are you, more majestic than the mountains full of prey.

Glorious. This is not a word we use much these days. It may speak to the loss of fascination with God. The psalmists seem to have a way of capturing the moment with phrases that make is easy to form images in our minds. So, too, is this verse.

Glorious are You (LORD). When you live off the land, and most of your meals come from the prey you are able to capture or kill, then seeing a mountain full of prey is glorious. Then, for the psalmist to apply this image to God helps us understand that they see God as their supply.

The Hebrew word, translated "glorious" in this verse, is "or". It means, "to be luminous". It refers to the breaking of dawn; that first light that gets the day started. This is prime time for hunting. Most animals of prey start foraging at daybreak. When *Glorious* appears as the breaking of dawn in our dark moments we can see the plenteous supply that He has prepared for us to meet every need.

Another meaning of this word, "or", is to "kindle, or set on fire." When surrounded by darkness, especially in the wilderness, a fire is a most welcomed sight. *Glorious* provides the means for our "fire" to be kindled, even when our wood is wet!

Let's find a way to work this word back into our vernacular. In your times of worship see God as *Glorious*. Give Him praise for the "prey in the mountains", and the light that shines in your dark times. Give Him praise for the warmth and light you have from the fire that He has kindled in your life.

He is *Glorious*!

Glorious Lord

> Isaiah 33:21 (ESV) But there the LORD in majesty (glorious) will be for us a place of broad rivers and streams, where no galley with oars can go, nor majestic ship can pass.

The previous post dealt with the name of God, *Glorious*. Even though today's name is similar there are some differences that warrant it being separated from the previous name.

Isaiah paints a picture in the verses above by describing God as a wide or broad river. Rivers and streams are symbols of blessing. God supplies the people of Israel with living water. The word "glorious" (KJV) or "majesty" (ESV) is translated from the Hebrew word "adar", which means "wide or large; powerful." This certainly is an accurate portrayal of God. He is the *Glorious Lord*.

In the analogy of the river, Isaiah points out that the Lord, Himself, is a river. Not one that large ships can traverse, but one that provides safe passage for His people, Israel.

Israel, for the most part in Isaiah's day, was desert. The main source of fresh water was the Jordan River. The people of this day would have understood the significance and importance of a river. By ascribing to God the image of being a wide river, or *Glorious Lord*, they easily pictured Him as the provider of good things in their lives.

Look around your world, or horizons, and see if there are things to help you envision or remember the presence of God in your life. He is there! The challenge is never, "Where is God?" The challenge is, "Are we looking for Him?" Use the names or attributes given to God in scripture to help keep God in your conscious thoughts. Never let too much time pass before looking around, or inward, and acknowledge His presence in your life. The more confident we become in knowing *Glorious Lord* is with us the more we can allow His grace to manifest in our lives.

Glory

> Psalm 3:3 (ESV) But you, O LORD, are a shield about me, my glory, and the lifter of my head.

So much of Christianity today is filled with references to I, me, my, etc. It is understandable, to some extent, because of the total lack of personal relationship fostered by the Dark Ages and organized religious traditions of clergy vs. laity. However, we must never lose sight of the fact that very little of the relationship we have with God is because of us.

The psalmist, David, is using personal pronouns, but not as a means of boasting about himself. He is exalting God above himself by declaring that God is *Shield*, *Glory*, and *Lifter of My Head*. Today we will look at one of these names: *Glory*. Look at this verse in the context of the entire Psalm.

> Psalm 3:1-8 (ESV) O LORD, how many are my foes! Many are rising against me; many are saying of my soul, there is no salvation for him in God. Selah
>
> But you, O LORD, are a shield about me, my glory, and the lifter of my head.
>
> I cried aloud to the LORD, and he answered me from his holy hill. Selah
>
> I lay down and slept; I woke again, for the LORD sustained me. I will not be afraid of many thousands of people who have set themselves against me all around.

Arise, O LORD! Save me, O my God! For you strike all my enemies on the cheek; you break the teeth of the wicked. Salvation belongs to the LORD; your blessing be on your people! Selah

Notice the progression. David starts by stating what others said about him, and his relationship to God. Then he stopped and considered those words (That's the meaning of Selah). After contemplating those comments with what the psalmist knew to be true of his God he then declares, "But You, O Lord ..." It is so important to know God: His character, His nature. That is why I'm pursuing the study of His names.

David knew the protection of God (*Shield About Me*) through his experience with the lion and the bear, and the Philistine, Goliath. David knew the *Lifter of My Head* through his experience in the cave. But, what about *Glory*? The Hebrew word used here is "kabod", and means "splendor." It comes from a root word that means "weight." I believe David is speaking of character in this particular instance. Based on the comments at the heading of this psalm, it was written when Absalom, his son, was seeking to David and inherit the throne of Israel.

David rested in the security of his God (shield), encouraged by Him (lifter), and confident in what God had done inside him (glory). When we face our enemy, or when we stand face to face with our God, we need to know from where our "glory" originates. If it is not *Glory* showing then we need to spend more "selah" time. We need to allow *Glory* to work His work in us until we can confess like David, "God is my *Glory*!"

A song lyric by Brian Littrell ("In Christ Alone") says it in a way only a song can:

> In Christ alone, I place my trust
> And find my ***glory*** in the power of the Cross
> In every victory, let it be said of me
> My source of strength,
> My source of hope is Christ alone[vii]

God is my *Glory*!

God of Gods

> Joshua 22:22 (NKJV) "The LORD God of gods, the LORD God of gods, He knows, and let Israel itself know--if it is in rebellion, or if in treachery against the LORD, do not save us this day.

While looking at the verse containing Lord of Lords I discovered a name for God that had been omitted from the list. It is similar, but also very different. The name is *God of Gods*.

There are two different Hebrew words used for God. The first is "el", which means "strength or mighty, especially the Almighty." The second word is "elohim", which means "gods (plural), in the ordinary sense." The English Standard Version gives a better translation of this verse, and more clearly explains this name for God.

> Joshua 22:22 (ESV) "The Mighty One, God, the LORD! The Mighty One, God, the LORD! He knows; and let Israel itself know! If it was in rebellion or in breach of faith against the LORD, do not spare us today

The Mighty One, God, the Lord! He truly is the God of Gods!

> Deuteronomy 10:17 (ESV) For the LORD your God is God of gods and Lord of lords, the great, the mighty, and the awesome God, who is not partial and takes no bribe.

He's the Lord, your God. In order for any of this to mean anything to you He must be your God. Without a relationship He is just a god, just a lord. When you embrace Him and receive the salvation provided through Jesus Christ then He becomes *God of Gods*, and Lord of Lords. He is everything. Above Him there is none other.

The reality is that He was there before you ever acknowledged Him as being God. Once you bow your will to His will He can then act on your behalf as your God. Let Him be *God of Gods* for you today.

God With Us

1 John 1:7 (ESV) But if we walk in the light, as he is in the light, we have fellowship with one another, and the blood of Jesus his Son cleanses us from all sin.

An earlier post looked at the name for God – *Emmanuel*, which means *God With Us*. If you haven't read it, please take time to look at it when you can. Even though these names are synonymous, I felt there were more things that could be said about this name for God. *Emmanuel* speaks more to when God came to be with man in a constant fashion in the form of the Son of Man, and then the Holy Spirit. However, God has been with mankind since the beginning in different ways.

God walked in the garden (Eden) in the cool of the day. (Genesis 3:8) Enoch walked with God: and was not; for God took him. (Genesis 5:24) Abram fell on his face: and God talked with him. (Genesis 17:3) Moses talked with God. (Exodus 3) There are many, many more examples of this in scripture. Even before the Holy Spirit came to abide in us, God is with us.

Not only has He been *God With Us* from the beginning, He is also God in us, as we saw in the post about *Abba*: He breathed life into us and we became a living soul. You cannot escape God's presence. David, in Psalm 139, said, "Where shall I go from your Spirit? Or where shall I flee from your presence. (vs. 7 ESV) He even went so far as to say, "if I make my bed in hell, you are there!" (vs. 8)

We can rest assured that we are never outside of God's presence. Even if you don't believe He is there, *God With Us*! Your lack of faith does change His faithfulness. Your disobedience does not change His steadfastness. Your anemia does not diminish His mighty power. Never mistake the feeling of being alone with the fact that you are not alone.

God With Us is closer than the air you breathe. *God With Us* is that *Friend Closer Than A Brother*. *God With Us* is not just here in our now-moment. He is already preparing our next step and will be *God With Us* in our next-moment, next-day, next-year, next- …

Our challenge is to become aware of His ever-presence in our life. I highly recommend a small book by Bro. Lawrence called, "The Practice of the Presence of God." It will give practical ways of acknowledging God's presence in every moment of our lives. *God With Us*. Nothing else can be more comforting to us.

Good

Psalm 145:7 (ESV) They shall pour forth the fame of your abundant goodness and shall sing aloud of your righteousness.

Everyone that knows God describes Him as being *Good*. He is so much more than just *Good*, but goodness is a quality that draws us toward Him.

My son, Nicolas, is a magnet for children. They are drawn to him. I believe it is because he is good. His gentleness is noticeable, even by small children. If he and children are in a crowded room, the young ones always find him.

Romans 2:4 tells us that "God's goodness leads men to repent." When we realize that God is *Good*, we become willing to open our hearts and confess our shortcomings. He, in turn, speaks truth to us, freeing us from the very thing that is holding us back: shame, lack of faith, and feelings of unworthiness.

How could God love me knowing all that I've done? That is the best part! He knows exactly what we have done wrong, and loves us anyway. Not only does He love us, He is the One showing goodness to us.

When I was young I remember foraging the kitchen, looking for something sweet to eat. It must have been close to shopping day because there was nothing sweet in the house. I ran across some semi-sweet chocolate. It was chocolate, and it said "sweet". I broke off a piece and popped it in my mouth expecting Hershey Bar chocolate. Boy, was I ever wrong. It was awful.

Psalm 103:5 (ESV) who satisfies you with good so that your youth is renewed like the eagle's.

Baker's chocolate did not satisfy my mouth with good. God is not like that. When He offers good it blesses; never curses. His good always encourages; never brings you down. His good always renews; never degrades.

Open yourself up to receive *Good*. The human soul is a complex thing. When we have been hurt emotionally it causes us to "close the door" to future hurt. It's a protection mechanism. The problem is you cannot pick and choose which emotions to "close off." You wind up closing off all emotional input. Our intent is close off the bad, hurtful things, but we also close off the love that people want to show to us. This includes the love of God.

In order for us to receive the love that God has we have to be willing to open up our emotional door. This can be a difficult thing, but that is where getting to know God comes in to play. Instead of making assumptions based on what others have said about God, read the scripture and find out for yourself. God is *Good*! His mercy endures forever.

Take a chance on *Good*. He never disappoints!

Good Shepherd

> John 10:11 (ESV) I am the good shepherd. The good shepherd lays down his life for the sheep.

Another name for God is *Good Shepherd*. There are many analogies given of what it means to be a shepherd. All are very interesting and are certainly descriptive of our Father's care for us, His sheep. This verse, however, goes beyond the simple job of shepherd.

The psalm of David that is quoted more than most of the Psalms speaks about this Good Shepherd.

> Psalm 23 (ESV) The LORD is my shepherd; I shall not want. He makes me lie down in green pastures. He leads me beside still waters. He restores my soul. He leads me in paths of righteousness for his name's sake. Even though I walk through the valley of the shadow of death, I will fear no evil, for you are with me; your rod and your staff, they comfort me. You prepare a table before me in the presence of my enemies; you anoint my head with oil; my cup overflows. Surely goodness and mercy shall follow me all the days of my life, and I shall dwell in the house of the LORD forever.

David surely had a revelation of the *Good Shepherd*. He himself was a shepherd. David understood what was involved in caring for sheep. But Jesus gives us an even deeper understanding of this One known as the *Good Shepherd*: He IS the *Good Shepherd*! Look at John 10:11 again. It does not say that the good shepherd is willing to lay down his life for the sheep, but instead the

Good Shepherd lays down His life. We looked earlier at God, the Friend That Sticks Closer Than A Brother.

A shepherd is one who keeps other peoples property. Normally the shepherd is not the owner of the sheep. He is a hireling. Any shepherd worth their salt would protect the sheep in his care at any cost, including being willing to die defending them. The *Good Shepherd* was given care over people, not sheep. He did lay down His life for them ... all of them, including you.

> John 15 (ESV) Greater love has no one than this, that someone lay down his life for his friends.

God counts you as a friend, not just a sheep. He gave the best He had, His Son, Jesus, to pay the ransom to redeem us from sin and death. When you allow the *Good Shepherd* to take care of you there will not be a need that goes unmet. Know that He loves you with a love like no other. He gave all to us so we can freely give ourselves back to Him.

Gracious

> Psalm 145:8 (ESV) The LORD is gracious and merciful, slow to anger and abounding in steadfast love.

I grew up using words that I did not understand until I was much older. As it turns out, some of them weren't even real words. I'm still not really sure which direction "yonder" is in, but many things are "over yonder." Sometimes words are used as exclamations, even though they really are not intended as such. Today's name for God is one of those words.

Whenever my mom was startled she would immediately say, "Gracious!" Sometimes other words would be added, such as "Gracious alive!", or "Mercy gracious!" I am not completely certain of the meaning of these phrases, but I would have to assume they were a declaration of thanksgiving to God for being *Gracious*; because without His graciousness we would not have survived whatever calamity might have befallen us at the time.

Even though the grace of God may have been involved in us avoiding the possible destruction by our circumstances, it is not really the meaning of this word *Gracious*.

When the writer spoke of God being *Gracious* he was describing something that God does on purpose. It is part of His nature and character. God is *Gracious*. It means that He "bends down, or stoops" in kindness; to "show us favor". The remainder of Psalm 145:8 explains the motivation behind this action: God abounds in steadfast love.

Another aspect of being *Gracious* is the understanding that the "kindness or favor" is not required to be given. The "bending or stooping" is a voluntary action shown toward "an inferior." *Gracious* does not have to show us "kindness and favor." But because of His great love for us, God chose to allow His only son, Jesus, to be sacrificed so that you and I could live. The fact that we have opportunity to know the living God is due to His graciousness toward us.

Do not allow this "kindness and favor" to be of no affect in your life. Acknowledge God as your Creator, receive the freedom from death, hell, and the grave available through the Lord's death, burial, resurrection, ascension, and seating at the right hand of God; then live a life submitted to Him. All of this is available because He is *Gracious*.

Great

Psalm 145:3 (ESV) Great is the LORD, and greatly to be praised, and his greatness is unsearchable.

Great, in the Hebrew sense of the word, is anything that is "more." I think that is a very fitting name for our God. The Imperials recorded a song back in the 1970's called "More (Than You'll Ever Know)", written by Danny Lee. I know there are many similar songs that are more current, but this one means a lot to me. Look at the lyrics.

If I could find the right words to say
To tell you just what Christ means to me
I'd say He's more than I could show
And more than you'll ever know

If you could have seen me just yesterday
You'd know why He's life and He's breath to me
You'd know why He's more than I could show
And more than you'll ever know

Christ means more to me
Than you'll ever know
Christ means more to me
Than I could possibly show
More, more, so much more,
He's more than you'll ever know[viii]

Regardless of what you think God is, He is more. The psalmist declared, "His greatness is unsearchable." I can imagine this exclamation coming after many hours of trying to fathom the greatness of God. That should not be a discouragement to us from trying to comprehend it. I think many of us live far beneath our covenant with God, the *Great*, because we do not realize how really great God is!

That is one of the reasons I embarked on this study of the names. I'm challenged by the words found in Daniel 11:32b (NKJV) "… but the people who know their God shall be strong, and carry out great exploits." We need to know just how great our God is, even if we can never fully understand His greatness. The further we look into Him, the more we will be able to conform to His image.

One of the first prayers I ever learned was "the blessing" at mealtime. It was such a simple prayer, but yet profound at the same time.

> God is Great; God is Good.
> Let us thank Him for our food.
> By His hands we all are fed.
> Thank you, God, for daily bread.
> Amen.

Even though, technically, this is not a prayer (spoken about God instead of to God), it would do us well to keep these words on our tongue; maybe not these exact words, but words that express awe of our Great God, and thanksgiving to Him for our very existence. By keeping a mind set on Him, God will in turn reveal more of His character and nature to us. This will only stir us to go deeper!

Guide

Psalm 48:14 (ESV) that this is God, our God forever and ever. He will guide us forever.

As long as people have traveled they have used a guide. In the Old West they always had a point-man known as a scout, who would direct the journey and also look for potential problems before the remainder of the party was affected. They would find the easiest, safest path for those making the journey.

After the advent of the automobile maps were made to assist motorist with their travel plans. These conveniently replaced the need for a human leader, providing directions and needed information, such as rest stops, hotels, etc.

Today we have real-time GPS systems that not only provide us with turn-by-turn navigation, but also alert us to potential delays due to traffic problems or road construction. They provide estimated arrival times based on current speed limits of the roads traveled.

Long before any of these means of traveler's aid ever existed, God was known as *Guide*. Throughout scripture we see examples of this. To Abraham the *Guide* said, "Go to a land that I will show you." To Moses and the people of Israel the *Guide* promised, "I will be a pillar of cloud by day and pillar of fire by night." The psalmist describes the *Guide* by saying, "Your Word is a lamp unto my feet." The Holy Spirit was sent to be our *Guide*. There are many, many more examples.

Here's the thing: maps, GPS, or a scout will only help us if we choose to follow them. Sometimes we choose not to follow because we do not trust the information being given to us. Often the directions are contrary to our internal instincts. Other times we just don't "feel" like doing things the way they say. Regardless of the reason, not following these means of guidance will usually end in wasted effort, longer travel times, or worse: getting lost.

The following may seem an out-of-place example, but I believe it fits. There is a foolproof method to traverse any maze. It always works regardless of how complex the maze, or how large. Here's the catch: you have to know when you are entering the maze. If, when you enter a maze, place your hand on either the right wall or the left wall. Once you have made contact with it never lift your hand. Either will work, but you cannot change sides in the middle of the maze or you could wind up hopelessly lost. If you follow this simple process you will always get out of the maze. It may not be the shortest, or quickest, but it is certain that you will make it to the other side.

That really is a good metaphor for life. God gave his people a choice by declaring, "I have placed before you life and death, blessing and cursing. Choose life!" The *Guide* was trying to help us traverse this maze called life. Pick a wall. Once chosen, stay with that wall and find your destiny.

Here is the really exciting part of this particular parable. For most of us, we don't actually come to the realization that we are in a maze until we have already entered the maze. Choosing a side is no longer an option to insure our safe exit at the end of our journey. That is where the *Guide* comes to our aid. He created the maze! He knows where you are, and the best way for you to proceed to get to the best outcome possible for you. If we spend our days looking at the walls around us to try and determine our path we will wind up wasting our effort, and could actually end up in a hopeless place. That is why we need to spend our time looking up at the Guide. He will direct our steps, order our way, make our paths straight.

Just as with the other means of directional assistance (map, GPS, scout, etc.) we have to decide if we can trust the advice given to us by the *Guide*. We must choose to follow His counsel. We must develop a trust that is unwavering and follow His lead even when we do not feel like it. If we can just keep in our minds that the *Guide* loves us more than we love ourselves, and wants the best possible outcome to our lives, it will be much easier to follow His lead.

Choose today to look up! Find the *Guide*. Follow Him. Live your best life ever!

Habitation

> Psalm 91:9-10 (ESV) Because you have made the LORD your dwelling place— the Most High, who is my refuge— no evil shall be allowed to befall you, no plague come near your tent.

Habitation, or dwelling place as given in the ESV, is another name for our God. Habitation defined is this: the state or process of living in a particular place. When we choose to make God our *Habitation* we take up residence in a place where evil cannot touch us. Sickness cannot come near us. It is a place of divine refuge.

The challenge is: how do we make God our *Habitation*? Bob Sorge produced a series of messages called "Secrets of the Secret Place." Bob shares the process of getting into the secret place, of *Habitation*, of God. It is something that we have to do. Look at these words of Jesus.

> Matthew 6:6 (ESV) But when you pray, go into your room and <u>shut the door and pray to your Father who is in secret.</u> And your Father who sees in secret will reward you.

In order to abide in the secret place we have to be willing to close out everything else. (I'm not speaking of becoming a monk; even though that is the motivation that leads some to adapt this lifestyle.) Taking time for prayer where the only focus is on God, this time becomes a *Habitation* for us. While in this secret place we can find communion with God in a way like we can in no other way.

Jesus indicated there would be a reward for dwelling in the *Habitation*. Isaiah spoke of this much earlier.

> Isaiah 45:3 (ESV) I will give you the treasures of darkness and the hoards in secret places, that you may know that it is I, the LORD, the God of Israel, who call you by your name.

God has a treasure that He has reserved for those willing to mine for it in the secret place. Time spent in private with the Lord, our *Habitation*, will yield amazing returns. God promises to reveal things about Himself, His nature, His character, His secrets, if we will only make room for Him. This is the true power behind living the Christian life to which we have been called. This is how Jesus learned of His calling. It is the same way that we will learn of our calling.

Psalm 91 begins with this promise.

> Psalm 91:1-2 (ESV) He who dwells in the shelter of the Most High will abide in the shadow of the Almighty. I will say to the LORD, "My refuge and my fortress, my God, in whom I trust."

Not only will this place be a place of revelation and reward. It will also be a place of refuge and safety. This is the place where we develop our trust in our Creator. As we share our heart, and He shares His, we learn to trust Him without reserve. He, in turn, releases His treasure without reserve. This is not a bad deal! All we have to do to begin the process is close the door.

Healer

Exodus 15:26 (ESV) saying, "If you will diligently listen to the voice of the LORD your God, and do that which is right in his eyes, and give ear to his commandments and keep all his statutes, I will put none of the diseases on you that I put on the Egyptians, for I am the LORD, your healer."

Sickness is not from the Lord. It is a result of sin. When man fell in the Garden the result was eventual death. Had Adam and Eve remained in covenant with God they would have eaten from the Tree of Life and lived eternally with the Lord. But, because of disobedience to God's command to not eat of the Tree of the Knowledge of Good and Evil, mankind fell from the divine plan God had purposed for them.

The verse cited above is not the only description of God as *Healer*. This is the first of such occurrences. We see here that even though sickness upon mankind was inevitable because of sin, God was willing to prevent sickness from coming on His chosen ones; adding to it, "I am the Lord, you *Healer*."

This is actually a double blessing. If they chose to walk in covenant with God He would keep sickness from them. As New Testament Christians, we have been given a better covenant than these. For those who have been identified with Christ, and have been baptized into Him, we now live under grace. *Healer* has made available to us the privilege of walking in divine health like He intended for Adam & Eve.

The Hebrew word translated "healer" is the word *raphah*, which means "to mend, cure, make whole." It always has been, and always will be, God's nature to heal. Jesus said it best when He drew the line in the sand, and set straight any misconceptions that existed about God, and His role in our life. Jesus said, "The thief comes to steal, kill, and destroy. I have come to give you a more abundant life."

Sickness comes because of sin in the earth, not necessarily your sin. But, through Jesus, we have access to health and healing in the middle of a sinful world. Jesus bore stripes on His back for our healing. 1 Peter 2:24 (ESV) "He himself bore our sins in his body on the tree, that we might die to sin and live to righteousness. By his wounds you have been healed." Some say this is only speaking of spiritual healing. I believe salvation affects every aspect of our being: spirit, soul, and body. Jesus redeemed us completely. Our spirit has re-born by the Spirit of God. Our soul is being transformed by the renewing of our mind. Our body is "made alive again" by His Spirit.

> Romans 8:11 (ESV) If the Spirit of him who raised Jesus from the dead dwells in you, he who raised Christ Jesus from the dead will also give life to your mortal bodies through his Spirit who dwells in you.

We will still die. But, because of Jesus, the sting has been removed from death. We have the promise of life-eternal with *Healer* in heaven, but that same *Healer* has promised a life of health here on earth.

Healer of Broken Hearts

> Psalm 147:3 (ESV) He heals the brokenhearted and binds up their wounds.

One of the primary roles Jesus came to fill was that of *Healer of Broken Hearts*. One of the main results of sin is a broken heart. Our heart is hurt by actions of others. Our heart may become broken because of our own actions. Either way, the hurt is real and the solution is not trivial. Many struggle with heart issues even after being saved. Until we allow Jesus to mend our hurting heart it will remain broken.

Jesus made this declaration when he stood in the synagogue to read:

> Luke 4:18-19 (NKJV) "The Spirit of the LORD is upon Me, Because He has anointed Me To preach the gospel to the poor; He has sent Me to heal the brokenhearted, To proclaim liberty to the captives And recovery of sight to the blind, To set at liberty those who are oppressed; To proclaim the acceptable year of the LORD."

This is a passage taken from Isaiah. Here is the text as Isaiah wrote it:

> Isaiah 61:1-3 (NKJV) "The Spirit of the Lord GOD is upon Me, Because the LORD has anointed Me To preach good tidings to the poor; He has sent Me to heal the brokenhearted, To proclaim liberty to the captives, And the opening of the prison to those who are bound; To proclaim the acceptable year of the LORD, And the day of vengeance of our God;

To comfort all who mourn, To console those who mourn in Zion, To give them beauty for ashes, The oil of joy for mourning, The garment of praise for the spirit of heaviness; That they may be called trees of righteousness, The planting of the LORD, that He may be glorified."

Good news to the poor, healing of broken hearts, freedom for captives, opened eyes for the blind, removing the weight of oppression, and favor from our God. This is what our God send His Son to earth to do for us. This is so much more than just praying a prayer and attending church on Sunday. *Healer of Broken Hearts* wants to restore you in every way. This is part of the "saving of your soul" spoken of in James 1:21.

Salvation is instantaneous; our spirit is recreated in us by the Spirit of God. Salvation is a process; the saving of our soul by the renewing of our mind. Salvation is a future event; eternity in heaven.

Allow the Lord to begin a work in your life by accepting the salvation provided through Jesus in His death, burial, resurrection, ascension, and seating at the right hand of God. Allow Jesus to continue His work in you to restore your soul (heart, mind, will, emotions, etc.) back to the way God created you to be. Allow the *Healer of Broken Hearts* to mend any wounds that keep you from becoming all that God has planned for you.

Helper

> Psalm 146:5-7 (ESV) Blessed is he whose help is the God of Jacob, whose hope is in the LORD his God, who made heaven and earth, the sea, and all that is in them, who keeps faith forever; who executes justice for the oppressed, who gives food to the hungry.

Imagine the God of the universe, Creator of all things, is your *Helper*. Do you think you could accomplish any task with that kind of help? Absolutely! The psalmist calls the person "happy, or blessed" whose help is the God of Jacob. God proved Himself faithful in Jacob's life, and his forefathers Abraham and Isaac. He was a present help in time of trouble, but also an ever-vigilant help when things were going well. *Helper* is not just something God does, it is who He is!

There is a "verse" that is often quoted, but is not in the Bible: "God helps those who help themselves." It sounds good to religious ears but it has never been part of our covenant with God. None of us are capable of helping ourselves. We can never fret enough to "add an inch to our height." (Matthew 6:27) We do not know where the wind comes from, or where it goes. (John 3:8) I love the lyric from a 2nd Chapter of Acts song that says, "You don't which way the wind blows, so how can you plan tomorrow."

God did not place us on earth and then step back to see how things go for us; quite to the contrary. He promised He would never leave us or forsake us. (Hebrews 13:5) This promise leads to one of the most faith-filled statements in scripture. "So we can confidently say, "The

Lord is my helper; I will not fear; what can man do to me?" (Hebrews 13:6) The Greek word for "helper" in this verse is "boethos," which means "to call and come running."

We serve a God, *Helper*, that is actively working ahead of our path to make ready every place that we will place our feet. And then, when we do not follow the path that He has prepared, is ready to come to our aid when we need Him. He is amazing God!

Helper of the Fatherless

Psalm 10:14 (ESV) But you do see, for you note mischief and vexation, that you may take it into your hands; to you the helpless commits himself; you have been the helper of the fatherless.

I love the psalmists. They always see more than most, looking into the facets of our Creator. In the previous post we looked at God as Helper. Today is more of the same, but with a specific mission: *Helper of the Fatherless*. The Hebrew word used here for "helper" is different from the previous post. The word here is "azar" and means "to surround, protect, aid." Couple that with "yatom", the Hebrew word for "fatherless", which means, "to be lonely, or bereaved."

What could be a bigger help to the fatherless than to surround them with protection and aid. The fear of being alone is one of the strongest of human emotions. When you add to loneliness the lack of provision, and the fear of being harmed, it makes for a miserable life. Unfortunately, many face this life every day. They need us to be the hands of God, *Helper of the Fatherless*, to render aid. In addition to our material help we also need to give them the greatest gift of all: the Good News of Jesus, and the path to restored relationship with their true Father, our Lord.

There are many that want to help, but only when it's convenient. They want to help on their own terms, their own timeframe, their own methods. The fatherless are not convenient. They do not plan on becoming orphans. They have no idea how to get beyond their circumstances. The Fatherless need more than just "help", they need someone to walk them through the process of "adoption into Christ."

Helper to the Fatherless is more than just pity. He is willing to give Himself to see that the orphaned are cared for in every way, until they can become "sons and daughters" again. This transformation is one that each of us must make in order to be restored to relationship with Father God. Sin separates us from God, leaving us as spiritual orphans. God, in all of His mercy and grace, gave His Son, Jesus, making Him in effect fatherless, so that we can now be made sons and daughters of the Most High.

Let us each take on the role of *Helper of the Fatherless* so that orphaned spirits can be brought back to the family, restored to right relationship with Father, and again enjoy the blessing of home.

Hiding Place

Psalm 32:7 (ESV) You are a hiding place for me; you preserve me from trouble; you surround me with shouts of deliverance. Selah

One of the greatest joys in my life is being a father. Being a man, the most fulfilling role was to provide safety for my family. I always wanted my children to feel like they were never in danger. As they grew older it became impossible for me to protect them all the time because they started school, would go places with friends, and began living their own lives. My hope was that they had learned some things along the way that would keep them out of trouble. Regardless of the distance, they always knew they could call me any time day or night and I would be there for them.

The desire I have to keep my children safe pales in comparison to the desire of our Father, the *Hiding Place*, to make sure His children live at peace. He is a place of refuge; a safe place. The psalmist, David, clearly had experienced *Hiding Place*. David sought refuge in the Lord often. He had been delivered from trouble many times during his life. He knew the sound of the "shouts of deliverance" from Father.

David's own testimony to Saul recounted the predicaments in which he found himself. He fought a lion and a bear. He then faced Goliath, and won. He escaped from Saul on several occasions. Toward the end of his life David's own children tried to kill him to take his place as king. Each time he turned to his Refuge, the *Hiding Place*, to find shelter from those trying to harm him.

We all need to learn to rest in *Hiding Place*. When Jesus came to visit Martha and Mary, the sisters of Lazarus, Mary found a *Hiding Place* at the feet of Jesus. She sat and listened to the wisdom Jesus shared, and Mary found solace in His presence. After Lazarus died Jesus came to visit the sisters. Mary immediately resumed her position at the feet of Jesus, and again found solace.

Like Mary let us develop the habit when things are going well to spend time in *Hiding Place*. When trouble comes we have a safe harbor that is familiar, and can rest assured of the sound of "shouts of deliverance" on our behalf.

High Tower

Psalm 144:2 (ESV) he is my steadfast love and my fortress, my stronghold and my deliverer, my shield and he in whom I take refuge, who subdues peoples under me.

A "high tower" is a place of safety. In movies you often see the one being pursued ascend to the highest place in the castle. Even though they are "backing themselves into a corner," it is much easier to defend from above your opponent. Also, these places have very limited access; usually just one way up to the "high tower."

In the Old Testament, the Hebrew word "misgab" is used to refer to a place of safety; usually speaking of God, our *High Tower*. Only once is it used in the negative.

A similar word is used in the New Testament only once; the Greek word "ochyroma." In 2 Corinthians 10:4 it is interpreted "strong holds," speaking negatively about the affect of the enemy's work in our life.

I believe the reason for the disparity of thought between the Old and New Testaments is the presence of the Holy Spirit. In the OT, the Spirit of God would "come on" people, but not permanently. The Spirit would come and go as needed. In the NT the Holy Spirit comes "into" people and abide with them forever.

The Believer has *High Tower* living inside them. They never have to "run" to find shelter; simply rest in knowing we live in a state of protected presence. Instead of the Believer waging battle to get into *High Tower*, the Lord is helping us wage war against the enemy to keep him from gaining a foothold in our life.

That is a totally different paradigm. If we can get to the place were we live in *High Tower,* and not continually trying to "run" into Him, we can walk in a new level of victory, tearing down any stronghold the enemy may try to bring into our life. "The weapons of our warfare are not carnal ..." (2 Corinthians 10:4)

What are the "weapons" of the Believer?

1. Love the Lord with all of your heart, soul, mind, and strength.
2. Love your neighbor as yourself.
3. Speak the truth in love.
4. Bear the fruit of the Spirit: love, joy, peace, patience, kindness, goodness, faithfulness, gentleness, and self-control.
5. Be a conduit for the gifts of the Spirit: Word of Wisdom, Word of Knowledge, Faith, Gifts of Healing, Working of Miracles, Prophecy, Discerning of Spirits,
6. Different Kinds of Tongues, and Interpretation of Tongues.
7. Prayer.

I'm sure there are many more. Maybe that will be the next "list" that we explore. If you have thoughts on any "weapons" at the disposal of the Believer please let me know.

Holy

Leviticus 19:2 (ESV) "Speak to all the congregation of the people of Israel and say to them, You shall be holy, for I the LORD your God am holy.

The Hebrew word translated as "holy" in this verse is "gadosh," which means "sacred."

"Sacred" has several meanings in the English language, but the one more closely aligned with "holy" in scripture is "dedicated, or set apart, for God." When God first gave the law to Moses after Israel left Egypt He said, "The Levites are to be separated from the other tribes and will be a 'holy' priesthood." He made this group of people "sacred" to Him, or holy.

Later after the initial giving of law to Moses, *Holy* added something else to it. The verse cited above says, "All of Israel will be holy." This is the primary reason the sacrificial system was implemented. Sin requires the shedding of blood. Holy set up a means by which Israel could be "made holy" by the priest making sacrifice one a year to atone for their sins. Because God is *Holy* the only way we can know Him fully is to be holy. Israel could not become holy themselves. That is why *Holy* intervened.

In the same way, you and I cannot become holy through our own effort. We must rely on the provision made by *Holy* God to bring us back into right relationship with Him. Jesus Christ came as a man, lived a sinless life to become the ultimate sacrifice for sin. He died, was buried, was raised from the dead, ascended to heaven, and was seated at the right hand of *Holy* God, where He now continually intercedes for us. If we, by faith, identify ourselves with Him in every way: die to self, bury the old nature, be raised again by God creating a new spirit in us, and live our lives mindful of the One by Whom we are saved, then God considers us "holy."

We are washed clean by the blood of Jesus. We can now stand before *Holy* God unashamed, in full relationship with Him, and live our lives from the power that He provides through the Holy Spirit. All of this is made possible because we serve a "holy" God.

Holy One

Isaiah 12:6 (ESV) Shout, and sing for joy, O inhabitant of Zion, for great in your midst is the Holy One of Israel."

Holy is a common word in scripture. We looked at this name in the last post. *Holy One* is a different name altogether. "One" implies singularity; there is only one.

When Jesus was on earth He proclaimed of Himself, "I am the Way, the Truth, and the Life." "The" is also singular. The *Holy One* came down from heaven where He existed eternally as The Word, part of the Trinity: Father, The Word, and The Holy Spirit. The gospel of John describes the miraculous transformation that took Christ from being The Word to being The Son of God, "The Word became flesh and dwelt among us, and we beheld His glory, the glory of the only Begotten Son of God, full of grace and truth."

The Divine Word was transformed into human flesh to become the Son of God, Jesus Christ. He was born of a virgin, He lived a sinless life to complete His journey to be the *Holy One*, the sacrifice that would pay, once for all, the sin of man. He then rose from the dead, ascended to heaven, and now intercedes to Father for us.

There is never a doubt in scripture that when *Holy One* is mentioned they are speaking of Jesus. Let us commit our lives to living for the *Holy One* by allowing Him to live through us. We cannot, of our own effort, live a holy life. However, with the power of the *Holy One*, the Holy Spirit, living in us we can show forth the praises of

Him that lives in us. That's all Jesus asks of us. Let us represent the *Holy One* to our world.

Holy Spirit

The *Holy Spirit* appears in scripture for the first time in the second verse in the Bible. Genesis 1:2 (ESV) "The earth was without form and void, and darkness was over the face of the deep. And the Spirit of God was hovering over the face of the waters."

The Hebrew word for "Spirit" is "ruah", which means "wind, or breath (as in exhaling)". In other words, the *Holy Spirit* is the "breath" that gives voice to the Word of God. The Hebrew word for "hovering (ESV)", or "moved upon (KJV)", is "rahap", which means "brood", as a hen sits on her eggs in order for them to hatch.

So, the first picture we have of the *Holy Spirit* is that of a mother hen waiting expectantly for Father God to speak. When He does speak, it becomes the Word of God, exhaled from Father and brought into existence by the power of the *Holy Spirit*; the *Holy Spirit* is the creative force of the Godhead.

It is the Holy Spirit that would "come on" men and women of the Old Testament to empower them to accomplish the purpose set before them by Father. The *Holy Spirit* was the one sent to "inhabit" believers in the New Testament. He would create a new spirit within the souls of men that became identified with Christ through His dead, burial, resurrection, ascension, and seating at the right hand of Father; some call this being "born again."

Just as Jesus is the Holy One (we looked at that last time), the *Holy Spirit* is also singular; there is only one! He is the third person of the Trinity: Father, Son (Word), *Holy Spirit*. He is every bit God, just as the Father, but has a unique role in the life of the believer. The *Holy Spirit* was given to empower believers to be witnesses of the saving work of Jesus Christ (Son of God) in order to reconcile mankind back to Father.

There are many facets to this empowerment. These include the fruit of the Spirit:

> Galatians 5:22-23a (ESV) But the fruit of the Spirit is love, joy, peace, patience, kindness, goodness, faithfulness, gentleness, self-control; against such things there is no law.

The *Holy Spirit* also works through gifts provided to believers:

> 1 Corinthians 12:4-11 (ESV) Now there are varieties of gifts, but the same Spirit; and there are varieties of service, but the same Lord; and there are varieties of activities, but it is the same God who empowers them all in everyone. To each is given the manifestation of the Spirit for the common good. For to one is given through the Spirit the utterance of wisdom, and to another the utterance of knowledge according to the same Spirit, to another faith by the same Spirit, to another gifts of healing by the one Spirit, to another the working of miracles, to another prophecy, to another the ability to distinguish between spirits, to another various kinds of tongues, to another the interpretation of tongues. All these are empowered by one and the same Spirit, who apportions to each one individually as he wills.

The *Holy Spirit* is a Helper to the believer:

John 14:26 (ESV) But the Helper, the *Holy Spirit*, whom the Father will send in my name, he will teach you all things and bring to your remembrance all that I have said to you.

All of this is given to the believer by our Father because He loves us and wants to see us re-formed into the image of the Trinity, just as Adam was in the Garden of Eden. Allow the *Holy Spirit* to complete the process that began at salvation.

Husband

Isaiah 54:5 (ESV) For your Maker is your husband, the LORD of hosts is his name; and the Holy One of Israel is your Redeemer, the God of the whole earth he is called.

The picture of marriage is used quite often in scripture to describe the relationship Believers has with Father God. The New Testament calls Jesus the Groom and the Church His bride. The Apostle Paul admonishes the Believers in Ephesus (Ephesians 5:25) by saying, "Husbands, love your wives, even as Christ also loved the church, and gave himself for it."

This imagery can be problematic for men. But, if you can remove the sexual component of marriage from being superimposed on our relationship with Father God, the marriage relationship metaphor is quite appropriate to give us a "worldly" (not sinful, but in our world) view of how God wants to interact with the Church.

In the passage cited above Isaiah refers to the Creator as our *Husband*. This is a term that simply means, "master," such as "the husbandman of a garden (i.e. the one that tends the garden)." God is our maker and is the most qualified to be our *Husband*; the one that watches over mankind, to care for us, to help us achieve our best life.

One issue that comes into play in our current society is the dysfunctional state of relationships; husbands abusing wives, fathers abusing children, etc. If you have been a victim to this type of abuse it becomes difficult to see our God as a *Husband* or a Father. The sad truth is that when we get offended by one so close to us as a spouse or parent we tend to close the door to our emotions as a protection mechanism; to limit the hurt that others might try to inflict upon us.

The problem is that the same door that lets in hurtful relationships is the very door that God wants to bring healing. When the emotional door is shut it keeps both hurt and love from penetrating our soul. The only way the love of the *Husband* can touch the pain is to open the door, become vulnerable, and allow Him to cleanse the hurt with His perfect love. I know that sounds like a bunch of religious jargon but it is the truth.

When we allow the love of God in, the hurt and hate that has festered in our soul making us angry and bitter will be displaced, allowing the *Husband* to lead us into the life He has prepared for us. So, take a deep breath, find the key to the lock that you buried years ago, and unlock the door to your soul so that the peace of God can come in. You will never regret it.

I recommend reading "The Shack," by William Paul Young. It is a fictional book, but it describes the process of emotional healing better than any I've read. Another suggestion: find someone that can help you through the process of praying a prayer of forgiveness for those that have wronged you. It is hard, but the results are beyond comprehension.

Husbandman (Gardener)

> John 15:1 (KJV) I am the true vine, and my Father is the husbandman.

We spoke last time of God being the Husband, but today's Name of God gets more specific: *Husbandman*. Jesus gives an amazing picture of the interaction between God the Father and God the Son. Jesus is the Vine. Father is the vinedresser. If you look at other descriptions of Jesus, the Church is the Body of Christ; hence the Vine.

As we are baptized into Christ by the Holy Spirit, we are in essence grafted into the Vine by Father, who is the *Husbandman*, or Keeper, of the Vine. That is a great view of the Godhead at work, together bringing about the saving of your soul.

The *Husbandman* has many roles. First of all, He decides the location of the garden, the size of the garden, and what will be planted in the garden. Preparing the plot for the garden is tedious to assure a successful planting. Trees, rocks, and any other debris must be removed in order to allow maximum root growth and development. Proper shaping of the slopes must be designed to prevent erosion of the soil and promote water retention.

Timing is critical when planning a garden. You must understand how weather will affect each type of growth planted. The *Husbandman* has to be knowledgeable of the local climate. Selection of plants that will thrive in the local climate of the garden will produce an abundant crop. You can't plant just any kind of plant in every garden and expect a crop. The *Husbandman* knows what is best for your garden.

Another role of the *Husbandman* is to care for the garden after planting. He removes weeds that will choke out the life of the plants. He protects the garden from creatures that would damage or pillage the fruit before it has been harvested.

The ultimate goal of the *Husbandman* is to make the garden of your life as large as possible, full of every kind of plant capable of producing in your life, and allow each crop to come to full term so that many can feed from your life.

In an actual garden, the plant has no control over anything that it does. All it can is respond to the stimulus provided in its environment. It cannot decide to uproot and move to another garden. It cannot decide to yield a different fruit than that which it was created to produce. It is totally dependent upon the *Husbandman*.

We each need to learn from this imagery given by Jesus about how the Godhead wants to bring each of us to a mature, productive garden. Father, the *Husbandman*, wants to bring the fruit (of the Holy Spirit) to maturity in your life as you abide in the Vine, Jesus. Learn to be like the plant mentioned above. Submit to the *Husbandman*. Don't try to move to a different garden, or produce a different fruit. In faith, trust Him to complete in you that which He started when you became a Believer.

I Am

> Exodus 3:14 (ESV) God said to Moses, "I AM WHO I AM." And he said, "Say this to the people of Israel, 'I AM has sent me to you.'"

Moses, born a Hebrew, grew up in Egypt, then fled to Median after killing an Egyptian guard, was tending sheep for his father-in-law basically minding his own business. Out of the corner of his eye he saw something that was not normal. A bush was burning but was not being consumed. I don't know if burning bushes were normal in those days, but scripture says he noticed this one was not being consumed.

As he approached to get a closer look a voice emanated from the bush. "Take your shoes off; this is holy ground." The story continues, and as I like to say, "the Reader's Digest version," or in the more current vernacular, "Yada, yada, yada," Moses is going to deliver Israel from Egypt.

Moses had some concerns about going, each one dismissed by God, the Voice from the bush. Finally, Moses asked, "If they ask who sent me, what shall I say? What is his name?" God replied, "*I AM THAT I AM!*"

This is a very curious replay. Throughout scripture names have been used for God in Hebrew: Jehovah, Elohim, Yahweh, etc. But when asked His name, God replied "*I AM.*" The phrase in Hebrew literally means, "I will be what I will be." God indicated to Moses that whatever is needed for the moment, He is; Pillar of Fire, manna from heaven, deliverance from Pharaoh's army, water from the rock, and on and on. Whenever His people were in need He became the solution.

The same is true of Jesus in the New Testament. When the soldiers came to arrest Jesus in the Garden of Gethsemane they asked, "Are you Jesus?" He replied, "*I AM.*" When He spoke these words the soldiers were knock backward and to the ground. Jesus came to bring *I AM* to earth in the form of a man so provide redemption from sin once for all. Jesus will be whatever we need: healing, peace, strength, comfort, and on and on. Whenever a Believer is in need *I AM* becomes the solution.

Whenever you have a need call out to *I AM*, because He still is!

In All

Ephesians 4:6 (ESV) one God and Father of all, who is over all and through all and in all.

One new-age concept of God is that He is simply the existence of all things. He is the trees, animals, plants, etc. This view of God is wrong, but I could easily see how one might get this perception. God in *In All*, but those things do not make up God.

Everything that we see consists by things that do not appear. (Hebrews 11:3) God is In All things, but He is bigger than all things. The theological term for this is omnipresent. God is everywhere. Consequently, He is *In All*, but larger than all.

The most encouraging thing about this is that He is in you and me. Imagine that. The Creator of all things is in you! He is in your spouse, your children, your neighbor, your boss; everyone.

Now, that does not mean that everyone is a Christian. You become a Christian when you yield your life to the complete control of God. You do this by becoming identified with Christ in His death, burial, resurrection, ascension, and seating at the right hand of God. When you accept the forgiveness of sin provided by Jesus on the cross, you are born again. The Holy Spirit creates a new spirit in you. The same God that is *In All* becomes one with your spirit. You are now living in complete unity with Him.

The desire of Him Who is *In All* is for everyone to come into unity with Him. So our job as Christians is to share the Good News with others that they can know God personally and become one with Him. This is the purpose of the Kingdom of God: to bring everything into right relationship with God.

Infinite Understanding

Psalm 147:5 (NKJV) Great is our Lord, and mighty in power; His understanding is infinite.

There is a theoretical limit in mathematics known as infinity. It is represented by this symbol: ∞. It is considered theoretical because we can never get there. We cannot count to infinity. We can never measure infinity.

However, our God contains infinity! He has *Infinite Understanding*. Anything you can imagine God understands. This is really good news for the believer. Any circumstance you face, any problem you encounter, any plan you need to make, God understands. What is even more exciting is that He wants to share this understanding with you.

When you pray express to God exactly what is needed for the situation in which you find yourself. While working as a software consultant in Atlanta, I had the responsibility for customer support of our Manufacturing Resource Planning system. A customer reported a problem that had me working for days to find a solution. One morning during my commute to work I prayed and ask the Lord to help me solve the problem.

Almost instantly a phrase came to my mind that I do not remember ever hearing before. It was "depletion indicator". That did not mean anything to me. As soon as I arrived at the office I went to our senior consultant to find out if he knew this term. He explained to me that it was a setting found within the inventory system that had a value of "Y" or "N", and then explained what happens with each setting.

This information solved the problem for the customer. We changed the depletion indicator from "N" to "Y" and everything worked as desired. When my supervisor inquired about the problem being resolved he asked, "How did you find that?" My reply surprised him. I said, "The Lord told me." He gave me a slight smirk and said, "Well, keep praying."

God understands computers. He is the creator of all things, even when a human is used in its creation. Technology, relationships, finances, science; He knows it all. He is *Infinite Understanding*. Do not hesitate to ask complex questions of our God. Just be ready to hear the answer, because it will come!

Jealous

Exodus 34:14 (ESV) (for you shall worship no other god, for the LORD, whose name is Jealous, is a jealous God),

This particular name for God is one that troubles American Christians. The word "jealous" has a very different meaning to our Western minds. Here is the current definition:

Adjective

> 1. Feeling resentment against someone because of that person's rivalry, success, or advantages (often followed by of): He was jealous of his rich brother.
>
> 2. Feeling resentment because of another's success, advantage, etc. (often followed by of): He was jealous of his brother's wealth.
>
> 3. Characterized by or proceeding from suspicious fears or envious resentment: a jealous rage; jealous intrigues.
>
> 4. Inclined to or troubled by suspicions or fears of rivalry, unfaithfulness, etc., as in love or aims: a jealous husband.
>
> 5. Solicitous or vigilant in maintaining or guarding something: The American people are jealous of their freedom.

Biblical jealousy is different. It's root word is "zeal", which means, "fervor for a person, cause, or object;

eager desire or endeavor; enthusiastic diligence; ardor." Zealous would then mean, "full of, characterized by, or due to zeal; ardently active, devoted, or diligent."

With this understanding, we can see that God is *Jealous* for us to become all that He created us to be. God has a strong desire to see us fulfill His wonderful plan for our lives. *Jealous* is not willing to accept anything less than His best.

The context here is clear. God is not "jealous" in sense of being threatened by any of the inhabitants of the land. He was concerned that His people would mistakenly enter into covenant with an enemy, thereby causing them to be led away from the plan that He had for them. *Jealous* did not want them to look on any other image that would cause them to be drawn away from the single purpose of God's best.

God is not "jealous" of another's success or advantage. He is all-powerful; no one is greater. He does not have the capability to be suspicious or be afraid; He is God. None of the "normal" ways we perceive jealousy can be applied to God.

Jealous has only one desire for us: to be conformed to the image of His Son, Jesus. He will be satisfied with nothing less. You were created in the image of God. His desire for us to live up to the standard of His best can only be described as jealousy. But, it is based in zeal; a passion for excellence. *Jealous* wants us to live our destiny.

Jehovah
(The Self-Existent One; I AM)

There is a phrase that is rather common these days that is used to describe a person that achieved success without having it given to them by their family. People will say, "He is a self-made man." We know what is being said, but the truth is the phrase is not accurate. No one is self-made. Everyone needs other people to help them achieve whatever success they may experience.

However, we were created by One that is not self-made, but self-existent, or eternal. *Jehovah* was not created. He IS! He always has been. He always will be. If He had been created then His creator would be god. Scripture states that when God wanted to swear an oath to Abraham He had to swear by His own name, because there was no one greater. (Hebrews 6:13 (ESV) "For when God made a promise to Abraham, since he had no one greater by whom to swear, he swore by himself,")

Luke 12:25 (NKJV) And which of you by worrying can add one cubit to his stature?

Can a man be self-made? I don't think so. Can *Jehovah* be self-existent? He has to be, or He is not God at all. We looked at "I AM" a few posts back. If you didn't read it then take a minute and check it out. The real meaning of that Name of God is important to understand. The only way *Jehovah* can be I AM is for Him to be self-existent. I AM in Hebrew literally means, "I will be what I will be." Whatever God needs to be in the moment is what He is.

The only way we as humans can live, and have being, is because our life is given to us by One who is greater: *Jehovah*. That is the reason we worship Him. He is worthy. Take time today to consider Him.

Jehovah-Elohim (The Lord God)

The next series of names we will look at are some of the most familiar. I've heard many teachings of the "Ten Hebrew Names of God." As you have already seen in this study, to date we have looked at 90 names of God found in scripture. There are approximately 202 names that we will address by the time we reach the end of this series.

Today we look at one of the most common names for God found in scripture: *Jehovah-Elohim*.

> Genesis 2:4 (ESV) These are the generations of the heavens and the earth when they were created, in the day that the LORD God made the earth and the heavens.

Whenever you find "LORD" (all caps) it is the word Jehovah. When you see the phrase "LORD God" it is usually *Jehovah-Elohim*. The word Elohim means, "gods" in the ordinary sense. However, when the writers of the Old Testament wanted you to know they were speaking of the Creator, God of Heaven, they would use *Jehovah-Elohim*.

Our God is not just a god. He is THE God. He is the Supreme Being. It is interesting that God is referred to in the plural, even though He is one God. This speaks to the triune nature of the Godhead: Father, Son (Word), Holy Spirit; each one God, but three different expressions.

A few years ago in a class of the School of the Spirit, the Trinity was being discussed. The teacher of the class was trying to explain that they are three different entities, but still the same God. One of the students responded with a phrase that encapsulates this theological teaching in plain English: "They're all God, but they ain't each other." That is a simple, yet profound, truth.

Jehovah-Elohim is typically used for emphasis. This may not have happened in your household, but when my mother meant business, instead of simply calling for me using my first name, she would couple it with my middle name. "Dudley Mack," meant come now or else. If the last name was ever invoked you were in big-time trouble.

It is interesting that in heaven, according to John the Revelator's story in the Book of Revelation, the elders around the throne refer to God as "Lord God Almighty." You can't get any more emphatic than this.

Let's give God praise as the Supreme God that He is, *Jehovah-Elohim*.

Jehovah-Jireh
(The Lord Will Provide)

Genesis 22:14 (ESV) So Abraham called the name of that place, "The LORD will provide"; as it is said to this day, "On the mount of the LORD it shall be provided."

When I first encountered the "Ten Hebrew Names for God," I made an assumption that these names each appear multiple times in scripture. I was very surprised not long ago to find that most only appears one time in scripture. Such is the case with this name: *Jehovah-Jireh*, which means, "The Lord will see to it." In the hay-day of the Charismatic movement this name appeared in songs, and was the topic of many sermons on Biblical Prosperity.

The name does mean "God will provide," but I feel to base an entire theology of finances on this one verse is a bit overstepping proper exegesis (interpretation of scripture). The name appears in the story of Abraham, as he was on his way to sacrifice the promised son, Isaac. If you're not familiar with the story you can read it in Genesis 22. As Abraham raised the knife to kill his own son, an angel stopped him. Abraham then looked over and saw a ram whose horns were caught in a thicket. The ram was then used as the sacrifice instead of Abraham's son, Isaac.

Abraham responded by naming the place *Jehovah-Jireh*: The Lord will provide. This does not have anything to do with prosperity. Abraham was a rich man. This does, however, speak to God's provision coming to us when we are obedient to His will. Everything we have need of is found in pursuing God's will for our life.

Larry Stockstill was speaking to a gathering at his church in Bethany World Prayer Center in Baker, LA. His topic was evangelism and missions. He encouraged churches that seemed to struggle finances. His counsel to them was this: "Everything you have need of is in the harvest." Winning souls will bring people into the Kingdom, and into your church. Along with those people will come giftings needed for ministry, finances for the mission, and eventually disciples to be sent out to complete the cycle.

Jehovah-Jireh is not an ATM. He is our provision. His ultimate provision came in the form of His own Son, Jesus. Just like Isaac, you and I should have been the sacrifice to pay for our sin. But like the ram, Jesus became the substitute sacrifice so that you and I could live. That is good news!

Now, through Him, *Jehovah-Jireh*, we have everything we need.

Jehovah-M'kaddesh (The Lord Who Sanctifies)

This name for God appears seven times in three chapters of Leviticus. Jehovah-M'kaddesh means "The Lord Who Sanctifies." When we think of the word "sanctify" we typically think of being cleansed, or forgiven, of sin. There is, however, a difference between being cleansed and being found clean.

I remember when our children were small bath time was a major ordeal. As the boys got older they were allowed to bathe themselves. Our second born was an expert at making it appear he had bathed. His mistake the amount of time he spent in the tub. He could bathe in about 2 minutes! We caught on to his trick of wetting his hair and declaring himself clean. He forgot that he still stunk.

When Jehovah-M'kaddesh completes His work in us we don't just have a wet head! He makes us so that we are found clean. His cleansing is absolute. There's no dirt left behind the ears (I've never actually understood why moms check behind your ears for dirt) or any scent of sweat. We are clean. Just like the three Hebrew boys saved from the fire, we don't even have the smell of the world on us any more.

The unfortunate part is that all of this cleansing occurs in our spirit, the part recreated by God when we are born again. The reason it is unfortunate is that we are still left with a soul (mind, will, emotions) that have to be renewed. Our soul is not re-born like our spirit. That is the reason Jehovah-M'kaddesh gives us the Holy Spirit. He helps us fight the battle with our soul, to bring it into submission to God's plan and purpose; to help us become conformed to the image of Christ Jesus, our Lord.

When we get the revelation that Jehovah-M'kaddesh has made us clean we can stop trying to act clean. We ARE clean. We are not dirty rotten sinners saved by grace. We were dirty rotten sinners, but now we are saved, by grace. There is a huge difference in those two statements. If you never get the revelation that you were made clean you will never see yourself becoming like Christ. That is the goal of every Believer. That is God's desire for everyone.

So, take your rest today, if you are a Believer, in knowing that you have been made clean by Jehovah-M'kaddesh, and He cleans to the uttermost!

Jehovah-Nissi
(The Lord Our Banner)

Exodus 17:15 (ESV) And Moses built an altar and called the name of it, The LORD Is My Banner,

This Hebrew name for God, *Jehovah-Nissi*, only appears one time in scripture. After seeing the Lord deliver Israel against Amalek he built an altar and named it "The Lord Is Our Banner." Banners, or flags, were used in battle to help communicate to the soldiers what they should do. If the one carrying the banner was injured, or worse, someone else would quickly step in to ensure the banner remained visible.

If you remember the story from Exodus, as Joshua led the army into battle, Moses, Aaron, and Hur went up on a hill to observe the conflict. Moses was instructed of the Lord to raise his rod up over his head. While the battle was raging, as long as Moses kept the rod (which the Lord had anointed when He called Moses) raised, Joshua and Israel prevailed.

However, Moses grew tired and had to drop his arms. When the rod was lowered Amalek began to take ground. Two men, Aaron (the high priest, representing worship ministry) and Hur (a Levite responsible for erecting and dismantling the Tabernacle when it was moved, representing helps ministry), went to assist Moses. They sat Moses on a rock and each man held one of Moses' arms to insure the rod remained raised. Israel, led by Joshua, destroyed Amalek.

After the battle Moses received instruction from the Lord to write these events down and rehearse them in the ears of Joshua so he will never forget that the Lord helped in the fight, and that He would "blot out the memory of Amalek from under heaven."

Moses responded by building an altar to the Lord, named it *Jehovah-Nissi*, and made this declaration.

Exodus 17:16 (ESV) saying, "A hand upon the throne of the LORD! The LORD will have war with Amalek from generation to generation."

"A hand upon the throne" indicated that God swore upon Himself (because there is no one higher). The next phrase is one that gives us God's intention for spiritual leadership. We must ensure that each generation has the understanding to allow God to fight the battles for us. We must pass the "banner" (or rod (God's anointing)) to those coming behind us. *Jehovah-Nissi* knew that Amalek would return and would continue trying to revenge this defeat to every generation.

Moses started the process by passing it from himself to Joshua (the next generation). It now falls upon each of us to ensure that we instruct the next generation regarding *Jehovah-Nissi's* presence in our life, and train them in the ways of warring against the enemies of God. Let's each do our part in raising the banner high so that others can clearly follow the battle plan God has given.

Jehovah-Rapha (The Lord Who Heals)

Exodus 15:26 (ESV) saying, "If you will diligently listen to the voice of the LORD your God, and do that which is right in his eyes, and give ear to his commandments and keep all his statutes, I will put none of the diseases on you that I put on the Egyptians, for I am the LORD, your healer."

This name for God, *Jehovah-Rapha*, also only appears one time in scripture. It is introduced at a rather odd time, considering the circumstances. The people of Israel came to a place with bitter water. As was their usual initial reaction, they began to complain to Moses. Moses' first response was to go to the Lord.

The Lord, as He always does, had a solution to the problem. He showed Moses a tree and told him to throw it into the water. The water became sweet, drinkable. The Lord then gives the people of Israel a revelation into another aspect of His character, His nature. The Lord promised them He would never place any of the diseases on them that had been placed on the Egyptians, because He is *Jehovah-Rapha*, the Lord Who Heals.

What does turning bitter water into sweet have to do with God being our Healer? Clearly the two being mentioned in basically the same breath makes it apparent the Lord thinks they are closely tied together.

When you examine the Hebrew words more closely you see something that might help us understand what *Jehovah-Rapha* is trying to communicate. I believe our current culture has again jaded our understanding of the word "heal." The Hebrew word "raphah", translated "heals" actually means, "to mend (by stitching), to cure (cause to) heal, repair, make whole." Every meaning except "heal" has an implication of a process rather than event. Instead of instantaneous healing, perhaps it more appropriate to say, "The Lord Who Causes Us to Recover."

In this story of Israel at Marah, couldn't God have instructed Moses to place his rod in the water? Or, perhaps, God could have had Moses lift his rod over the waters? The reality is God could have had Moses do anything, including nothing, to make the water drinkable. He is God!

It is possible that God wanted to demonstrate to His people that He could bring about a cure in them through "natural" means. Consider this:

Moringa oleifera

One of the most remarkably useful trees is one being cultivated heavily for use in the Sudan. The Food and Agriculture Organization of the United Nations said that village women had successfully used the tree Moringa oleifera to cleanse the highly turbid water of the River Nile. After trying other moringa species in Egypt, Namibia, Somalia, and Kenya, they too have shown properties that clarify water quickly.

When moringa seeds are crushed and poured into a pot or bottle of dirty water, the water turns transparent within seconds. The seeds' anti-bacterial properties can turn low, medium, and high turbidity waters into tap-water quality in an hour or two.

Studies on the effectiveness of moringa seeds for treating water have been done since the 1970s, and have consistently shown that moringa is especially effective in removing suspended particles from water with medium to high levels of turbidity (muddiness or dirtiness).[ix]

What if this is the tree that God "showed" Moses? What if the water turned from bitter to sweet without any "miraculous" input from God? Does that make it any less a miracle? Consider Naaman (told to wash in the Jordan seven times to cure leprosy); Jesus - spit on the ground, made mud, and told the man to go wash and be healed; ten lepers – told to go show themselves to the priest (all were cleansed). These were not "instantaneous" healings, but the end result was they all recovered. God brought about a cure to each one.

As we saw in an earlier post, God is I AM. He will be whatever He needs to be. It's no problem for God to heal instantly, just as He could have instantly cleaned the water at Marah. But the more I learn of God's character and nature I realize that He is a God of process. Why take six days to create the universe, when one word could have made the whole thing?

Please do not think I have moved away from my charismatic theology. I still believe in laying hands on the sick and praying for healing. However, think about the verse where we get the phrase, "lay hands on the sick." The rest of that verse says, "... they will recover." It does not say they will instantly be made whole. This does not dilute my faith in God's ability to heal, or His desire to heal. He is *Jehovah-Rapha*, The God Who Causes Us to Recover. If anything it gives me reason to rejoice because God does not change.

Whatever the reason for "healing" the water at Marah and God's promise of no diseases being connected, we can be sure that *Jehovah-Rapha* can handle any situation we face. All we have to do is listen for His instruction and then follow it.

Jehovah-Rohi
(The Lord My Shepherd)

Rohi is a variant spelling of Raah. I'm not sure why Rohi became the preferred name in the list of Hebrew names for God. I just mention it here for the sake of complete disclosure.

> Psalm 23:1 (ESV) The **LORD is my shepherd**; I shall not want. (*Jehovah-Rohi*)

The name for God, *Jehovah-Rohi*, only appears one time in scripture. A similar name for God is found in other places in scripture.

> Genesis 48:15 (ESV) And he blessed Joseph and said, "The God before whom my fathers Abraham and Isaac walked, the **God who has been my shepherd** all my life long to this day, (Elohim-Rohi)

In Psalm 23 we see the heart of the Shepherd revealed through the pen of a shepherd. David wrote the 23rd Psalm from the revelation he had received while tending the sheep that God had entrusted to him. Even though he was king of Israel he never stopped allowing Jehovah-Rohi from being his Lord. Much earlier we see one of David's forefathers making the same declaration. When Jacob (or Israel as he was later called) had not heard the name Jehovah. God revealed that to Moses and the Hebrew nation that bore his name, Israel. (Exodus 6:3 (ESV) I appeared to Abraham, to Isaac, and to Jacob, as God Almighty, but by my name the LORD I did not make myself known to them.) Jacob knew his Shepherd as Elohim.

Regardless of the name by which they knew Him, God showed Himself to be One that cared for those with whom He has relationship. His heart is to Shepherd.

There are many good books on this subject so I will not try to fully describe the role of the shepherd, but the short version is this: sheep are relatively helpless, much like a human baby. They have to be led to pasture, to water, and protected from predators. *Jehovah-Rohi* is a good shepherd.

Take time to read Psalm 23. Let the words sink in as you imagine each phrase being the character and nature of God. You will know why David and Jacob both chose Shepherd as the way they describe their God; Jehovah or Elohim doesn't matter. He is still *Rohi*, or Shepherd.

Jehovah-Sabaoth (Lord of Hosts)

1 Samuel 1:3 (ESV) Now this man used to go up year by year from his city to worship and to sacrifice to the LORD of hosts at Shiloh, where the two sons of Eli, Hophni and Phinehas, were priests of the LORD.

The name we look at this time is almost in direct contrast to the last one of the "Jehovah" names for God. Previously we dealt with Jehovah-Rohi: The Lord Is My Shepherd. That is a very personal name. Even though everyone can call Him Jehovah-Rohi, it still implies a one-on-one relationship.

The name we consider today is Jehovah-Sabaoth: The Lord of Hosts. Hosts describes a multitude; a mass of people. God is the God of one, but He is also the God of many, all at the same time. This title for God appears in both the Jehovah and Elohim forms about 285 times in scripture. It is the most common of the "Jehovah" names. That really makes sense, because God is the God of the people. He came to redeem all of mankind. That is quite a large number of folks.

This also implies that Jehovah-Sabaoth is familiar with every walk of life; rich/poor, male/female, black/white/yellow/brown/red/and every shade in between, white/blue collar, educated/simple. He can identify with the "multitude" because He created them. One of the top priorities with God is relationship. After creating man, God came and "walked with them in the cool of the day." He appeared to individuals time and again, but would also display His mighty acts before many.

Another name we considered earlier in this study was Captain of the Hosts. I believe this to be Jesus Christ, the Messiah. He leads the Hosts of Jehovah. This should give us great comfort in knowing that God is able. He has a host that He commands to do His bidding. God calls us with a calling and has everything needed to ensure that we are able to accomplish it.

Let's fall into ranks and take our place in the Hosts of Heaven, behind our Savior, Jesus, and get to work with Jehovah-Sabaoth as He directs us.

Jehovah-Shalom (The Lord Our Peace)

Judges 6:24 (ESV) Then Gideon built an altar there to the LORD and called it, The LORD Is Peace. To this day it still stands at Ophrah, which belongs to the Abiezrites.

Here again is a name for God, *Jehovah-Shalom*, that only appears one time in scripture. There's a clear pattern to these "unique" names. Each one is given to an individual that either has faced, or is facing, a major circumstance in their life.

Gideon was approached by an "angel" that gave him an unusual proposition. He was called to deliver Israel from Midian bondage. Gideon was very apprehensive by the proposal. He asked the "angel" for a sign, to give him a feeling of certainty that what he was hearing was real. He referred to the "angel" as Lord. I believe this was a pre-incarnate visitation of Jesus, known as The Word (John 1:1) in heaven.

The Angel did as Gideon requested. The sacrifice Gideon prepared was placed on a rock, and then it was consumed by fire that came up from the rock. Being convinced he had witnessed a "sign" Gideon proclaimed, " I have seen the angel of the Lord face to face." They Lord then said, "Peace be to you."

Gideon built an altar and named it *Jehovah-Shalom*: The Lord Is Peace. Gideon found a peace that would sustain him through many trying times. After this encounter he knew the Lord, *Jehovah-Shalom*, was with him.

As Christians we have this promise.

> Philippians 4:7 (ESV) And the peace of God, which surpasses all understanding, will guard your hearts and your minds in Christ Jesus.

This stems from a promise that Jesus gave before He ascended to heaven to be seated at the right hand of Father. He said, "John 14:27 (ESV) Peace I leave with you; my peace I give to you. Not as the world gives do I give to you. Let not your hearts be troubled, neither let them be afraid."

One of the most important benefits to the Holy Spirit's indwelling the spirit of the Believer is peace. God's presence gives us the ability to rest, knowing that He has everything under control.

If you have never encountered *Jehovah-Shalom* then now is the time; today is the day of salvation. Identify with the death of Jesus on the cross where He shed His blood for our forgiveness. Identify with His burial and resurrection, then subsequent ascension and seating by Father. Once you are born again the Holy Spirit comes to live in you. This is Peace!

Jehovah-Shammah (The Lord Is Present)

> Ezekiel 48:35 (ESV) The circumference of the city shall be 18,000 cubits. And the name of the city from that time on shall be, The LORD Is There."

With the last word Ezekiel penned when describing Jerusalem he gave it a new name: *Jehovah-Shammah* – The Lord Is Present. It's the only time the name appears in scripture.

Jerusalem is where Israel was instructed to build the temple. It's where the Ark of the Covenant was housed. It's where the glory of God dwelt.

Things have gone full circle with mankind pertaining to the presence of God. After Adam and Eve sinned, shame drove them away from God's presence.

> Genesis 3:8 (ESV) And they heard the sound of the LORD God walking in the garden in the cool of the day, and the man and his wife hid themselves from the presence of the LORD God among the trees of the garden.

Imagine walking with God! Adam and Eve were in complete union with *Jehovah-Shammah*. They dwelled in His presence! That had to be an amazing feeling; to stand before the Creator without any reservations. There was nothing between them. Each one able to fully express to the other the love they had, and to be totally open and honest about everything.

Then sin came. And so did the hiding. Adam and Eve experienced shame for the first time and caused them to flee from the *Jehovah-Shammah*. God was still there. They were not. From that event until the cross God was working a plan to get mankind back to a place where they could walk with Him once again.

However, in between The Garden and The Cross, man was left outside of God's presence because of sin.

> Exodus 33:20 (ESV) But," he said, "you cannot see my face, for man shall not see me and live."

The reason was sin. When The Law was given to Moses God devised a plan to where He and man could come together. The Law was given to make man aware of the need for atonement of sin. The entire religious system that The Law created was simply to show man that God wanted to be with them, but it had to be on His terms.

The Lord God began to speak through His prophets of the solution to man's problem of separation from Him.

> Isaiah 7:14 (ESV) Therefore the Lord himself will give you a sign. Behold, the virgin shall conceive and bear a son, and shall call his name Immanuel.

The meaning of the name Immanuel is, "God With Us". We looked at this name previously using the spelling found in the New Testament: The Names of God – Emmanuel. Go back and read that on if you've not read it yet. Isaiah spoke of a time when God would once again be "with" His people. The Angel shared this with Joseph when prophesying the birth of Jesus through Mary. It was a promise Joseph longed to see fulfilled. I'm sure his heart melted to hear that he would be a part of bringing Messiah to the earth.

Fast forward to Jerusalem. The temple was built to house the Ark of the Covenant. God's presence was there because of the Mercy Seat that sat atop the Ark. That is where Grace and Mercy met sin and death. The priest would apply the blood to the Mercy Seat and God would forgive Israel's sin. So in Ezekiel's description of Jerusalem he described it as *Jehovah-Shammah*: The Lord Is Present. And under The Law, that was the only place His "presence" was found.

All of that changed at The Cross. When Jesus died as the Perfect Sacrifice, He forever dealt with the issue of sin keeping us from God's presence. The veil of the temple that hid the Ark of the Covenant, and the presence of God, was torn into, revealing the presence of God to all who would come. Now, through Jesus' atonement, we can once again "walk with God in the cool of the day." He is still *Jehovah-Shammah*. His presence is now with the Believer always. We can now have open fellowship with Him and experience His love fully, without shame, because we have been washed clean by Christ.

Thank you, Lord, that you are here!

Jehovah-Tsidkenu
(The Lord Our Righteousness)

> Jeremiah 23:6 (ESV) In his days Judah will be saved, and Israel will dwell securely. And this is the name by which he will be called: 'The LORD is our righteousness.'

The last of the "Jehovah" names for God is *Jehovah-Tsidkenu*: The Lord Our Righteousness. This is a prophetic name used in reference to a Righteous Branch that would come from David to reign as King. This is none other than Jesus Christ!

As we saw in a previous name, Jehovah-M'kaddesh (The Lord Who Sanctifies), it the God who makes us clean. It only by the blood of Jesus that we can be cleansed of sin that was in our nature when we were born. *Jehovah-Tsidkenu* then comes to make return us into right standing with God. He stands in our place when judgment tries to come against us. Whenever a charge is brought against a Believer, *Jehovah-Tsidkenu* pronounces us innocent.

As we dwell with Him in this place of absolute acceptance we enjoy the fellowship with our Father. He can speak to our hearts the truth of Who He is, and also the truth about who we are in Him. Once you have been identified with Christ in His death, burial, resurrection, ascension, and seating at the right hand of Father, you have been baptized into Christ by the Holy Spirit. Now, as far as the Lord is concerned, when He looks at you He sees Jesus, *Jehovah-Tsidkenu*: The Lord Our Righteousness.

This is why Paul could write the following: Galatians 2:20 (ESV) I have been crucified with Christ. It is no longer I who live, but Christ who lives in me. And the life I now live in the flesh I live by faith in the Son of God, who loved me and gave himself for me.

That is a great place to be; covered by Righteousness.

Jesus

Matthew 1:21 (ESV) She will bear a son, and you shall call his name Jesus, for he will save his people from their sins."

I couldn't believe it. As I was working through the "R"s on the Names of God list, it suddenly occurred to me that the name *Jesus* was omitted. How could that be?

Then a few thoughts came to me. First of all, it is the most familiar name for God that we know. Every thing from lullabies to epic movies has the name of *Jesus* in them.

Secondly, it is also a name that many avoid because the mere mention of the name evokes a response. For Believers it triggers gratitude. For non-believers it brings conviction. For others it brings anger because of the hardness of their heart.

C. S. Lewis summed up men's response to *Jesus*. He said, "He is either Lord, liar, or lunatic." *Jesus* is either the Son of God as He claimed, a liar for making such a claim, or a lunatic that has no idea what he is saying. "But," as Lewis continued, "You cannot call Him just a good man."

You can speak of "God" to most people and they will politely oblige your conversation, but when you mention Jesus their heart is almost certainly revealed in their response.

We just completed the Christmas season where you see and hear more of the name of *Jesus* than at any other time (at least in the Western culture). It is after all, the time we celebrate His birth. But *Jesus* is so much more than a baby in a manger. Even the name Mary was told to give Him at His birth implied there was much more to this child than any before Him.

Since the fall of man in the Garden of Eden, God had been working a plan of redemption; a way to bring man back into a right relationship with his Creator. The one that would "crush the head of the serpent" became a baby in a manger; helpless, vulnerable, the embodiment of God's love. His name, however, caused satan and his kingdom to fear. The Second Adam had been born. The Second Joshua had come to deliver God's people (this time all of them) from the grasp of sin and darkness that kept them in bondage.

Jesus. His name is from the Hebrew word interpreted as "Joshua," and means, "Jehovah-saved." The first Joshua completed the journey of Israel out of bondage from Egypt to Canaan. The Second Joshua, *Jesus*, paid the penalty for sin and gave mankind a way to escape the second death.

Call out to Him now. Receive the forgiveness provided through the death, burial, resurrection, ascension, and seating of *Jesus*. Identify yourself with Him in baptism. Receive the Gift He sent to abide in us until He returns: the Holy Spirit. You life will never be the same.

Judge

> Genesis 18:25 (ESV) Far be it from you to do such a thing, to put the righteous to death with the wicked, so that the righteous fare as the wicked! Far be that from you! Shall not the Judge of all the earth do what is just?"

This post brings us to the halfway point on the journey to explore all the Names of God mentioned in scripture. The list stands at 202 different names. The list has actually expanded during this study. Hopefully it will continue to expand as we delve deeper into our discovery of how wonderful our God truly is, and allow our minds to be stretched beyond our preconceived ideas of who He is. Now, for today's name.

Judgment. It's a word that brings very mixed emotions. To the one who is guilty, judgment is not welcomed; he cries for mercy. To the one who has been wronged judgment is something longed for in order to right the wrong. The character of the judge determines whether a fair verdict is rendered.

This name for God, *Judge*, causes many to cower in fear at the thought of God passing judgment on them. After all, God knows everything. We know that we are guilty. Therefore, God will have to rule with a guilty verdict and sentence us to death. In this passage, and others, in describing God as Judge, the writer states that He will "do what is just."

Here is the reality. God cannot overlook sin. It must be judged, and the penalty for disobeying The Law of God is death. However, because God is also Loving and

Merciful, He provided a way of escape from the harsh penalty of The Law. The fact is, the only reason God gave The Law was to show mankind that they could never be good enough to appease Him by human effort. We do not have the capability of performing at a level worthy to be called Righteousness.

As we saw in a previous post, The Lord Is Our Righteousness. In order to accomplish this in our lives there had to be payment for the penalty for sin. Sin cannot, and will not, go unpunished. Here is the plan God devised. He would come to earth as a man (not as God, but human in the form of Jesus), live a perfect life as a man (empowered by the Holy Spirit), and then die in our place on the cross (as a man, shed human blood) and pay the price for sin once for all.

All that remains for us to have this payment applied to our account is to become identified with Jesus Christ, in His death, burial, resurrection, ascension, and seating at God's right hand. This is called Salvation. It results in our being made right with God concerning our sins against His Law, and removes the penalty of death (spiritually) from the sentence that will handed down on Judgment Day.

God is the *Judge*, and He will *Judge*. He must *Judge* every person. For those who have been identified with Christ (saved) will be spared the punishment that we deserve, and will be granted mercy instead. This is truly the act of a *Righteous Judge*.

Judge of the Widows

> Psalm 68:5 (KJV) A father of the fatherless, and a judge of the widows, is God in his holy habitation.

We just saw in the previous post that God is also Judge. In Psalm 68:5 God is referred to in a specific role: Judge of the Widows. The word used for "judge" in this case is the Hebrew word "dayyan", which means "judge or advocate." It is derived from another Hebrew word "din", which means, "rule, or judge; also to strive, contend, execute judgment."

I believe the meaning is quite clear. As Judge, God will execute judgment on all mankind. However, in this case He is acting as an advocate on behalf of the widows, unlike the "unjust judge" mentioned in Luke 18:1-5.

> Luke 18:2-5 (ESV) He said, "In a certain city there was a judge who neither feared God nor respected man. And there was a widow in that city who kept coming to him and saying, 'Give me justice against my adversary.' For a while he refused, but afterward he said to himself, 'Though I neither fear God nor respect man, yet because this widow keeps bothering me, I will give her justice, so that she will not beat me down by her continual coming.'"

This is not a parable about our Father God, Jehovah. He is not unjust in any way. Jesus gave this parable to show how much more grace and mercy God would show toward the widow than this unjust judge showed. The unjust judge only relented and gave in to her request because she was persistent. God, the Righteous Judge will vindicate the widow because He loves them and has promised to care for them.

It is amazing how in our society so many take advantage of the widow. They are overcharged for car repair, home repair, or tricked out of their money through various schemes. Unfortunately, this is not a new phenomenon. That is the reason God gave commands to care for the widows; first to the people of Israel and then to the Church.

God commanded the Church to care for the widows in 1 Timothy 5. James states it even more clearly by saying, "Religion that is pure and undefiled before God, the Father, is this: to visit orphans and widows in their affliction, and to keep oneself unstained from the world. James 1:27 (ESV)"

The *Judge of the Widows* steps in when necessary to make sure that their cause is heard, and that their welfare is assured.

Just

Isaiah 45:21 (NKJV) Tell and bring forth your case; Yes, let them take counsel together. Who has declared this from ancient time? Who has told it from that time? Have not I, the LORD? And there is no other God besides Me, A just God and a Savior; There is none besides Me.

The modern definition of the word "just" has lost something from when the Hebrew word "saddiq" was used in reference to God.

Modern definition:
Just - based on or behaving according to what is morally right and fair.

Hebrew definition:
Saddiq – from the root word sadaq; to be right; to make right.

God does not simply behave according to what is morally right and fair. His behavior is the standard by which "just" is measured. He is a Just God. There is no one else that can be compared to Him.

In many types of measurements there are exact standards by which things are governed. Every country has a set of Standard Weights and Measurements by which trade is conducted. It is designed to make things fair for everyone involved, but mostly to protect the consumer from unscrupulous acts of vendors.

However, in anything other than weights and measures the process of measurement becomes a little less precise. It then falls to the standard of "best practices," such as accounting procedures or manufacturing processes. This is somewhat subjective because it is left up to interpretation as to how to apply these "best practices" to every situation. A few decades ago there was an international effort to try to standardize EVERYTHING, called ISO 9000. Governments jumped on board and started refusing to do business with anyone that was not ISO 9000 compliant.

I worked for 2 such companies, both of which became ISO 9000 compliant while I was employed. I understand the process and the purpose for the process. Here is a simplified version.

1. Define with precision how you complete every process in your company.
2. Devise methods to measure the accuracy by which you complete the processes.
3. Track your success rate of compliance.
4. Adjust the definition of the process, or the way in which it is measured, when necessary to ensure continued compliance.

Bottom line: ISO 9000 was smoke and mirrors to be able to continue to obtain government and private contracts for goods and services. It was "the emperor's new clothes" all over again. There were advantages to completing the certification, but these were simply unplanned side-affects from the main objective.

"Why did you say all of that?", you may ask. Simple. Without an independent standard by which to measure, all measurements become meaningless. When you "self-impose" standards then you are simply justifying your actions as being "right."

God, Himself, is Just. He has not been found "compliant" to some arbitrary set of rules or regulations. He is the standard by which everything else is measured. Because there is no one His equal, there is nowhere to look for an alternative standard. There is no cosmic ISO 9000 so we can conceive our own set of operating procedures. We must use the measures given by our Just God in order to know if we are making progress. Just gave us His guide for us to use. His name is Jesus.

God's desire for every human is for us to become conformed to the image of Jesus Christ. With the help of the Holy Spirit we can renew our minds (soul) to think like Jesus, act like Jesus, and be like Jesus. Anything else falls short of the Just measure of God.

Keeper

Psalm 121:5 (ESV) The LORD is your keeper; the LORD is your shade on your right hand.

According to Miriam-Webster, the definition of "keeper" is, "a person whose job is to guard or take care of something or someone; something or someone that is worth keeping; something or someone that is good, valuable, etc."

The Hebrew word "shamar" from which we get "keeper" means, "to hedge about (as with thorns), i.e. guard; generally to protect, attend to, etc." Previously we considered the name for God of Husbandman. I believe this name, *Keeper*, certainly is applicable. God not only created us, He is always actively "keeping" us as we learn to walk with Him.

Keeper is not a jail cell attendant. He is more like the Secret Service. The Secret Service goes ahead of the president to scope out potential threats that might endanger him. They pursue any information that implies intent to harm the president. They travel with the president to assure his safety at all times. The Secret Service does not limit the activity of the president, but is there to assist in keeping him safe at every turn. This describes *Keeper* somewhat, but there is no way the Secret Service or any other human attempt could replicate our God's ability to "keep" us.

Psalm 139:5 (ESV) You hem me in, behind and before, and lay your hand upon me.

In addition to safety, our God, *Keeper*, sees to our wellbeing, making certain that we are cared for emotionally, spiritually, and in every other way imaginable.

When you become a Believer through being identified with Christ you also acknowledge the Keeper's role in your life. Through Christ, by the leading of the Holy Spirit, you will be directed into an abundantly fulfilling life with God, our *Keeper*. Learn to rest in Him. He cares for you.

King of All the Earth

Psalm 47:7 (ESV) For God is the King of all the earth; sing praises with a psalm!

King of All the Earth! That has been the desire of men since The Fall in the Garden. Once man realized they were separated relationally from God because of sin, they have set out to become a god. The sad truth is that regardless of the "success" they have in their quest they will never overtake the One that still rules and reigns: *The King of All the Earth*.

Nero came close. Rome ruled most of the known world. Napoleon tried. Hitler tried. Islam is now trying! Regardless of their success God still reigns Supreme. If man would submit to the lordship of Christ, allow our hearts to be changed from stone to flesh, allow our minds to be renewed to the Gospel of Jesus, and prefer one another in the love of God, we would be able to live at peace under our God's rule.

Because God is *King of All the Earth* He is worthy to receive our worship. As the psalmist put it, "sing praises with a psalm." Our lives should be a praise to Him that loves us.

I had a conversation with some folks this week on this subject. Paul, in his letter to the Ephesian Church, gave this command.

Ephesians 1:12 (ESV) so that we who were the first to hope in Christ might be to the praise of his glory.

"Be to the praise of His glory." That is a daunting task. What about command he gave to the Church at Thessalonica?

> 1 Thessalonians 5:17 (ESV) pray without ceasing,

Consider that. How can you pray without ceasing? The *King* is certainly worthy of our unending attention. Here is how I have come to terms with these two verses. I believe that all praise is prayer, but not all prayer is praise. Given this, then if we live our lives as praise to God (i.e. "be to the praise of His glory") then we are living our lives as a prayer to Him (i.e. unceasing prayer). We don't have to agree on this to have fellowship together. It's just where I've come to on the subject.

Because we live as Sons and Daughters of the *King of All the Earth* we have privileges in the Kingdom not afforded to those outside of this relationship with The King. I visited Buckingham Palace on one of the trips through London. Our tour was very limited, with ropes at many doors, preventing us from access to these areas. However, as part of the Royal Family, they could go anywhere in the Palace they desired to go. *King of All the Earth* has given His Children access to the whole earth.

Consider this:
> Deuteronomy 11:24-25 (ESV) Every place on which the sole of your foot treads shall be yours. Your territory shall be from the wilderness to the Lebanon and from the River, the river Euphrates, to the western sea. No one shall be able to stand against you. The LORD your God will lay the fear of you and the dread of you on all the land that you shall tread, as he promised you.

Please understand that I am not implying a militant take over of the world by Christians. However, I am saying that anywhere the *King of All the Earth* directs us to go, we can go. Follow His direction. He is King over all. He has a plan to redeem the earth and all that is in it. Let us be part of the process, not a hindrance to the plan.

The *King of All the Earth* reigns, and we reign with Him through Jesus Christ. Just as man lost his position with the King in the Garden, we have regained our status through Jesus Christ.

> Romans 5:17 (ESV) For if, because of one man's trespass, death reigned through that one man, much more will those who receive the abundance of grace and the free gift of righteousness reign in life through the one man Jesus Christ.

So let's embrace our place in the Kingdom of our King as Believers and enjoy the privileges that come with being Royalty. Live free as a Son or Daughter of *The King of All the Earth*.

King of Glory

Psalm 24:1-10 (ESV) The earth is the LORD's and the fullness thereof, the world and those who dwell therein, for he has founded it upon the seas and established it upon the rivers.

Who shall ascend the hill of the LORD? And who shall stand in his holy place? He who has clean hands and a pure heart, who does not lift up his soul to what is false and does not swear deceitfully. He will receive blessing from the LORD and righteousness from the God of his salvation. Such is the generation of those who seek him, who seek the face of the God of Jacob. Selah

Lift up your heads, O gates! And be lifted up, O ancient doors, that the King of glory may come in. Who is this King of glory? The LORD, strong and mighty, the LORD, mighty in battle! Lift up your heads, O gates! And lift them up, O ancient doors, that the King of glory may come in. Who is this King of glory? The LORD of hosts, he is the King of glory! Selah

This psalm has within it a brief look at the complete Gospel. He starts by declaring, "The earth is the Lord's and the fullness thereof ..." We looked this last time in the name *King of All the Earth*. The earth is the Lord's, and all that is in it belongs to Him. We must acknowledge the King.

The psalmist, David, in this case, then asks, "Who shall ascend the hill of the Lord?" In other words, who can have fellowship with this "Lord of everything?" Only those who are clean can approach Him. David is prophesying of The One that is coming that will bring a "blessing" and "righteousness" so that we can "seek the face of God." Through Jesus, we can be made "right" again in our relationship with the *King of Glory*.

After completing this thought of approaching the King, David uses the word "selah", which means, "pause and think about that." It is worth considering. When you realize the *King of Glory* wants to have fellowship with you, it is important to try to figure out how to get to that place of fellowship.

The third section of this psalm is dedicated to the *King of Glory*. He is saying in essence, "Let everything that has breath praise the *King of Glory*." The psalmist then asks a great question. "Who is this *King of Glory*?" I believe it to be Jesus Christ. This was mentioned when I looked at the name *Captain of the Hosts*.

In the city of London, and others, they have huge ornate gates. The main one that comes to mind is the Admiralty Arch at the end of the street leading up to Buckingham Palace. No one passes through this arch except the queen. David was giving notice with his psalm. Open up the gates! The King is coming! The Lord of Hosts, the *King of Glory*, is here!

And then again, "Selah", or pause and think about that. It is truly worth considering. Let us take time to open up the gates, even the ancient doors, and let in the *King of Glory*.

Lamb That Was Slain

Revelation 5:11-12 (ESV) Then I looked, and I heard around the throne and the living creatures and the elders the voice of many angels, numbering myriads of myriads and thousands of thousands, saying with a loud voice, "Worthy is the Lamb who was slain, to receive power and wealth and wisdom and might and honor and glory and blessing!"

The Book of the Revelation of Jesus Christ, commonly referred to as Revelations, was written by John the Beloved, an apostle called by Jesus. The book, according to John, is a single revelation. (Revelation 1:1) One of the images portrayed in this revelation is that of Jesus as *The Lamb That Was Slain*. The Greek word "arnion", interpreted "lamb", is almost exclusively used to refer to Jesus. The remainder of the phrase comes from the Greek word "sphazo", which means "to butcher, slaughter, main."

When we consider these two words used to coin the phrase *The Lamb That Was Slain* we see that Jesus did not just die. His death was not accidental. His death was intentional and brutal. All the narratives given of the crucifixion of Jesus tells us it was a gruesome event. From the psychological ridicule and taunting at the mock court, the slapping and hitting and pulling His beard, to the beating (known as scourging) where flesh was torn from His back, to finally carrying His own cross to Golgotha and being nailed to it, we see that Jesus died a horrific death. He was butchered in every sense of the word. Through the shedding of His blood, The Lamb paid the price necessary to satisfy the requirement for sin for all mankind.

Jesus, as we see in Hebrews, then ascended to Heaven and placed His own blood on the TRUE Mercy Seat in Heaven. Jesus was the only One qualified to enter the TRUE Holy of Holies in Heaven and place the propitiation needed to fulfill the requirement of The Law. (See Hebrews 10)

That is why He, *The Lamb That Was Slain*, is worshipped unceasingly in Heaven. As those that surround the Throne of God in Heaven declare, Jesus is worthy "to receive power and wealth and wisdom and might and honor and glory and blessing" forever and ever. That is why we should worship Him now. Without His sacrifice we would still be lost without hope of ever being restored relationally to our Creator.

Take time to consider this. Let's have a "selah" moment. Pause and think about it. He alone is worthy.

Lawgiver

Isaiah 33:22 (ESV) For the LORD is our judge; the LORD is our lawgiver; the LORD is our king; he will save us.

One of the reasons the founders of the United States of America put in place three Branches of government is to prevent, or at reduce, injustice. There is one body given charge with writing laws; the Legislative Branch. The Executive Branch is given the charge of enforcing the laws. Another, the Judicial Branch, is given charge of judging those accused of breaking the law.

When you give one person, or body, complete control of all three of these functions we call them a dictator. These people are usually psychopaths that have no regard for anything except their own pleasure. All of this is humanly speaking. This occurs because man has a sinful nature.

God, on the other hand, can be our *Lawgiver* and Judge without any fear that He will be impartial or selfish in His rule. He is perfect Love. He is Justice. He is Righteous.

It is interesting how the word *Lawgiver* was derived from the Hebrew word "haqaq." The word means, "to hack; engrave." Just as God Himself did on the mountain when He gave The Law to Moses, it was common practice for laws to be carved into stone or metal. By doing so it made it difficult for someone to alter the original text.

Men's hearts require rigorous means to protect others from becoming a victim of their ill intent. If left to their own devices, men will cheat and lie in order to get their way. Again, this is not so with God.

With God as our *Lawgiver* we can rest assured that any law written will be for our benefit; either to protect something that is ours, or to protect us from harm. The only reason He gave The Law was to show mankind that we needed God to help us. It is impossible for us to keep The Law without transgression. The penalty for transgression is death. But, God is also our Judge. He understands our inability to keep The Law. Therefore, He made provision for us to be found innocent by allowing a substitute to take our punishment. His name is Jesus. We just looked at the name, Lamb That Was Slain. Jesus paid the price for our freedom.

So, let's give praise to the Righteous *Lawgiver*, because He not only defined what was wrong, but He also gave us a way of escape. Praise Him!

Lifter of My Head

Psalm 3:3 (ESV) But you, O LORD, are a shield about me, my glory, and the lifter of my head.

This has been one of my favorite images of God for a long, long time. I have always picture our Father as one that would come to the aid of the downtrodden; the underdog, the one that seemingly was out of the race. One of the first things that happen when we sense that failure is about to be the result is that we drop our head. Watch the sidelines at a football game. When the other team scores what is most likely the winning touchdown every head on the sideline drops in disappointment. There is no longer the expectation of winning.

Life is hard. Life has times that are called "troubles" for a reason. When it seems that there is nowhere else to go, *The Lifter of My Head* comes and gives new hope. One vivid example of this is in the life of Abram, later known as Abraham. When God first came to Abram and presented His plan of a son, God gave Abram a visual aid. He said, "Abram, your offspring will be as the sands on the seashore." Years passed and no son.

God came to Abram again, this time giving him a new name: Abraham – Father of a multitude. God also gave him a new visual aid. God asked, "Can you count the stars? So shall be your offspring." Abraham started looking upward. God had "lifted His head" to see the possibilities that faith can produce. (You can find the whole story in Genesis 14-18)

Another picture of God being *The Lifer of My Head* is in the story of the woman caught in the very act of adultery. (John 8) It is said that the religious leaders of the day brought the woman to Jesus to see what He would have them do with her. The Law required her to be stoned, but they had heard Jesus' teaching on love and forgiveness.

After pondering the situation Jesus spoke up and said, "He that is without sin cast the first stone." One by one, the multitude left the scene until only Jesus and the woman remained. Jesus then asked the woman, "Where are your accusers? Has no one condemned you?" She replied, "No one, Lord."

Jesus then said, "Neither do I. Go, and sin no more." He had just lifted her head, given her hope of a better day. I'm sure in that moment, especially when they brought her to Jesus, the shame and ridicule that she endured was horrifying. She probably wanted to die. But after the encounter with Jesus, she left, able to hold her head up and look for a new possibility at life.

Jesus is still raising heads today. He still comes to each of us and says, "No one condemns you. Go and sin no more." Listen to *The Lifer of My Head* say these words to you, regardless of where you are, or where you've been. He loves you absolutely, and has redeemed you completely.

Light

Psalm 27:1 (ESV) The LORD is my light and my salvation; whom shall I fear? The LORD is the stronghold of my life; of whom shall I be afraid?

The Lord is my *Light*. John put it this way: 1 John 1:5 (ESV) This is the message we have heard from him and proclaim to you, that God is light, and in him is no darkness at all.

Not only is He my *Light*, He is light. There is no darkness in Him. In Revelation it gives this account: Revelation 21:23 (ESV) And the city has no need of sun or moon to shine on it, for the glory of God gives it light, and its lamp is the Lamb.

Light is always a welcomed thing when there is trouble. An unexpected noise in the dark brings all kinds of imagined dangers that could be lurking about, only to be relieved when the light comes on to find it was nothing.

We have a promise from John, 1 John 1:7 (ESV) But if we walk in the light, as he is in the light, we have fellowship with one another, and the blood of Jesus his Son cleanses us from all sin.

Just like Adam, we can walk in complete fellowship with God, *The Light*. It is interesting that the first thing God spoke into being was light. (Genesis 1:3) The same Hebrew word for light is used in both Psalm 27:1 and Genesis 1:3.

I find it interesting that God commanding light to come did not eliminate darkness. In Genesis 1:4 God divided the light from the darkness. That is difficult for our minds to comprehend. A similar thing occurred in Egypt when God was dealing with Pharaoh to release the people of Israel. One of the plagues brought on Egypt was darkness. However, even though darkness covered Egypt, the place where Israel dwelt was light.

Both of these give us a great metaphor by which we can picture God, *Light,* at work in our lives. Jesus described the world as being darkness. Those who choose to be His followers are called "the light of the world." With God, *The Light*, inside us we can show forth His light to all with whom we have contact. The Lord is my *Light.*

As a young child I remember singing the song, "This Little Light of Mine." I understand the point of the song, but the lyrics really downsize the effect God has on the life of the Believer. Our lives should be spent living as *Light* in a dark world. This is no small light. When present it will shine. It's not optional. The only thing that limits the brightness with which *The Light* can be seen through the Believer is the degree to which he has submitted himself to *The Light.*

Let us strive, or contend, with our soul to allow more of *The Light* to shine through us. The struggle is real, but the results are eternal. The Lord is my *Light*!

Light of the World

> John 8:12 (ESV) Again Jesus spoke to them, saying, "I am the light of the world. Whoever follows me will not walk in darkness, but will have the light of life."

Jesus came to earth, sent by His Heavenly Father, to reveal God to mankind. He demonstrated the Father's love by having compassion, by healing hurts, and by giving hope to the hopeless. He fulfilled The Law of God by living a sinless life. Jesus came to be *The Light of the World*.

The Greek word "phos" is translated "light" in this verse. It means, "to shine, or make manifest." Jesus came to manifest the Word of God.

> John 1:1-5 (ESV) In the beginning was the Word, and the Word was with God, and the Word was God. He was in the beginning with God. All things were made through him, and without him was not any thing made that was made. In him was life, and the life was the light of men. The light shines in the darkness, and the darkness has not overcome it.

Genesis 1 was the physical manifestation of "light" in the earth. John 1 is the manifestation of spiritual "light" to man. The Law had created a sense of hopelessness because man found it impossible to live a perfect life. That was the intent of The Law from the start. Jesus came to show mankind the solution to The Law. It would be salvation by grace.

You cannot hide light in darkness. Even the dimmest candle can illuminate a room that is totally dark.

Jesus came as the breaking of dawn on the longest night ever. It had been 4000 years since man sinned in The Garden. Now the Light of Heaven was shining as *The Light of the World*. For the first time since Adam men were able to touch and see God, hear His voice, and know His love.

All Jesus did while on earth was to invite us to follow Him. His disciples were only asked to do what He had done. Jesus only expected His followers to go where He had already been. He took His closest followers, Peter, James, and John, to places that no one else could in order to reveal more of His Father's heart to them. He asked His followers then, and He is asking us today: "Follow Me!"

Being a Believer in Jesus really is that simple, but it means completely walking away from everything, which can be difficult. Light and darkness is before us. Let us choose Light!

Lily of the Valleys

Song of Songs 2:1 (ESV) I am a rose of Sharon, a lily of the valleys.

Our God is always found in places where He is least expected. People expect to find God in the stained glass cathedrals and in the steepled churches. You expect to encounter God when spending time with others in prayer or worship. However, when things are not going as planned, or when the unexpected comes, we have to start "looking" for God, because we do not expect Him to be there.

This is one of the reasons fear seems to overwhelm us in these moments. Since this is bad God cannot be here. Today's name for God says otherwise. He is *The Lily of the Valleys*. The Hebrew word for lily is "shushan", which means, "white." It comes from another Hebrew word, "sus", which means, "bright."

The second word in this title is the Hebrew word "emeq", which means, "darkness, depression." Solomon, when he wrote this "Song" about the Lord he calls Him "*a Lily of the Valleys.*" David, Solomon's father, put it this way in Psalm 23:4 (ESV). "Even though I walk through the valley of the shadow of death, I will fear no evil, for you are with me; your rod and your staff, they comfort me."

God is in the valley just as He is on the mountaintop. The difference is our perception of Him. God will shine as a *Lily of the Valleys* during our dark, depressing times. We simply have to look for Him. He has promised to be a Light to Our Path.

Psalm 119:105 (ESV) Your word is a lamp to my feet and a light to my path.

The focus of this promise is more about the path than the light. If we are not on the path He has for us then we will not have the light. But just as today's name implies, we can look around in the darkness and find the *Lily of the Valleys* shining, run to Him, and return to the lighted path He has prepared.

This is a wonderful promise we have from our God. Regardless of the level of darkness we can rest assured that there will always be a *Lily of the Valleys* shining brightly to guide us onward toward our destiny.

Living Water

Jeremiah 2:13 (ESV) or my people have committed two evils: they have forsaken me, the fountain of living waters, and hewed out cisterns for themselves, broken cisterns that can hold no water.

This name comes from two Hebrew words. The first is "hay" which means, "alive, raw, fresh, strong: life." The second word is "mayin" which means, "water or juice." From that you get the name *Living Water*, or the essence of life.

In this verse Jeremiah is lamenting over the fact that Israel had chosen leave the fresh flow of *Living Water*, and instead drink from cisterns, or pots made from carved out stone. The water in a cistern is typically rainwater that has been captured. There is no flow of the water, causing it to become stagnant and putrid.

The same thing happened with the manna in the wilderness. God commended them to gather it daily. Some decided that was too much trouble so they gathered more on one day so they would have some left over for the next day. The next morning it was wormy. God's provision is always fresh, intended for the moment. He is *Living Water*.

It is interesting that this is considered two evils. In our minds it would just be one error. But in the mind of God, not drinking from *Living Water* is a sin. Drinking water from another source is a different sin. This indicates it is not enough to just NOT do the wrong things. We must also DO the right things. Living a carnal (fleshly) life is not acceptable for a Believer. It is not acceptable just to live a file free from sin, but we must also be in pursuit of our God, the *Living Water*.

> Isaiah 12:3 (ESV) With joy you will draw water from the wells of salvation.

> John 7:37-38 (ESV) On the last day of the feast, the great day, Jesus stood up and cried out, "If anyone thirsts, let him come to me and drink. Whoever believes in me, as the Scripture has said, 'Out of his heart will flow rivers of living water.'"

God has provided *Living Water* for us from which we are to draw our life. He in turn will then flow from us as Living Water to become a source of life for others. When we are born again, or baptized into Christ by the Holy Spirit, *Living Water* comes to abide in us. As we commune with Him and He in us, the *Living Water* flows from us.

Let us be the fountainhead of *Living Water* for those around us. We encounter thirsty people every day that could use a drink of the fresh *Living Water*. Once they drink from it they will never thirst again.

Longsuffering

> Numbers 14:18 (ESV) 'The LORD is slow to anger (longsuffering) and abounding in steadfast love, forgiving iniquity and transgression, but he will by no means clear the guilty, visiting the iniquity of the fathers on the children, to the third and the fourth generation.'

Many people's view of God is that of Him sitting on His throne in Heaven with His finger on the red button waiting to zap us the first time we step out of line. Others see Him as a tyrant that bullies people into doing His will using any means necessary, including inflicting them with sickness and disease. These folks have never encountered the love of God.

Our God is *Longsuffering*, full of loving kindness and tender mercies.

The verse above troubled me for a while before I heard Craig Hill explain it in this fashion.

> When we see someone that is clearly not living for God but not encountering what we would view as "His judgment or wrath" we get frustrated. In the light of this verse in Numbers we see that God "by no means clear the guilty", but is waiting for a generation that will repent.

> He simply postpones judgment until someone in the future, even three or four generations later, will realize their need for God's love and forgiveness. This is actually a demonstration of the grace of God.

Longsuffering is more concerned with repentance than punishment for sin. He does not excuse the sin. There are still consequences when we sin. However, God is looking for an opportunity to forgive. If we could only see Him for the loving Father that He is, desiring for us, His creation, to realize the relationship that is available if we will simply accept His forgiveness provided through His Son, Jesus.

When Paul gave us the wonderful "love chapter" in 1 Corinthians 13 he started his description with, "love is patient." Remember, God IS love. How could He be anything but patient, or *Longsuffering*.

Today let us live our life knowing that God is not looking for an opportunity to whack us with a big stick, or zap us with the plague, but instead "looking for someone whose heart is pure toward Him so that He can show Himself strong on our behalf." (2 Chronicles 16:9)

Lord

> Genesis 15:1 (ESV) After these things the word of the LORD came to Abram in a vision: "Fear not, Abram, I am your shield; your reward shall be very great."

The most common name for God in all of scripture is *Lord*. It is the sum total of everything God is, and everything that we need from Him. When you speak this name you are confessing your submission to Him in everything, and you are acknowledging Him as your source for everything.

To sincerely speak this name requires something more than we have in us.

> 1 Corinthians 12:3 (ESV) Therefore I want you to understand that no one speaking in the Spirit of God ever says "Jesus is accursed!" and no one can say "Jesus is Lord" except in the Holy Spirit.

God set this up in the beginning to make it possible for man to once again walk with God as Adam did in the Garden of Eden.

> 1 John 4:19 (ESV) We love because he first loved us.

We did not even know God, but He sent His love to us, to give us the ability to love Him. The Holy Spirit is the One that baptizes us into Christ.

Here's the bottom line. This is what *Lord* means to me.

Romans 11:36 (ESV) For from him and through him and to him are all things. To him be glory forever. Amen.

Here is Mary's simple confession.

Luke 1:38 (ESV) And Mary said, "Behold, I am the servant of the Lord; let it be to me according to your word." And the angel departed from her.

When you call Him *Lord* you declare to yourself and to the world that He is your God, and you are His child; end of story.

Lord God Omnipotent

> Revelation 19:6 (NKJV) And I heard, as it were, the voice of a great multitude, as the sound of many waters and as the sound of mighty thunderings, saying, "Alleluia! For the Lord God Omnipotent reigns!

How fitting it is that this name for God would be announced in such a dynamic fashion. John heard something that had to sound like the loudest roar ever given by a stadium full of fanatics yelling. However, instead of war cries for the local team these voices were lifting up the name of God: *Lord God Omnipotent*! I've never been to Niagara Falls, but they say the sound of the waterfall is deafening because the water crashes down with such force.

John describes what he heard as the sound of many waters. Add to that the sound of mighty thunderings and you have quite a loud proclamation. This great multitude had reason to be excited. They were giving praise to their God. The name used for God, *Lord God Omnipotent*, comes from three Greek words: kyrios – supreme in authority; theos – supreme Divinity; and pantokrator – from two words meaning all + dominion or might. This is one of the most powerfully condensed phrases in scripture. All three together attempts to describe just how powerful our God is.

Here's the part that should give every Believer extreme excitement. All of this power lives in you! The Omnipotent God has chosen to live inside each person willing to lay down their own power in exchange for His. Salvation has been described as The Great Exchange. This is why. We give God all of our weakness, shortcomings, and failures and in exchange we get the *Lord God Omnipotent*, able to save to the uttermost. That is one good deal.

When you trust your life to the One that has all power, you are in good hands. Because He has all power, there is no power that can ever remove you from His grasp; and He has promised to never leave us or forsake us. Let us take heart in knowing how secure we are once we place our trust in the *Lord God Omnipotent*.

Lord of Hosts

> Psalm 24:10 (ESV) Who is this King of glory? The LORD of hosts, he is the King of glory!

This name for God is like God Himself: multifaceted. The Hebrew word for Lord is "Jehovah" which we've looked at several time. It is a formal name used for God throughout the Old Testament. However, the Hebrew word for Hosts has within it multiple applications that speak to the nature of God.

The word is "saba", and usually means "a mass of persons." When you apply this word to organized war the meaning changes to "army." We saw this when we looked at the name Captain of the Hosts. This word can then have the implication of a specific "campaign", which is used to describe a military action. Lastly, this word is also interpreted as "appointed time."

When you look at all of these meanings you see a name that brings hope to those who have trusted in God. The *Lord of Hosts* leads an army that will wage war on your behalf when the need arises.

It's one thing to have a massive army. It's another thing altogether to use that army strategically in battle against an enemy force. But when you add in the timeliness of the action you have a Delta Force or Seal Team 6-kind of response to the things that have risen to oppose the purposes of God

This gives added meaning to the psalm. The psalmist is crying out for others to give praise to the One for Whom honor is due.

Psalm 24:7-10 (ESV) Lift up your heads, O gates! And be lifted up, O ancient doors, that the King of glory may come in.

Who is this King of glory? The LORD, strong and mighty, the LORD, mighty in battle!

Lift up your heads, O gates! And lift them up, O ancient doors, that the King of glory may come in.

Who is this King of glory? The LORD of hosts, he is the King of glory! Selah

When you consider our God you quickly realize He is worthy of all praise. The *Lord of Hosts*, He is the King of Glory!

Lord of Lords

> Deuteronomy 10:17 (ESV) For the LORD your God is God of gods and Lord of lords, the great, the mighty, and the awesome God, who is not partial and takes no bribe.

I love the clarity by which our God communicates with His people. This verse leaves no room for doubt. The Lord your God is ... *Lord of Lords*! The same Hebrew word is used twice for emphasis. The word is "adon", where we get Adonai, a name for God that we have already seen. This word means "sovereign, controller." When you take this in context it means that of all the sovereigns, of all the masters, our God is Lord of them.

> Acts 17:22-27 (ESV) So Paul, standing in the midst of the Areopagus, said: "Men of Athens, I perceive that in every way you are very religious. For as I passed along and observed the objects of your worship, I found also an altar with this inscription, 'To the unknown god.' What therefore you worship as unknown, this I proclaim to you.

The God who made the world and everything in it, being Lord of heaven and earth, does not live in temples made by man, nor is he served by human hands, as though he needed anything, since he himself gives to all mankind life and breath and everything. And he made from one man every nation of mankind to live on all the face of the earth, having determined allotted periods and the boundaries of their dwelling place, that they should seek God, and perhaps feel their way toward him and find him.

Paul gave a description of something that those present could not comprehend because they had never met Jehovah. All of the other gods represented by monuments were simply that; monuments. *Lord of Lords* was not even acknowledged among them, but reigns over all other gods.

This is still true today. Many people have allowed things to be elevated as gods in their life. But the One True God is still the *Lord of Lords*, even if He is not acknowledged as such. One day He will be recognized as Lord, and every knee will bow to Him. Let us learn as Paul did and allow Him to be Lord of all … now!

Lord of the Sabbath

> Luke 6:5 (ESV) And he said to them, "The Son of Man is lord of the Sabbath."

What exactly is the Sabbath? The Hebrew word "shabbat", where we get Sabbath, literally means "intermission." It comes from another Hebrew word "shabat", which means "to repose, i.e. desist from exertion; (cause to, let, make to) cease."

Sabbath takes on new meaning, or importance, when you use it in the phrase "The Sabbath Day." That is where the religious context is derived and what we find used in the Ten Commandments.

> Exodus 20:11 (ESV) For in six days the LORD made heaven and earth, the sea, and all that is in them, and rested on the seventh day. Therefore the LORD blessed the Sabbath day and made it holy.

Here we see that Israel was to follow the model that God used when He created the universe. For six days He "made heaven and earth, the sea, and all that is in them." Then He took an intermission, and rested. He wasn't tired, but He ceased from His activity to repose.

Why would an Almighty God, that "never sleeps or slumbers," take a rest break? I believe God was demonstrating the need for margin. There must always be margin in our lives; room in which we can make adjustments along the way. We need margin in every area of our life. Jesus modeled this for us as well. He would often pull away from the crowd to pray.

Just like the rest of The Law, The Sabbath Day is no longer something we have to keep. We each have relationship with God and therefore do not have to go the "the priest" to obtain forgiveness. It has already been provided by Jesus. Once we are identified with Christ we walk in His forgiveness. Every day is "the Lord's day."

Some ministers use The Sabbath Day concept in order to get Christians into the church building. Speaking of their Sunday services they dogmatically declare, "Remember The Sabbath Day, and keep it holy." Here's the thing: Sunday is not The Sabbath Day! It is still Saturday, the last day of the week.

There's an entire denomination founded on the Old Testament law, "Remember The Sabbath Day." They still regard Saturday as a holy day, and forgo many activities just like the nation of Israel was commanded to do. We are no longer under The Law. If we are, we need to build a temple, complete with laver, brazen altar, table of shewbread, candles, and an ark ... oh yeah, where will we get an ark? And then keep the WHOLE Law if we have hope of being redeemed by keeping it. Man has already proven he cannot. That's why God sent Jesus, to redeem us and restore us to relationship with Himself, without The Law.

Jesus came and fulfilled all righteousness, removing the need to keep The Law once we are in Christ. He is now *Lord of the Sabbath*. Our Sabbath is now found in Him, perpetually, as we live our lives out in fellowship with Him. We now allow margin in our life for prayer, study of God's Word, and worship. It's not a "day," it's every day!

Lord on High

Psalm 93:4 (ESV) Mightier than the thunders of many waters, mightier than the waves of the sea, the LORD on high is mighty!

This name for God is probably one of the most misleading, and usually misunderstood, names we find in scripture. The name comes from two Hebrew words. The first we have seen many times in this study: Yahweh, one of the formal names for God. The second word is "marom", which means "altitude, an elevated place, on high, or most high." All of these things are true of God in the proper context.

When some think of the *Lord on High* they picture God way off somewhere, in heaven, seated on a throne in a galaxy far, far from here. He can communicate with us because He is God, but we could never see Him or experience His presence. This causes many to never attempt to have a true relationship with God.

This image is not accurate. God is to be *Lord on High* in the sense that He is exalted above all other gods. He is in an elevated place spiritually as our Creator, Father, and Lord. He is the Most High and He reigns on high. But He is also the Breath You Breathe. If you're a Believer then He lives inside you in the form of the Holy Spirit. He is not far, far away. He is closer than life itself. He is your Life.

We need to see *Lord on High* as a position, not a location. He is to be Above All. He is to reign over every aspect of our life. But, He does it, not at a distance, but closer than anything else you can experience in this life.

Love

1 John 4:8 (ESV) Anyone who does not love does not know God, because God is love.

One of the most ubiquitous names for God is *Love*. When you say, "love," one's mind easily can think of God. This makes sense, because God is Love. When you realize this it can change your entire perspective on how you relate to God, and how you interpret His words and behavior concerning you.

One of the hardest experiences I ever had as a parent occurred at the hospital in Marietta, GA. One of our children had climbed up onto the kitchen counter and opened the cabinet where we kept the medicine. When we found him he was standing there with an opened bottle of Children's Tylenol. There were a few drops on the counter, the bottle almost empty. We had no idea how much had been ingested so we took every precaution and rushed to the emergency room.

Initial blood tests showed the drug was in his system, but only at a "therapeutic" level. Since it was not known exactly how long it had been since the medicine was ingested the doctors decided to pump the child's stomach. The nurse asked us to wait in the hallway while they performed the procedure. They found it tends to reduce the stress on the child. When they attempt procedures like this with the parents in the room the child tends to struggle more violently trying to get to the parents. When they are absent the child seems to be more cooperative.

We were able to watch through the window as they strapped our child to a board, securing his head with a restraint and then wrapped him in something like a swaddling blanket so his legs and arms were immobilized. They then ran a tube up the nose, into the stomach, and pumped out the contents in order to eliminate any more of the medicine from being processed into the blood stream.

As soon as the procedure ended we were allowed in to comfort our son and assure him of our presence, and that we had not forsaken him. Fortunately, everything came back clear on subsequent blood tests and we returned home.

This story speaks of God's love to me in several ways. First of all, as a parent I felt such love for my son and wanted to do everything possible to ensure his safety. What he did to get into this situation was irrelevant. I just wanted him to be well. How much more can our Father God move heaven and earth, if needed, to bring help to us when needed because of His love for us.

Secondly, as we peered through the window watching the procedure, our son had locked eyes with a nurse that was assisting. I saw the love she showed for our son as they worked to help him. Our son was comforted by her presence as she gazed at him, reassuring him with her calm voice and gentle touch. *Love* wants to have this kind of intimate relationship with us, where we gaze into Him and feel His love being poured into us.

1 John 4:19 (KJV) "We love Him, because He first loved us."

Lastly, this shows that even when we mess up and do something that God never intended for us, He comes to bring us peace and comfort by being *Love* to us.

Romans 5:8 (ESV) but God shows his love for us in that while we were still sinners, Christ died for us.

I shared all of that to say this: regardless of what you perceive to be God's activity in your life, know that if it is Him then He is doing it in love. God is *Love*. If you encounter something that is not love, then it is not God. God cannot separate Himself from love because He is *Love*. It's simple, yet profound. Remember that every day and in every way, God loves you!

Lover of My Soul

This name for God is not found in scripture, however it is very easy to see how one could regard Him as such. The title became well known when Charles Wesley penned a hymn with this title.

> Jesus, lover of my soul,
> Let me to Thy bosom fly,
> While the nearer waters roll,
> While the tempest still is high.
> Hide me, O my Savior, hide,
> Till the storm of life is past;
> Safe into the haven guide;
> Oh, receive my soul at last.
>
> Other refuge have I none,
> Hangs my helpless soul on Thee;
> Leave, ah! leave me not alone,
> Still support and comfort me.
> All my trust on Thee is stayed,
> All my help from Thee I bring;
> Cover my defenseless head
> With the shadow of Thy wing.
>
> Wilt Thou not regard my call?
> Wilt Thou not accept my prayer?
> Lo! I sink, I faint, I fall—
> Lo! on Thee I cast my care.
> Reach me out Thy gracious hand!
> While I of Thy strength receive,
> Hoping against hope I stand,
> Dying, and behold, I live.
>
> Thou, O Christ, art all I want,

More than all in Thee I find;
Raise the fallen, cheer the faint,
Heal the sick, and lead the blind.
Just and holy is Thy Name,
Source of all true righteousness;
Thou art evermore the same,
Thou art full of truth and grace.

Plenteous grace with Thee is found,
Grace to cover all my sin;
Let the healing streams abound;
Make and keep me pure within.
Thou of life the fountain art,
Freely let me take of Thee;
Spring Thou up within my heart;
Rise to all eternity.[x]

Some have a difficult time with the term "lover", primarily because of the current vernacular. It is usually given to a person that is engaged in sex outside of marriage. I realize it's not the only use, but it is the most common in today's lingo. However, Wesley had nothing like this in mind when he penned his song.

Charles Wesley clearly had a deep relationship with God, and felt so much love from Him that these words became the overflow of that bond. One of the Twelve Disciples Jesus chose was referred to as John the Beloved, because there was such a strong bond between them.

This kind of love is rare, especially for men. A man today would be considered a homosexual if he were to refer to another man as a lover. The reason is that the term "lover" today speaks totally in the physical sense. *Lover of My Soul* is not a physical intimacy. It is a strong emotional and mental bond that goes beyond mere pleasantries. It penetrates to the deepest part of our human intellect and emotion to connect us in ways that words cannot even describe.

I believe that is where Wesley and others found themselves. When we have fellowship with our God where words just will not express the emotions, we are experiencing Him as *Lover of My Soul*. This is God's desire for every Believer. He wants to connect with us beyond surface relationships, but it will require us to become vulnerable with Him. The good news is this: He is trustworthy!

Open your heart to *Lover of My Soul* and let Him begin to love you in ways that only He can.

Lovingkindness

> Psalm 51:1 (NKJV) Have mercy upon me, O God, According to Your lovingkindness; According to the multitude of Your tender mercies, Blot out my transgressions.

This name is not a title for God, but it is a characteristic that is attributed to Him throughout scripture. It comes from the Hebrew word "hesed", which means "kindness, merciful."

King David, as you remember the story, was in the palace "when kings go out to battle." Instead of leading his men in war he was watching Bathsheba take a bath. He then had Bathsheba's husband killed in battle and took her for his wife.

Nathan, the prophet, came to David and confronted him with his sin. David repented and was met with God's mercy.

Psalm 51 was the result of this experience. David begins by crying out to God, reminding him of His nature. He uses two phrases to describe God, lovingkindness and tender mercies, both of which are covenant terms. Take a look at the following explanation of the Hebrew word used for lovingkindness. There really is not an English equivalent.

> Loving-Kindness. This is a biblical word, invented by Miles Coverdale, and carried over into the English versions generally. It is one of the words he used in the Psalms (23 times, plus Hosea 2:19) to translate the Hebrew "hesed" when it refers to

God's love for his people Israel. Otherwise he used 'mercy,' 'goodness,' and 'great kindness' in the Psalms for God's attitude to man; and, outside the Psalms, such words as 'mercy,' 'goodness,' 'favour' for God's attitude to man, and 'kindness' for man's attitude to man. It is important to notice that Coverdale takes pains to avoid using the word 'kindness' of God's attitude to man, though he is not followed in this respect by the Authorized Version and the Revised Version.

There is one case in the Psalms (141:5) where the word 'hesed' is used of man's attitude to man, and even here Coverdale avoids 'kindness' (so AV and RV), but has 'friendly.' The nearest New Testament equivalent to the Hebrew 'hesed' is 'charis' (grace), as Luther realized when he used the German Gnade for both words.[xi]

David knew God loved him. David knew he had offended that love. If we can grow in our relationship with God to know Him as *Lovingkindness* then we will be less prone to do anything that would grieve Him.

The more we know *Lovingkindness*, the more His nature will be reflected in our lives. The longer we gaze into Him, the more we will act like Him. The world needs *Lovingkindness* like never before. Commit with me to pursue Him.

Majesty

Psalm 145:5 (ESV) On the glorious splendor of your majesty, and on your wondrous works, I will meditate.

This name used to describe God is so fitting. Majesty comes from the Hebrew word "hod", which means "grandeur, an imposing form and appearance."

Moses asked to see God's glory. God responded by allowing Moses to see His back, but said, "You cannot see my face, for man shall not see me and live." Exodus 33:20 (ESV) God's form is so imposing that man cannot see it and live.

I believe God is speaking of the human nature of man. Because of sin we were separated from God both spiritually and relationally. The sin in man could not survive the presence of our Holy God. It would kill the flesh that contains our spirit.

The good news of the gospel of Jesus Christ brings hope for us. When we are identified with Christ our spirit is recreated. The Spirit of God comes to live in us, restoring our fellowship with God. We still cannot see Him, but we are able to know and experience His presence in our life on a daily basis. We actually become a manifestation of His *Majesty* in the earth.

We encounter His *Majesty* when we realize our need for God. We behold His *Majesty* in our worship. Others behold His *Majesty* in us because of our worship of Him. That is the real circle of life in the Spirit.

The writer of Hebrews describes it like this:

Hebrews 1:3 (ESV) He is the radiance of the glory of God and the exact imprint of his nature, and he upholds the universe by the word of his power. After making purification for sins, he sat down at the right hand of the Majesty on high,

If you have been identified with Christ, baptized into Christ by the Holy Spirit, then you are also seated, with Christ, at Majesty's right hand. We live from that position as Believers. Never allow your mind to minimize the importance of this. We reign WITH CHRIST in the earth.

Maker of Heaven and Earth

Psalm 115:15 (ESV) May you be blessed by the LORD, who made heaven and earth!

If anyone ever mistakes someone else for God, there is a simple way clear up the confusion. Our God is the *Maker of Heaven and Earth*. There's a funny anecdote that accentuates this fact. You may have heard this before. But in case you haven't, here it is.

One day a group of scientists got together and decided that man had come a long way and no longer needed God. So they picked one scientist to go and tell Him that they were done with Him.

The scientist walked up to God and said, "God, we've decided that we no longer need you. We're to the point that we can clone people and do many miraculous things, so why don't you just go on and get lost."

God listened very patiently and kindly to the man and after the scientist was done talking, God said, "Very well, how about this. Let's say we have a man making contest." To which the scientist replied, "OK, great!"

But God added, "Now, we're going to do this just like I did back in the old days with Adam."

The scientist said, "Sure, no problem" and bent down and grabbed himself a handful of dirt.

> God just looked at him and said, "No, no, no. You go get your own dirt!"

It is a silly notion that man could consider His surroundings and come to the conclusion there is no God. I recently read an article on Quantum Entanglement that fascinated me. You can read the whole article at the link found in the endnotes.[xii] Without reiterating things I'll share the conclusion of one noted scientist.

> A fundamental conclusion of the new physics also acknowledges that the observer creates the reality. As observers, we are personally involved with the creation of our own reality. Physicists are being forced to admit that the universe is a 'mental' construction. Pioneering physicist Sir James Jeans wrote: 'The stream of knowledge is heading toward a non-mechanical reality; the universe begins to look more like a great thought than like a great machine. Mind no longer appears to be an accidental intruder into the realm of matter, we ought rather hail it as the creator and governor of the realm of matter. Get over it, and accept the inarguable conclusion. The universe is immaterial-mental and spiritual.'" – R.C. Henry, Professor of Physics and Astronomy at Johns Hopkins University[xiii]

The thing that amazes me about this is they have just proven scripture. The writer of Hebrews said, "By faith we understand that the universe was created by the word of God, so that what is seen was not made out of things that are visible." Hebrews 11:3 (ESV)

The deeper man attempts to look into creation the more they find that there is "nothing there." At least nothing that they can see! Modern science does not threaten my faith. It increases it. *Maker of Heaven and Earth* watches with patience for man to come to the end of himself. Once that happens He can act.

Go ahead and acknowledge Him as Lord. Let *Maker of Heaven and Earth* make your life into something beautiful.

Man of War

> Exodus 15:3 (ESV) The LORD is a man of war; the LORD is his name.

We have seen many names for God that are related to this name, *Man of War*. We know God as Captain of the Hosts and Lord of Hosts. He is our Defense. There is no doubt of His prowess in battle.

Even though the context is clearly that of waging war, today's name is a little different than what it might appear. *Man of War* had just shown Himself faithful by delivering the people of Israel from the Egyptian army. After seeing His hand save them, and seeing the enemy drown in the sea, Moses led the people in a song, declaring,

> Exodus 15:1-2 (ESV) Then Moses and the people of Israel sang this song to the LORD, saying, "I will sing to the LORD, for he has triumphed gloriously; the horse and his rider he has thrown into the sea. The LORD is my strength and my song, and he has become my salvation; this is my God, and I will praise him, my father's God, and I will exalt him.

Then they extol the Lord by calling Him, "*Man of War*." This name is derived from two Hebrew words. The first is "ish", which most commonly interpreted as "man." However, the root meaning of the word is "extant," which means "still in existence; surviving." The second Hebrew word is "milhama", which means, "destroying in battle." When you combine these words you see that God is the one still standing when the dust settles. He destroys but is not destroyed.

This is reflected in the life of the New Testament Believer in the letter Paul wrote to the Corinthian church.

> 2 Corinthians 4:7-10 (ESV) But we have this treasure in jars of clay, to show that the surpassing power belongs to God and not to us. We are afflicted in every way, but not crushed; perplexed, but not driven to despair; persecuted, but not forsaken; struck down, but not destroyed; always carrying in the body the death of Jesus, so that the life of Jesus may also be manifested in our bodies.

Jesus promised there would be tribulation in this earth. But, we have the Spirit of the *Man of War* living in us. We are afflicted but not crushed, perplexed but not drive to despair. When the dust settles we are still standing because God is with us. Let us learn to allow our God to help us persevere through everything that might try to keep us from being salt and light in the earth.

Man of War, the extant fighter, is always standing; the enemy, always defeated.

Master

Matthew 22:16 (KJV) And they sent out unto him their disciples with the Herodians, saying, Master, we know that thou art true, and teachest the way of God in truth, neither carest thou for any man: for thou regardest not the person of men.

Greek tradition was for the more learned individuals to develop followers that would immerse themselves in their teaching. One of the terms of endearment used for these teachers was "master." The Greek word used is "didaskalos", which means "instructor."

Some of those that followed Jesus referred to Him as *Master*. They saw Him as a good teacher of things regarding God. There was no real commitment by these followers. They liked His company. They liked the way He cared for them.

The tradition of baptism was applied to these Greek teachers. They would actually baptize those that wanted to commit themselves to learning the teaching of the master. They would follow him everywhere and serve him in hopes of one day themselves becoming a master.

This is a great type, or picture, of the process of discipleship. Christian discipleship is when one commits to Jesus Christ as their *Master* and begins to learn His ways, so much so, that they become like Him. This is the will of God for every human.

There is another Greek word that interpreted as "Master" in the New Testament. That word is "rhabbi."

Mark 9:5 (KJV) And Peter answered and said to Jesus, Master, it is good for us to be here: and let us make three tabernacles; one for thee, and one for Moses, and one for Elias.

There is a huge difference between these two words. *Master* (teacher) is someone you enjoy hearing. People would sometimes follow many teachers, never really committing themselves to a single discipline. *Master* (rhabbi) is more correctly interpreted "my master." This is the term Peter used when referring to Jesus.

When first called by Jesus, Peter followed him as "didaskalos", a teacher. But after spending time with Jesus, Peter's view of Him changes from "teacher" to "rhabbi", "my *Master*." Peter was willing to die for the cause to which Jesus had called Him. This is Christian discipleship.

The choice today is clear. Many regard Jesus as a teacher, but do not see Him as their rabbi. Let us commit our life to Jesus and make Him *Master*, my Teacher, so that He can transform us into His image.

Merciful

Ephesians 2:4 (ESV) But God, being rich in mercy, because of the great love with which he loved us,

Second only to Love, the most beloved name for God is *Merciful*. Whenever we have problems we cry out for God's mercy. When others have wronged us we call on God for justice. We should be very glad to know that God does not respond to our whims. Both God's mercy and justice are doled out from a position of Love.

Paul spells it out here in the letter to the Church at Ephesus. "God is *Merciful* because of the great love He has for us." This statement is a precursor to the greatest act of mercy that God ever showed toward mankind. Even while we were dead in sin God made us alive together with Christ, by grace.

Consider these two verses.

Psalm 103:8 (ESV) The LORD is merciful and gracious, slow to anger and abounding in steadfast love.

Malachi 3:6 (ESV) "For I the LORD do not change; therefore you, O children of Jacob, are not consumed.

God is *Merciful*. He will always be *Merciful*. It's His nature. Just as He is Love, He is also *Merciful*. His justice will come, but only for those who have never been identified with Christ. Through Jesus, we obtain mercy because of God's love.

Let the truth of this sink in if you are a Believer. Take rest knowing that *Merciful* God loves you.

Messiah

Many of the names that we have seen thus far only appear a few times in scripture. This is another one. *Messiah* is probably one of the most familiar names used by modern writers and theologians when referring to Jesus. We speak often of the Jewish people waiting on their *Messiah* to come.

The proper name of *Messiah* only appears in scripture two times; both times in Daniel 9:25-26. However, the Hebrew word interpreted "*Messiah*" is used many other times. The word "mashiah" means "anointed." When the Bible speaks of The Anointed One, it means The *Messiah*, which is Jesus.

There is an equivalent word in Greek, "Christos", which also means, "anointed." Of course, this is where the word Christ originates. When the name Jesus Christ appears in scripture it literally means Jesus, The Anointed One. I encourage you to go back and read The Names of God – Anointed One. It gives more insight into this name in particular.

From the time of Adam there has never been more anticipation for anyone to be born than Messiah. The hope for all of mankind rested squarely on His shoulders. Through Him mankind would again have access to God.

Since His coming, those who have been identified with Him, Believers, are now empowered with that same anointing by the Holy Spirit. We have been given the charge to help others find *Messiah* today. There are still those waiting on The Anointed One to invade their life with His love, acceptance, and forgiveness.

Isaiah 61:1-3 (ESV) The Spirit of the Lord GOD is upon me, because the LORD has anointed me to bring good news to the poor; he has sent me to bind up the brokenhearted, to proclaim liberty to the captives, and the opening of the prison to those who are bound; to proclaim the year of the LORD's favor, and the day of vengeance of our God; to comfort all who mourn; to grant to those who mourn in Zion— to give them a beautiful headdress instead of ashes, the oil of gladness instead of mourning, the garment of praise instead of a faint spirit; that they may be called oaks of righteousness, the planting of the LORD, that he may be glorified.

Believers are now the vessels used to deliver this Anointing, *Messiah*, to our world.

Mighty

Luke 1:49 (ESV) for he who is mighty has done great things for me, and holy is his name.

This is an amazing verse. He who is *Mighty*, holy is His name. There are many people in our world that could be considered mighty. However, when you consider the circumstances in which this statement is made you realize there can only be one conclusion.

Mary, a teenage girl in Israel, a virgin, was just asked to become the mother of God's Son, Jesus. Can you imagine what must have been going through this young lady's mind? Based on what we know about her background Mary most likely understood The Law. She had heard that a Messiah was coming to redeem Israel – through a virgin. She also understood the penalty for pregnancy outside of marriage – death by stoning.

When the angel appeared Mary was surprised by the words spoken to her, yet she was willing to be obedient to God's will for her life. "Let it be according to your word." This one moment was both a pinnacle of excitement beyond her wildest dreams – to be the mother of God's Son – and the deepest pit of dread – dying as an unwed mother.

She had to ask some questions: What would Joseph think? What would her parents think? What would the priest do to her? In the end her answer was, "Yes!" Once the decision was made and sealed by her confession to the angel, Mary began to see the gravity of her agreement. She just said yes to God. That is when she began her "song" as theologians call it.

The verse cited above is part of Mary's Song. He who is *Mighty* has done great things FOR ME. Unlike others that were encountered by God that could not find it within them to say, "Yes," because of what it would cost them, Mary said, "Great things were done for me!" Mary realized that *Mighty* God had just entered her through the Holy Spirit. As far as we know from scripture, Mary became the first person filled with the Holy Spirit.

It resulted in her conceiving Jesus in her womb; God now becoming flesh. Jack Hayford, in his book "The Mary Miracle" describes this event as the "fountainhead of all miracles." Because Mary recognized God as *Mighty*, and allowed Him to perform His plan through her, she became blessed among women.

Each of us has a choice today. Do we say, "Yes," to God and His plan by allowing *Mighty* to do great things FOR US, or do we rebuff the One who loves us most?

Mighty and Terrible

Deuteronomy 7:21 (KJV) Thou shalt not be affrighted at them: for the LORD thy God is among you, a mighty God and terrible.

Deuteronomy 7:21 (ESV) You shall not be in dread of them, for the LORD your God is in your midst, a great and awesome God.

Language evolves over time. Communication is difficult at best, but is greatly hampered when the words being used are not clear. One of the best examples of this is the word "gay." At one time "gay" meant, "happy, carefree." In today's language "gay" refers to a homosexual man. In the same way some words used in the King James Version of the English Bible no longer have the same meaning. Such is the case with today's name for God.

Mighty and Terrible would be great adjectives used to describe some sci-fi creature like Godzilla or Swamp Creature. We usually do not ascribe Terrible to our God. The reason is the meaning has changed over time. As you can see in the two versions of the verse from Deuteronomy, *Mighty and Terrible* have become Great and Awesome; same meaning just different vernacular.

The Hebrew word "gadol" is interpreted "mighty (great) in any sense: far, high, long, loud, more, much, very." All of these are true of God. Most any adjective you consider to apply, God is greater than. This is very good news for the Believer. Anything you face in life that is considered an obstacle, God is Greater!

The Hebrew word "yare" is interpreted "terrible (awesome)." When applied to God it means He is to be revered, shown reverence, and feared in the sense of respect. For the Believer, this is our motivation to worship our God.

When you look at this combination of names, *Mighty and Terrible*, ascribed to God by Moses, you find One that is able to save us to the uttermost and worthy of all of our praise. Our response is faith to believe that God can do anything beyond what we could ask or think (Ephesians 3:20), and worship Him because there is none other above Him (John 3:31).

Mighty and Terrible or Great and Awesome, either way He is our God, and we will live for Him.

Mighty in Wisdom

One of the prophetic names used when telling of the coming Messiah was Wonderful Counselor. Our God would send nothing but the best to represent Him and all that He is. One of Job's friends, Elihu, was trying to encourage Job in the middle of his trials. He was speaking truth about God trying to build Job's faith.

> Job 36:1-5 (ESV) And Elihu continued, and said: "Bear with me a little, and I will show you, for I have yet something to say on God's behalf. I will get my knowledge from afar and ascribe righteousness to my Maker. For truly my words are not false; one who is perfect in knowledge is with you. "Behold, God is mighty, and does not despise any; he is mighty in strength of understanding.

Strength of understanding. The King James Bible says, *"Mighty in Wisdom."* The Hebrew word used here is "leb", which means, "the heart, the will and intellect, the center of everything." At His very core (wisdom), our God is Mighty. Everything He does comes from this place.

I'm sure you have heard about Job. I'll not take the time to tell it here. Job was a man of God. He was faithful in His worship of Jehovah. Through a series of events Job lost everything he had except his life. His family was killed, his possessions destroyed or stolen, and even his health was diminished to the point of death, yet Job remained faithful to God.

During this time of trials Job had many "friends" come to him to give counsel. Fortunately, Job knew his God and would not believe the lies spoken to him by some.

But Elihu came with the truth about God and encouraged Job by building his faith in the One who is *Mighty in Wisdom*. Job believed, and in the end was blessed by God more abundantly than before all of the tragedy.

Where are You with your trust in God's wisdom for your life? In "the center of everything" God directs our paths with *Mighty Wisdom*. His plan for each of us is beyond anything else we could imagine. Regards of the level of trials in which you may find yourself God's heart for you is for good and not evil. His plan for you is to lift you up and never let you down. His Strength of Understanding will direct your steps from wherever you are back to right standing with Him.

Mighty in Wisdom. Let Him be your Wonderful Counselor.

Miracle Worker

Matthew 19:26 (ESV) But Jesus looked at them and said, "With man this is impossible, but with God all things are possible."

His day began like it did every day. He crawled out of bed and waited. He spent most of his life waiting. He waited for a friend to carry him to the porch by the Pool of Bethesda. "Maybe today will be the day," he hoped. But like every day before someone made it to the pool before him.

It was believed that an angel would come and stir the water. If you got in the water while it was "stirred" you would be healed. He could never get there in time. Now, I don't know if anyone was ever healed by getting in the water after it was "stirred," but they kept trying.

However, today would be different. This day the One who could heal was there by the pool. The *Miracle Worker* happened by and inquired of the man. "Do you want to be healed?", Jesus asked. What kind of a question is that? "Of course I want to be healed," the man replied, "but no one will help me in the water." Jesus simple spoke to him and said, "Get up, take up your bed, and walk." At once the man was healed. (John 5:2-9)

We all face circumstances that seem insurmountable. Even then, we still try to figure out a way to solve the problem ourselves. This man did not know the Miracle Worker was right beside him. Instead of asking for healing, the man expected Jesus to help him in the water. The man had a plan.

The verse cited earlier from Matthew has Jesus making a statement that was given to boost our faith in God. "With man this is impossible, but with God ALL THINGS are possible." (Matthew 19:26) When we face impossibility we need to rest in God's possibility. Our struggle will not make it any more possible; only faith in the *Miracle Worker*.

Today's challenge is this: let's not wait until it is "impossible" before we seek the Lord's help. His best for us is to live a life of submission to Him, but He is still the *Miracle Worker* when needed.

Most High

> Daniel 7:27 (ESV) And the kingdom and the dominion and the greatness of the kingdoms under the whole heaven shall be given to the people of the saints of the Most High; his kingdom shall be an everlasting kingdom, and all dominions shall serve and obey him.'

As a child there were many arguments over many things, but none so frequent as: "Mine is bigger. Mine is better. Mine is stronger. Mine is best." It really didn't matter the topic, the goal was to be better.

Childish competition is just that; childish. However, there are times when you really need to know that yours is better. When it comes to God, He is the Most High. There is none above Him. He created all. No creation has ever risen above its creator. He is Most High.

We looked at a Name of God similar to this one. El Elyon means "God Most High." This verse in Daniel uses the Hebrew word "elyon", which simply means "most high." The meaning is clearly a reference to God.

Daniel was giving a prophetic view of the Kingdom of God. It will be an everlasting Kingdom, and all dominions shave serve and obey Him (the Most High)." Here's the best part. It will be given to the people (saints) of the Most High! The Believers are the Kingdom of God.

The following verse describes the final step in the process of salvation for the Believer.

> Ephesians 1:20 (ESV) that he worked in Christ when he raised him from the dead and seated him at his right hand in the heavenly places,

When we identify with Jesus in His death, burial, resurrection, ascension, and seating at God's right hand we are saved. We must become identified with every step. Repentance is not enough. Turning from sin is not enough. Baptism in water is not enough. It is only when we make it through each stage of identification, including being seated at God's right hand, we are still trying to make Heaven by works of the flesh.

The seating is where we gain our authority. God rules, and we are at His right hand, ruling with Him. Until we see ourselves there we cannot experience the fullness of God's salvation. We must live from that position.

> Colossians 3:2 (ESV) Set your minds on things that are above, not on things that are on earth.

Paul gave the Christians at Rome the command to "be transformed by the renewing of our mind." When our mind is renewed we see things from a Heavenly perspective.

So now when the enemy attempts to have you live beneath the life that Jesus died to bring to you, simply proclaim, "God is bigger than ..." We serve the Most High!

Near

Psalm 145:18 (ESV) The LORD is near to all who call on him, to all who call on him in truth.

The psalmist, David, is speaking from his experience when he proclaims, "The Lord is near." The Hebrew word used is "qarob" which means, "near in location, relationship, or time." It is derived from a word which means, "to approach." This could not be any more true about our God.

When we face struggles our first response is usually to seek help. When help is close it gives us hope that the struggle will be short, easily overcome. For those who are aware of God's presence, the Believer, we call out to Him because He is *Near*. He is always ready to act, and is actually already working, to bring about a good outcome to our situation.

The sad truth is that He is *Near* to everyone, not just the Believer. God's desire is that everyone would call out to Him. David spoke of this very thing. "He is near to all who call on Him." His is already *Near*. He's just waiting on the call.

Consider the other aspects of God being *Near*. The word can also be applied to relationship. Proverbs 18:24 speaks of "a friend that is closer than a brother." I believe this was speaking of our God. He is *Near*. Not just in location, but in relation.

Galatians 4:6-7 (ESV) And because you are sons, God has sent the Spirit of his Son into our hearts, crying, "Abba! Father!" So you are no longer a slave, but a son, and if a son, then an heir through God.

We are not strangers. We are sons and daughters once we have been identified with Christ. *Near* by relationship.

The last way inferred by the word used for *Near* is in time. So many speak of the sweet by and by, when we all get to Heaven. It is our future to be in Heaven with God. But, we do not have to wait until then to be near Him. He is *Near*, now! There is never a time that He was not *Near*. From the moment you are conceived until that day you do see Heaven, God is *Near*.

Moses said it this way:
> Exodus 33:15 (ESV) And he said to him, "If your presence will not go with me, do not bring us up from here.

David said it this way:
> Psalm 139:7-10 (ESV) Where shall I go from your Spirit? Or where shall I flee from your presence? If I ascend to heaven, you are there! If I make my bed in Sheol, you are there! If I take the wings of the morning and dwell in the uttermost parts of the sea, even there your hand shall lead me, and your right hand shall hold me.

You cannot go anywhere that God is not *Near*. You cannot have any relationship closer than you can with Near. You cannot lag behind or run ahead of *Near*. He is always there: location, relation, time.

Try it now. Reach out to Him, because He is *Near*.

Never Changing

James 1:17 (ESV) Every good gift and every perfect gift is from above, coming down from the Father of lights with whom there is no variation or shadow due to change.

We have a little dog, a Maltese, named Bee. She is a joy to our household. She is so tiny, yet acts as though she is a Rottweiler. One of the things that triggers her bark is a change in light; a reflection, or "shadow due to change." The slightest change draws her attention.

Our God is so steadfast, so immovable, that there is no change in His shadow. *Never Changing* has a character that cannot be affected by outside stimulus. He emanates, not reflects. He is a voice, not an echo. He is the original, never a copy.

James is assuring us regarding this attribute of God in relation to the gifts that come from Him. "Every good and perfect gift comes from above." When bad things come, you should never be tempted think of it as coming from God. Pride leads us to try to "spiritualize" bad things as somehow being a "test or trial" from God. This verse should eliminate that thinking.

When it comes to good gifts, perfect gifts, God is *Never Changing*. He only knows how to bless. Anything from *Never Changing* will be good and perfect. This should build our faith. If what you face is not "good or perfect" then look to *Never Changing* for what He has available for you. He will bring light to your path to bring you back into the blessing He has provided.

Here's the thing. If this is true, and it is, it means we can live our lives on purpose knowing that *Never Changing* will always love us, always lead us, always provide for us, and will never leave us. He redeemed us from sin and death through the sacrifice of His Son, Jesus, and adopted us as sons and daughters with full inheritance to His Kingdom, Heaven, and has empowered us with His Spirit to lead us into all truth and knowledge of Him. And it will never change!

Allow this to settle into your spirit. Imagine how this can change your life. Now, let it change you, because God is *Never Changing*!

Never Weary

> Isaiah 40:28 (ESV) Have you not known? Have you not heard? The LORD is the everlasting God, the Creator of the ends of the earth. He does not faint or grow weary; his understanding is unsearchable.

One of the most comical scenes in scripture is when Elijah took on the prophets of Baal atop Mt. Carmel. If you don't know the story you can read it in 1 Kings 18. The story is quite interesting, where Elijah propositions the followers of Baal, asserting that which ever God responds by fire, him will they serve.

Elijah allows the others to go first. Here's what happened.

> 1 Kings 18:26-29 (ESV) And they took the bull that was given them, and they prepared it and called upon the name of Baal from morning until noon, saying, "O Baal, answer us!" But there was no voice, and no one answered. And they limped around the altar that they had made. And at noon Elijah mocked them, saying, "Cry aloud, for he is a god. Either he is musing, or he is relieving himself, or he is on a journey, or perhaps he is asleep and must be awakened." And they cried aloud and cut themselves after their custom with swords and lances, until the blood gushed out upon them. And as midday passed, they raved on until the time of the offering of the oblation, but there was no voice. No one answered; no one paid attention.

"Is he using the bathroom?" "Maybe he's asleep." Elijah taunted them to the point they began to harm themselves to get Baal to respond.

It is difficult for us to see these events in light of the New Testament. This certainly does not seem like something Jesus would have done. Elijah was being led by the Holy Spirit. Elijah knew God was *Never Weary*.

In Psalm 121, one of the Psalms of Ascent, one of the statements Israel would proclaim this as they went up the steps to the temple was, "Behold, he who keeps Israel will neither slumber nor sleep."

This is not just some circumstance that led these people to believe this characteristic of God. It is part of His nature. God is *Never Weary*. He has no need of rest. God is life. He upholds all things. He gives life to everything in our world. He is *Never Weary*.

Regardless of the your circumstance God can bring you through it. We do not have to act like the prophets of Baal to earn, or in any way garner God's attention.

> 2 Chronicles 16:9 (ESV) For the eyes of the LORD run to and fro throughout the whole earth, to give strong support to those whose heart is blameless toward him.

He is ever vigilant and is searching for ways to act on your behalf. God is *Never Weary*.

Omnipresent

> Psalm 139:7-10 (ESV) Where shall I go from your Spirit? Or where shall I flee from your presence? If I ascend to heaven, you are there! If I make my bed in Sheol, you are there! If I take the wings of the morning and dwell in the uttermost parts of the sea, even there your hand shall lead me, and your right hand shall hold me.

Just a few days ago we looked at The Names of God – Near. This verse was used to explain that God is Near you, regardless of where you go. The reality is this: He is everywhere! You cannot go anywhere that He is not. Our human minds cannot comprehend that, but it is the truth.

The word *Omnipresent* is not in scripture. To my knowledge, there is no Hebrew or Greek word that means *Omnipresent*. The word is derived from Latin. However, you can clearly find the principle of this truth.

> 1 Kings 8:27 (ESV) "But will God indeed dwell on the earth? Behold, heaven and the highest heaven cannot contain you; how much less this house that I have built!

The heavens cannot contain God. He is *Omnipresent*. He is bigger than the whole.

> Deuteronomy 4:7 (ESV) For what great nation is there that has a god so near to it as the LORD our God is to us, whenever we call upon him?

He fills the heavens but is closer to us than the air we breathe. He hears us when we call out to Him. He is everywhere at the same time. He is *Omnipresent*.

Again, our finite minds cannot contain infinity. We can complete theoretical computations using infinity ("∞") as a parameter but we cannot fully fathom the ramifications. We measure space but we never reach the "end" of space. It is unfathomable. Yet, as broad as our universe, and expansive as any space we can imagine, God fills all of it. He is *Omnipresent*.

This should greatly increase our faith. We need to allow this truth to settle in our consciousness until we can proclaim like the psalmist, "Where can I go from Your Spirit?" It will calm the fight-or-flight in us. When we realize God is here we don't need to run. Conversely, regardless of where we run, God is there. He is *Omnipresent*.

Remember this the next time you need to pray. You don't have to look for God. You don't have to go and find Him. He is here!

One Who Hides Himself

> Isaiah 45:15 (ESV) Truly, you are a God who hides himself, O God of Israel, the Savior.

This is one of the most intriguing verses of scripture to me. We just looked at The Names of God – Omnipresent. If He is everywhere, and He is, how can He hide Himself?

First of all, the Hebrew word used for "hide" is "satar," which means, "hide by covering, keep close (secret), or conceal." We have already seen that God is Almighty. Clearly He is able to do anything He wants, including become "hidden" while filling all of creation.

Keith Moore gave one of the best messages on Faith that I've ever heard. Part of that message included this verse. He described it this way. "God is not hiding from us, but for us." This certainly makes sense when you consider Jesus' words."

> Matthew 7:7-8 (ESV) "Ask, and it will be given to you; seek, and you will find; knock, and it will be opened to you. For everyone who asks receives, and the one who seeks finds, and to the one who knocks it will be opened.

If God is in plain sight why would we have to "seek" Him. Moses gave this admonition to Israel.

> Deuteronomy 4:29 (ESV) But from there you will seek the LORD your God and you will find him, if you search after him with all your heart and with all your soul.

Searching with "all of your heart and soul" sounds like effort. The promise is that you will find Him if you search for Him. There is something about having to search for something that makes finding it more special.

Read the Song of Solomon. This is a picture of the husband/wife dynamic, but is a type of Christ and The Church. In this story, The Church is the one seeking after the Bridegroom. Once found, the joy of the fellowship they enjoy totally replaces the anguish experience in the search.

The same is true of our God. We are to spend the remainder of our days, once we are Born Again, seeking to know more fully the God that saved us. We can never exhaust the knowledge of God, the fellowship with our Lord Jesus, or the blessings brought by the Holy Spirit. Further more, our human minds could not fully comprehend the Godhead.

God told Moses, "No man can see Me and live." He hides for our sake. We cannot handle "seeing" Him, but He reveals more and more as our spirits grow, and as we become conformed to the image of Christ more fully.

So, rest assured, you will see God; just not all at once. Keep asking, seeking, and knocking.

One Who Sanctifies

> Numbers 8:17 (ESV) For all the firstborn among the people of Israel are mine, both of man and of beast. On the day that I struck down all the firstborn in the land of Egypt I consecrated them for myself,

From the very beginning God has always kept something for Himself. In the Garden of Eden God gave mankind everything they needed. But there was one thing God commanded mankind to leave alone – The Tree of the Knowledge of Good and Evil. That tree was "sanctified" unto the Lord.

Fast forward to the giving of the Law of Moses. God told Moses that the tribe of Levi would be set apart from the other twelve. They were consecrated to the Lord – sanctified. They would spend their lives in service to God and the people of Israel. All the priests that served in the Tabernacle were Levites. They became the go-between for God and man.

The Hebrew word used here is "qadash", which means, "to be set apart or consecrated."

There is an equivalent word in Greek, "hagiazo", which means basically the same thing, "treat as holy, set apart." Sanctification is part of the process God takes us through as Believers.

> 1 Corinthians 6:11 (ESV) And such were some of you. But you were washed, you were sanctified, you were justified in the name of the Lord Jesus Christ and by the Spirit of our God.

What does this mean for the Believer? Look at what Paul says in the verse above. As a Believer that has been baptized into Christ by the Holy Spirit, God has done several things: 1) washed you (removed sin from you by the blood of Jesus), 2) sanctified you (set you apart for His own), 3) justified you (made you righteous – completely restored into fellowship with God).

As Believers, we are then called to live a "separated" life. This is not a command to join a monastery and become secluded from mankind. It simply means we are to live our lives only for our God. We are His, so everything we do should be in response to His Spirit's leading.

When giving the Ten Commandments God told Moses, "I am a jealous God." He wants what is His, and will not share the "sanctified things" with anyone. That give us great assurance that as Believers we are in the best place possible, because we have been "sanctified", set apart for God alone.

Our Strength

Psalm 46:1 (ESV) God is our refuge and strength, a very present help in trouble.

I heard a funny story about a conversation between a children's Sunday School teacher and a young boy in her class. The story of the day was on telling the truth. The teacher asked, "Johnny, do you know what the Bible says about a lie? Little Johnny replied, "A lie is an abomination unto the Lord, … and a present help in time of trouble."

The reality is this: God is "a very present help in trouble." He is *Our Strength*. When trouble comes to the Believer the first response should be to cry out to *Our Strength*, God. We have seen many names for God during the study, but none are more important in times of trouble than *Our Strength*. We need to know we have shelter from the storm, a Rock that will is higher than ourselves.

Just like little Johnny, when faced with a circumstance where he felt compelled to lie in order to avoid trouble, we often come across situations that leave us feeling vulnerable or threatened. In these times we need a foundation that is immovable. We need someone who can help us carry our burden, or resist the temptation to act out of our flesh. *Our Strength* will always be there to help, teach, guide, comfort, and empower us to make it through.

The Hebrew word used here is "oz", which means, "strength in various applications (force, security, majesty, praise). God demonstrates strength in every area of His existence. Through our relationship with Him as Believers, God extends His strength toward us in many ways; primarily His love for us. His love compels us to Him. His love constrains us to serve Him. His love sustains us through every circumstance. His love empowers us to love others.

God is *Our Strength*. God is *Love*. Let us learn to relate to Him in both of these aspects of His character.

Peacemaker

Proverbs 16:7 (ESV) When a man's ways please the LORD, he makes even his enemies to be at peace with him.

Peace. It is what war-torn regions have been shouting for centuries. It's what young mothers crave after a hard day with the children. It's what spouses long for when marital strife is raging. In all of these circumstances, peace seems to be something out of reach. We are incapable of bringing about peace ourselves. Thank God, He is the *Peacemaker*!

This promise from Proverbs tells us that when we are in fellowship with our Lord, and walk in His ways, He, the *Peacemaker*, will make other be at peace with us. The thing that messes us up so often is our own attempts to bring about peace.

Look at Abram and Sarai. All they wanted was peace but their disobedience to wait on God's promise produced an illegitimate result. Instead of peace it brought about a conflict that still rages today.

Look at the Hebrew word used for "peace" in this verse. It's the word "shalem", which means, "to be safe (in mind, body or estate); to be completed; by implication to be friendly; by extension to reciprocate."

When we seek peace we just want the problem to go away. God doesn't just want the absence of conflict. *Peacemaker* wants things to be brought to a safe place; a place of wholeness; a place of completion. When the dust settles He doesn't just send us to our respective corners where we steam over what the other has done. That is not peace.

Peacemaker's first desire is for us to be at peace in ourselves – "When a man's ways please the Lord." Our spirit must be at peace with our soul in order for us to walk this way. Without that God cannot bring peace because we are not capable of living at peace.

But when we are in a place of peace with God, He brings about the peace in others. We cannot change another person's will. That place is God's alone. He is the *Peacemaker*. The good news is that when He has completed His work we are safe; in mind, body, and spirit. That's the way to live.

Physician

> Psalm 103:2-5 (ESV) Bless the LORD, O my soul, and forget not all his benefits, who forgives all your iniquity, who heals all your diseases, who redeems your life from the pit, who crowns you with steadfast love and mercy, who satisfies you with good so that your youth is renewed like the eagle's.

Today's name for God, *Physician*, is never actually attributed directly to Him. It is extremely easy to justify the use of the name, usually shown in writings as "The Great Physician."

Jesus did prophecy that others would refer to Him by the name Physician.

> Luke 4:23 (ESV) And he said to them, "Doubtless you will quote to me this proverb, 'Physician, heal yourself.' What we have heard you did at Capernaum, do here in your hometown as well."

Jesus also boldly proclaimed that He was the Messiah by reading from Isaiah, asserting that He was anointed with healing power. You can see both the original text in Isaiah and how Luke recorded the event in his Gospel.

> Isaiah 61:1-3 (ESV) The Spirit of the Lord GOD is upon me, because the LORD has anointed me to bring good news to the poor; he has sent me to bind up the brokenhearted, to proclaim liberty to the captives, and the opening of the prison to those who are bound; to proclaim the year of the LORD's favor, and the day of vengeance of our God; to

comfort all who mourn; to grant to those who mourn in Zion— to give them a beautiful headdress instead of ashes, the oil of gladness instead of mourning, the garment of praise instead of a faint spirit; that they may be called oaks of righteousness, the planting of the LORD, that he may be glorified.

Luke 4:18-19 (ESV) "The Spirit of the Lord is upon me, because he has anointed me to proclaim good news to the poor. He has sent me to proclaim liberty to the captives and recovering of sight to the blind, to set at liberty those who are oppressed, to proclaim the year of the Lord's favor."

Even though we looked earlier at the name *Healer*, there is something more implied by the name *Physician*. The Greek word used for "physician" is "iaomai", which means, "to cure, heal, make whole." Not only is God our *Healer*, He is also our *Physician*. Healing sickness and disease is needful; being healthy is the way God intended us to live. He provides both for us.

The passages from Isaiah and Luke above give us more insight into God's desire for us. He brings "good news to the poor", "binds the brokenhearted", "liberty to captives", "freedom to the imprisoned", and "favor with God." Furthermore, our Physician "comforts when we mourn, giving us beauty for ashes and the oil of gladness", "He leads the weary in praise", all so that He will be glorified.

That is some *Physician*. The main reason people do not recover under a physician's care is they do not follow his instructions. The same is true for the *Great Physician*. We must follow His direction, and He has promised to bring us to a place of, not only healing, but health, which is far better.

Potter

> Isaiah 64:8 (ESV) But now, O LORD, you are our Father; we are the clay, and you are our potter; we are all the work of your hand.

This name for God, *Potter*, is one of the most poetic in scripture. Many songs have been written using the imagery of God as the *Potter* and us as clay. It is even used other places in scripture.

> 2 Corinthians 4:7 (ESV) But we have this treasure in jars of clay, to show that the surpassing power belongs to God and not to us.

When you look at the account of creation in Genesis 2 you find the origin of this type (imagery) of the relationship of God as *Potter* and man as clay.

> Genesis 2:7 (ESV) then the LORD God formed the man of dust from the ground and breathed into his nostrils the breath of life, and the man became a living creature.

God's judgment is also viewed through the *Potter* metaphor.

> Psalm 2:9 (ESV) You shall break them with a rod of iron and dash them in pieces like a potter's vessel."

> Isaiah 30:12-14 (ESV) Therefore thus says the Holy One of Israel, "Because you despise this word and trust in oppression and perverseness and rely on them, therefore this iniquity shall be to you like a breach in a high wall, bulging out, and about to

collapse, whose breaking comes suddenly, in an instant; and its breaking is like that of a potter's vessel that is smashed so ruthlessly that among its fragments not a shard is found with which to take fire from the hearth, or to dip up water out of the cistern."

Jeremiah 19:10-11 (ESV) "Then you shall break the flask in the sight of the men who go with you, and shall say to them, 'Thus says the LORD of hosts: So will I break this people and this city, as one breaks a potter's vessel, so that it can never be mended. Men shall bury in Topheth because there will be no place else to bury.

The most important message using the *Potter*/clay picture is that of the Believer being shaped into the image of Jesus.

Romans 9:19-20 (ESV) You will say to me then, "Why does he still find fault? For who can resist his will?" But who are you, O man, to answer back to God? Will what is molded say to its molder, "Why have you made me like this?"

2 Timothy 2:20-21 (ESV) Now in a great house there are not only vessels of gold and silver but also of wood and clay, some for honorable use, some for dishonorable. Therefore, if anyone cleanses himself from what is dishonorable, he will be a vessel for honorable use, set apart as holy, useful to the master of the house, ready for every good work.

1 Thessalonians 4:3-4 (ESV) For this is the will of God, your sanctification: that you abstain from

sexual immorality; that each one of you know how to control his own body in holiness and honor,

There are more verses related to each of these images. This typology is where the Calvinists get their theology that God is in complete control, and man is subjected to God's discretion without any involvement of man's will.

The Armenians would interpret it a different way. Man must choose to put themselves on the *Potter*'s wheel and allow God to do His work; hence the "breaking, melting, molding" that is found in poetic verse.

I tend to lean more toward the Armenian approach, in that we have a choice as to whether we submit to the will of God for our life. Once we are identified with Christ, part of that identification is death to self (buried with Him), and then being raised to a new life in God (resurrection).

Regardless of how one gets on the *Potter*'s wheel, the result is the same: the clay is subjected to the Master's desire for the outcome. The outcome, by the way, is the same for everyone: we are to be conformed to the image of Christ.

Powerful

> Psalm 66:6-7 (ESV) There did we rejoice in him, who rules by his might (power) forever, whose eyes keep watch on the nations— let not the rebellious exalt themselves. Selah

For anyone who believes that God exists will acknowledge His power. He created the universe. He created you and me. He is *Powerful*. The psalmist, David, declares, "He rules by his might (power)." The Hebrew word used here is derived from "gabar" which means, "to be strong, prevail." God is *Powerful*.

There is a verse in the New Testament that uses four different Greek words for power to describe one act by God. That act was when He brought Jesus back from the dead. It is by far one of the most defining acts of God's power described in scripture.

> Ephesians 1:19-20 (KJV) And what is the exceeding greatness of his <u>power</u> to us-ward who believe, according to the <u>working</u> of his <u>mighty power</u>, Which he wrought in Christ, when he raised him from the dead, and set him at his own right hand in the heavenly places,

Four words are used to describe what God did in raising Jesus from the dead; "greatness of His power, working, mighty, and power".

> Greatness – Greek word "megethos", which means, "magnitude."

> Power – Greek word "dynamis", which means, "force, miraculous power." Our English word "dynamite" is derived from this word.

When you put these words together we get the phrase used to describe the damage that can be caused by explosives: megaton = 1 million pounds of TNT.

> Working – Greek word "energeia", which means, "efficiency." We get the word "energy" from this.

> Mighty – Greek word "ischys", which means, "force."

> Power – Greek word "kratos", which means, "vigor."

Paul used every way he could imagine to express the amazing display of power, might, and dominion that God had when He brought Jesus back from the dead.

When we think of that moment we resign ourselves to say, "Yes, but that was Jesus. Of course God did that for Him."

Here's the amazing part. Paul is describing what God did in the resurrection of Jesus to help us understand that God did the exact same thing for YOU when He saved you. Look at Ephesians 2:1:

> Ephesians 2:1 (KJV) And you *hath he quickened*, who were dead in trespasses and sins;

You may already know this, but when words are italicized in the KJV it means they are not actually in the original text. In other words, "hath he quickened" does not appear in the Greek text written by Paul. Because of the chapter and verse divisions added by the interpreters for reference purposes, they add some language to make Ephesians 2:1 a complete sentence.

They have done us a terrible injustice in this case. Because of the chapter break we assume Paul has started a new thought, but he has not. This is a continuation of the statement made in chapter one concerning Jesus being raised from the dead. The verse should rightly read:

> Ephesians 2:1 And you, who were dead in trespasses and sins.

To put it in context consider this restatement of the verses. I've omitted some of them because they make up a parenthetical thought that Paul inserts during his description of the resurrection of Jesus.

Remember, this is a prayer that Paul is describing for us that he prays over the Church.

> Ephesians 1:15 – 2:1 (KJV) Wherefore I also, after I heard of your faith in the Lord Jesus, and love unto all the saints, Cease not to give thanks for you, making mention of you in my prayers;
>
> Prayer Point 1: That the God of our Lord Jesus Christ, the Father of glory, may give unto you the spirit of wisdom and revelation in the knowledge of him:
>
> Prayer Point 2: The eyes of your understanding being enlightened;

Prayer Point 3: that ye may know what is the hope of his calling, and what the riches of the glory of his inheritance in the saints,

Prayer Point 4: And what is the exceeding greatness of his power to us-ward who believe, according to the working of his mighty power, Which he wrought in Christ, when he raised him from the dead, And you, who were dead in trespasses and sins;

Parenthetical thought: (and set him at his own right hand in the heavenly places, Far above all principality, and power, and might, and dominion, and every name that is named, not only in this world, but also in that which is to come: And hath put all things under his feet, and gave him to be the head over all things to the church, Which is his body, the fulness of him that filleth all in all.)

When you see it this way, you realize that God expended the same amount of effort to bring about your salvation as He did in bringing Jesus back from the dead!

That is why our God is called *Powerful*! Let us do like David, the psalmist in our text verse, said: Selah! Take some time and think about that.

Prince of Peace

Isaiah 9:6 (ESV) For to us a child is born, to us a son is given; and the government shall be upon his shoulder, and his name shall be called Wonderful Counselor, Mighty God, Everlasting Father, Prince of Peace.

Wow! How appropriate that this name for God shows up today. In the aftermath of the bombings in France and Lebanon it is difficult to imagine a world at peace. Isaiah prophesied that there was One coming that would be *The Prince of Peace*. This phrase is made up of two Hebrew words: "sar", which means "a head person (of any rank or class)", and "shalom", which means "safe."

When Jesus came as Messiah, He also came to demonstrate to us how to be safe, how to live at peace with everyone. Our mission is to bring as many into this "peace" as possible, by introducing them to The Prince of Peace, Jesus Christ.

There is much confusion (I choose to say that, even though it may be blatant ignorance) among many politicians and members of the media. They speak of Islam as a "peaceful religion." They arrive at this notion by asking imams and other Islamic leaders questions like, "Is this a peaceful religion?" To which, they always reply, "Yes, we strive for peace will all people."

Here's the truth. In Islam there is only one goal: for Allah to rule the world. Within that premise, there are only two states of being for a region. If Allah rules it is considered a "house of peace", but where Allah is not acknowledged as god, it is a "house of war." The "war" is aimed at ANYONE that does not bow to Allah. The notions of "houses" or "divisions" of the world in Islam such as Dar al-Islam and Dar al-Harb does not appear in the Quran or the Hadith. Early Islamic jurists devised these terms to denote legal rulings for ongoing Muslim conquests almost a century after Muhammad. (http://www.jewishvirtuallibrary.org/jsource/History/daralislam.html)

You cannot come to any other conclusion when looking at the barebones truth of Christianity and Islam. They cannot coexist. We cannot be "tolerant" of Islam. What is our recourse as Christians? Evangelize!! It is not our purpose to oppose them with force. That is the role of governments and the military. (I do not support the notion that Christians should not be involved in politics or the military.) Our job as the Church is to win them for Christ. We must tell them of *The Prince of Peace*, because that is the reality for which their hearts are searching.

Let us join the world in mourning for France and Lebanon. Let us also join together to pray for those blinded by Islam that they would see The Prince of Peace, the one known to them as Isa, and receive Him as the Messiah for which they seek.

Promise Keeper

> Isaiah 46:11 (ESV) calling a bird of prey from the east, the man of my counsel from a far country. I have spoken, and I will bring it to pass; I have purposed, and I will do it.

There is a common phrase used with speaking on the subject of integrity and accountability. Its source is unknown, but it says: A man's word is his bond. A bond is something you put up to assure the other party that you will do what you have agreed to do. If you do not fulfill your obligation you forfeit the bond. When ones word is all that is on the line, the other party has to trust you unwaveringly.

The only one that can truly use His word as bond is God. He is the *Promise Keeper*. In the passage above Isaiah makes a bold statement about God. Quoting the Lord's words, "I have spoken, and I will bring it to pass; I have purposed, and I will do it."

In today's world even an ironclad contract can be challenged in court. Depending on how cunning your attorney, the outcome is somewhat up for grabs. There are always "loop holes" in a contract. For a former president it came down to what the definition of "is" is. When you have to rely on the definition of "is" you are certainly grasping at straws.

Fortunately, our God lives at a whole level above anything mankind could muster in terms of keeping His word. Consider a few verses. The do not contain the phrase "*Promise Keeper*", but you can clearly conclude that it is a valid attribute that describes our God.

> Hebrews 1:3 (KJV) Who being the brightness of his glory, and the express image of his person, and upholding all things by the word of his power, when he had by himself purged our sins, sat down on the right hand of the Majesty on high;

Imagine that. Everything is upheld by the Word of God.

> Malachi 3:6 (KJV) For I am the LORD, I change not; therefore ye sons of Jacob are not consumed.

If God ever went back on His word everything that exists would be destroyed. If God ever changed His mind life would end.

> James 1:17 (KJV) Every good gift and every perfect gift is from above, and cometh down from the Father of lights, with whom is no variableness, neither shadow of turning.

Look at this. There is nothing that wavers in God, or even a slight change in His shadow. You can trust the *Promise Keeper* without reserve. You can trust Him with your most valuable asset or possession. You can trust Him with your life.

> Hebrews 6:13 (KJV) For when God made promise to Abraham, because he could swear by no greater, he swore by himself,

Truly, God's word was His bond. There was nothing greater than His word. Would that we would develop character to the degree that our word would be more valuable than our net worth. God, the *Promise Keeper*, can help us develop this kind of character. Trust Him.

Provider

> Matthew 6:31-33 (ESV) Therefore do not be anxious, saying, 'What shall we eat?' or 'What shall we drink?' or 'What shall we wear?' For the Gentiles seek after all these things, and your heavenly Father knows that you need them all. But seek first the kingdom of God and his righteousness, and all these things will be added to you.

Probably the most common attribute given to God is that of *Provider*. There have been more prayers of petition prayed that any other type. No one has a problem asking God to give them things. Many do not believe He will, but they ask anyway.

When we made the decision to move to Florence in 1998, we prayed and asked the Lord to be true to His word concerning us. We found a promise in scripture that became our focus.

> Mark 10:29-30 (ESV) Jesus said, "Truly, I say to you, there is no one who has left house or brothers or sisters or mother or father or children or lands, for my sake and for the gospel, who will not receive a hundredfold now in this time, houses and brothers and sisters and mothers and children and lands, with persecutions, and in the age to come eternal life.

We asked that everything we would need to be provided, including friends for our children, school, housing ... everything! And He did! We knew we were pursuing God's will and had complete confidence that He would provide.

Here's the truth concerning God's role as *Provider*. He has promised to supply every need that we have as Believer's. He is not a spiritual ATM, nor is He Santa Claus or the Easter Bunny. He is our Creator and takes responsibility for keeping us well. Our job is to seek after the things that He considers important. In the process of seeking after Him, He will in turn supply us with everything we need.

If you haven't read the entry on Jehovah Jireh I encourage you to do so (or re-read it). It helps clarify this attribute of *Provider*.

Misunderstandings arise from a lack of knowledge on what God "provides."

> Genesis 22:8 (ESV) Abraham said, "God will provide for himself the lamb for a burnt offering, my son." So they went both of them together.

> Abraham was following God's direction for his life. He was about to sacrifice the very son God had promised him. An "angel" stopped him, and instead a ram whose horns were caught in the bushes became the sacrifice.

> Joshua 1:13 (ESV) "Remember the word that Moses the servant of the LORD commanded you, saying, 'The LORD your God is providing you a place of rest and will give you this land.'

God promised to take Israel into the land He provided. It would be a place where they would live in God's rest as they served Him.

Philippians 4:19 (ESV) And my God will supply every need of yours according to his riches in glory in Christ Jesus.

The key word in this verse is "need." When we purse God's will for our life, the *Provider* makes sure that we have everything needed for the journey. His provision is always more than enough so that we can bless others along the way.

1 Peter 4:11 (ESV) whoever speaks, as one who speaks oracles of God; whoever serves, as one who serves by the strength that God supplies—in order that in everything God may be glorified through Jesus Christ. To him belong glory and dominion forever and ever. Amen.

Provision is not just material things. *Provider* also gives us strength to help us pursue His will. He gave us the Holy Spirit to empower us to be witnesses for Him. If you experience any lack consider this. What is God's plan for you? Are you pursuing that plan? I realize this is simplistic, but sometimes we miss out on the big picture because of little things.

The bottom line is that God is faithful. He will provide. Look for His provision. He is *Provider*.

Ready to Forgive

> Psalm 86:5 (NKJV) For You, Lord, are good, and ready to forgive, And abundant in mercy to all those who call upon You.

For many, forgiveness is not the first image that comes to mind when thinking of God. Instead they see Him as one ready to smack them in the head when they mess up. This is a very wrong view of God. He is Love. Remember that one? The psalmist, David, knew the true nature of God. David is referred to in scripture as a man after God's own heart.

> Acts 13:22 (ESV) And when he had removed him, he raised up David to be their king, of whom he testified and said, 'I have found in David the son of Jesse a man after my heart, who will do all my will.'

David had experienced God's forgiveness many times. God is always *Ready to Forgive*.

One of the most interesting passages of scripture is found in Genesis 18. God had pronounced judgment on the cities of Sodom and Gomorrah. Their sin was seen as a flagrant attempt to stand against God and His purpose. Abraham "stood before the Lord" and challenged God's plan to destroy everyone the two cities.

> Genesis 18:22-33 (ESV) So the men turned from there and went toward Sodom, but Abraham still stood before the LORD. Then Abraham drew near and said, "Will you indeed sweep away the righteous with the wicked? Suppose there are fifty

righteous within the city. Will you then sweep away the place and not spare it for the fifty righteous who are in it? Far be it from you to do such a thing, to put the righteous to death with the wicked, so that the righteous fare as the wicked! Far be that from you! Shall not the Judge of all the earth do what is just?" And the LORD said, "If I find at Sodom fifty righteous in the city, I will spare the whole place for their sake."

Abraham answered and said, "Behold, I have undertaken to speak to the Lord, I who am but dust and ashes. Suppose five of the fifty righteous are lacking. Will you destroy the whole city for lack of five?" And he said, "I will not destroy it if I find forty-five there." Again he spoke to him and said, "Suppose forty are found there." He answered, "For the sake of forty I will not do it." Then he said, "Oh let not the Lord be angry, and I will speak. Suppose thirty are found there." He answered, "I will not do it, if I find thirty there." He said, "Behold, I have undertaken to speak to the Lord. Suppose twenty are found there." He answered, "For the sake of twenty I will not destroy it." Then he said, "Oh let not the Lord be angry, and I will speak again but this once. Suppose ten are found there." He answered, "For the sake of ten I will not destroy it." And the LORD went his way, when he had finished speaking to Abraham, and Abraham returned to his place.

Some read this story and come to the conclusion that God "changed" His mind. Here is the truth regarding this dialog. I heard this from my former pastor, Mike Harrison, years ago. God did not change because of Abraham's pleading. God was simply acting according to

His nature. He is always *Ready to Forgive*. Because Abraham, someone God knew to be a righteous and just man, asked something of God, God did it. He wanted to show mercy to the people. Even though God knew there were none righteous in the cities, He was willing to spare them because of Abraham's intercession.

Let us learn to trust God and be willing to ask Him for mercy and forgiveness, not only for ourselves, but also for others. Imagine how our world could be different if we, like Abraham, interceded on behalf of others who are clearly outside of God's plan and purpose. God is willing and *Ready to Forgive*.

Reconciler

> 2 Corinthians 5:17-19 (ESV) Therefore, if anyone is in Christ, he is a new creation. The old has passed away; behold, the new has come. All this is from God, who through Christ reconciled us to himself and gave us the ministry of reconciliation;

These are two of the first verses I remember memorizing. When I understood the revelation found here I could not have been more excited. To realize that the moment I became a Christian God created a new spirit in me. Then, what He just accomplished in me, He commissioned me to go and do the same for others. He gave me "the ministry of reconciliation."

God is a *Reconciler*. His first desire for every person is be restored to right relationship with Him. We became separated from fellowship with God because of sin. The transgression against God's law caused the spirit of man to die. Through Jesus, God made a way back to life and fellowship with Him.

Redeemer

Isaiah 54:5 (ESV) For your Maker is your husband, the LORD of hosts is his name; and the Holy One of Israel is your Redeemer, the God of the whole earth he is called.

Of all the names we have looked at thus far, this name is one of the most important. It is a good thing that God is our Creator, that He is Awesome, Above All, Conqueror, Wonderworking, Everlasting, etc. But without a relationship with Him, our life is still nothing. There are powerful people in the earth, people of wealth, people of fame. But unless you are related to them through blood or friendship you will never benefit from them in any way.

That is where God is different. He came to us to bring us back into relationship with Him. He is *Redeemer*.

This word has lost meaning in our Western culture. Webster's defines the root word, "deem," as follows:

Deem – to think of (someone or something) in a particular way

transitive verb
: to come to think or judge : consider <deemed it wise to go slow>
intransitive verb
: to have an opinion : believe

To think of Redeemer in this way would mean that God chose to believe in us again, or changed His opinion of us. Neither of these reflects the Hebrew meaning of the word.

The Hebrew word used here is "gaal", which means, "redeem." But to the Eastern mind this is the process whereby property that once belonged to a relative is bought back by the next of kin. The practice also included a brother, or other male relative, would marry the widow if there were no children by the first marriage.

The story of Ruth gives us the picture of this process. Boaz was a kinsman redeemer. He bought the property from Naomi, and married Ruth. Both were acts of a redeemer. Both give us a picture of what God, The *Redeemer*, has done for us.

We were created as sons and daughters of the Most High God. Because of sin, we chose to leave Him and be joined with the devil. We lost everything we had coming from our birthright. But God did not leave us in this state. He sent our Brother, Christ Jesus, to redeem us. It cost Him is life in order to pay the ransom for our souls. He also reclaimed everything we had lost by overcoming death, hell, and the grave. He then betrothed Himself to us (The Church), and is coming again to be joined with His Bride.

With out this act of redemption we would all be lost, without hope. But thank the Lord, He is *Redeemer*. God has restored us to right relationship with Him, and has returned our birthright of blessing. So be thankful. We have a *Redeemer*.

Refiner

> Malachi 3:3 (ESV) He will sit as a refiner and purifier of silver, and he will purify the sons of Levi and refine them like gold and silver, and they will bring offerings in righteousness to the LORD.

The last name we looked at was one of the most welcomed names of God; that of *Redeemer*. Today's name probably one of the least welcomed. The same God that redeemed us also works as *Refiner*. God's plan each of us is to be conformed into the image of His Son, Jesus. He never forces His will upon us. We must be willing to allow the *Refiner* to do His work.

The process begins by the Lord, Himself, drawing us by the Holy Spirit. When we decide to become identified with Christ in His death, burial, resurrection, ascension, and seating at the right hand of the Father, the *Refiner* then begins His work. He begins by creating in us a new spirit, one that is alive to His voice and sensitive to His ways. We arc immediately made righteous and placed in right standing with God.

We develop a hunger for His word, the Bible, which begins to wash away the impurities of soulish habits and impure thought patterns. We begin a dialogue, prayer, where we share our thoughts with our Creator and He in turn shares His heart, the heart of the Father.

As with any good father, our Father brings correction, or refining, when needed; not to punish but to perfect. In Christ, we have been redeemed from the curse that comes from the law. We have been spared the punishment for sin by the sacrifice of Jesus' blood on the cross, the conquering of death, hell, and the grave by His resurrection, and have been given authority over sin by being seated at the right hand of God with Christ. Punishment is not needed for the Believer. Refining, however, is the constant work of the Holy Spirit until we have become the image of Christ.

We live in a fallen world. Our flesh will eventually become a victim of the consequence of sin. However, our spirit, created in us by God at salvation, will live forever. Our soul is being renewed as we learn to yield more fully to the Holy Spirit, and apply more completely the Word of God.

The completed work of the refiner is to remove all impurities. Usually this involves heating the substance, which causes impurities to either sink to the bottom or float to the top. The unwanted substance can then be skimmed off the top, or the purified substance can be poured out, usually into molds for further processing. Either way, things are removed, making the remaining material more valuable, and also more usable for the purpose for which it was created.

You are the most valuable thing in God's eyes. His only desire for you is that you become the best "you" possible. Willingly allow Him to be *Refiner*. You will never regret it.

Refuge

> Psalm 46:1 (ESV) God is our refuge and strength, a very present help in trouble.

We just looked at a similar name last time, but this one is different. It is good to know that God is the *Refuge from the Storm*. However, there does not have to be a storm for us to refuge in Him. He is also *Refuge*.

The same Hebrew name is used here. The word "mahseh" means, "shelter, hope." From the moment we are returned to right relationship with our Father God, He resumes His roll of *Refuge*. Psalm 91 describes it this way.

> Psalm 91:1-2 (ESV) He who dwells in the shelter of the Most High will abide in the shadow of the Almighty. I will say to the LORD, "My refuge and my fortress, my God, in whom I trust."

God is not just some place we run to when trouble comes. His presence is a continual covering for us. It is part of the Covenant that we have through Christ. When God sent the Holy Spirit to abide in us, He became much more than just a crisis manager. He is present to keep us in every way: spiritually, emotionally, physically.

> Psalm 3:3 (ESV) But you, O LORD, are a shield about me, my glory, and the lifter of my head.

This was part of Paul's prayer for the Church at Rome.

> Romans 15:13 (ESV) May the God of hope fill you with all joy and peace in believing, so that by the power of the Holy Spirit you may abound in hope.

The modern day definition of refuge gives us an accurate picture of God's nature as our *Refuge*.

> Refuge: 1) a condition of being safe or sheltered from pursuit, danger, or trouble.
> 2) something providing shelter.

I believe St. Patrick understood some things about God as *Refuge*. Look at this prayer written by Patrick.

> As I arise today,
> may the strength of God pilot me,
> the power of God uphold me,
> the wisdom of God guide me.
> May the eye of God look before me,
> the ear of God hear me,
> the word of God speak for me.
> May the hand of God protect me,
> the way of God lie before me,
> the shield of God defend me,
> the host of God save me.
> May Christ shield me today.
> Christ with me, Christ before me,
> Christ behind me,
> Christ in me, Christ beneath me,
> Christ above me,
> Christ on my right, Christ on my left,
> Christ when I lie down, Christ when I sit,
> Christ when I stand,
> Christ in the heart of everyone who thinks of me,
> Christ in the mouth of everyone who speaks of me,
> Christ in every eye that sees me,
> Christ in every ear that hears me.
> Amen

If we awoke to this revelation every day, there is nothing the enemy could do to stop us. God is our *Refuge*!

Refuge from the Storm

Isaiah 25:4 (ESV) For you have been a stronghold to the poor, a stronghold to the needy in his distress, a shelter from the storm and a shade from the heat; for the breath of the ruthless is like a storm against a wall,

Everyone needs help. Everyone. Hard times come, be it physical, mental, spiritual, financial, emotional, ... When those times come it is good to know we have a God that is the *Refuge from the Storm*. He is not moved by our circumstance. He is there to give us an unmovable rock to which we can cling. The winds will blow, the rains will come, the ground will shake, but God is faithful still.

The word "refuge" comes from the Hebrew word "mahseh", which means "a shelter, hope." It comes from a root word, which means, "flee for protection." Aren't you glad God did not leave us to fend for ourselves, to face life alone. He is the *Refuge from the Storm*.

A few years ago I found myself in a bad place. For the first time in my life I sought counseling to help me through the circumstance. I went through a prayer ministry called Sozo, where the facilitator helps you voice the issues you face and allow the Holy Spirit to speak to those issues.

As I was talking through the things going on in my life, I described it as "hitting the wall." During the process of praying through this image the Lord showed me that what I ran into was not a wall, but a rock; The Rock, who is Jesus. He reached down and pulled me up above the circumstances and let me find rest, *Refuge from the Storm*.

I am so grateful to know that regardless of how hard the storm, how big the challenge, God is bigger still. In these busy days full of bad news and frustration, hatred and violence, let us find our hope in God. Let's seek the *Refuge from the Storm*.

Repairer of the Breach

Isaiah 58:12 (ESV) And your ancient ruins shall be rebuilt; you shall raise up the foundations of many generations; you shall be called the repairer of the breach, the restorer of streets to dwell in.

As part of the human race, you were born with a hole in your soul. Your spirit was dead to the things of God because of the sin nature you inherited from Adam. But, God made provision to fix you from the beginning because He is the *Repairer of the Breach*.

The Hebrew word for "repairer" means, "to wall in or around, close up." The word for "breach" simply means, "a break, gap."

There is a common birth defect where a child is born with a hole in their heart. Every baby has one when they're born. It's how blood flows through the body, bypassing the lungs, since babies in the womb do not breath. Soon after birth, most children continue developing normally, and the hole closes, creating normal blood flow through the four chambers of the heart.

In the same way, our soul has a hole in it when we are born. The only way this hole can be filled is by allowing the *Repairer of the Breach* into our lives. We do this by being identified with Christ in His death, burial, resurrection, ascension, and seating at the right hand of the Father. We acknowledge that Jesus is the Son of God, that He was born of a virgin, He lived a sinless life, He died as payment for sin, was resurrected from the death, and now lives to intercede for us. This is what is known as salvation.

As we live life, things happen along the way. Things catch us off guard and in effect blow holes in our plans, or crash through the walls we have erected around our life. Again, the *Repairer of the Breach* is there to help us get back on our feet. He provides peace in the storm and then courage to exit the bunker and start rebuilding. He strengthens us, physically and spiritually, and gives faith to know there will be a better future.

Keep your faith in the *Repairer of the Breach*. He is for you, and not against you. He wants you to win at life. He wants you to be "planted by rivers of water" (Psalm 1:3) so you can be a help to others. During these holiday times be aware of others that may be experiencing a "breach" in their life. Help lead them to the *Repairer of the Breach* so they can be made whole.

Rescuer

> Daniel 6:27 (ESV) He delivers and rescues; he works signs and wonders in heaven and on earth, he who has saved Daniel from the power of the lions."

Today's name for God is an uncommon one. This English word is only used in the book of Daniel. It occurs three times. I almost chose to omit this name from the list because of this, but since it is used to refer to God, I included it. The name is attributed to God by King Darius, who was a non-believer. The name is *Rescuer*. It comes from the Hebrew word "nesal", which means, "to extricate." It comes from the root word "nāsal", which means, "to snatch away."

The reason I was hesitant to include this name is because it does not reflect God's nature as described in other places. It seems that most of the ways that God chooses to "extricate" His children is through "delivering" them. It is a subtle difference, but an important one. The word "rescue" implies an unexpected danger that came suddenly, requiring immediate assistance. The life of the Believer is to be lived in such a way that this never occurs.

With that being said, I understand we all get into circumstances where we feel overwhelmed. It seems like an "unexpected danger," but is usually a result of bad choices, or the fruit from bad seeds sown. God is still ready to help us in these times, but normally does so through "deliverance" by way of a process. So many treat God, *Rescuer*, as a "get out of jail free" card. They live life any way they choose and cry out to Him in times of trouble. That is the problem with referring to God as *Rescuer*.

This is not the case with Daniel. He was living his life with purpose with his actions being an example for all. Because of this, men schemed to destroy him, which led to him being thrown into the lion's den. King Darius then described the event from his perspective as God "rescuing him," when in fact God did not "extricate" Daniel from the den, but delivered him from harm IN the lion's den.

I know this may seem like an insignificant difference, but it makes a huge difference in how we live our lives. Rescue implies panic. Deliverance is a result of faith. Let us live with intentional trust that God will direct our steps and will provide an escape, deliverance, when we stray. However, regardless of the circumstance, our God is faithful, and will if necessary, be our *Rescuer*.

Revenger

> Psalm 94:1 (ESV) O LORD, God of vengeance, O God of vengeance, shine forth!
>
> Romans 12:19 (ESV) Beloved, never avenge yourselves, but leave it to the wrath of God, for it is written, "Vengeance is mine, I will repay, says the Lord."
>
> Deuteronomy 32:35 (ESV) Vengeance is mine, and recompense, for the time when their foot shall slip; for the day of their calamity is at hand, and their doom comes swiftly.'

Most of the names given to God are easy to consider. How could anyone not want to speak of God being Love, Forgiving, Kind, Mighty, Awesome, Creator, or Friend? We love those attributes, and it what draws us to Him in the first place. We love Him because He first loved us.

However, there are other names that we don't like to discuss, but are just as much a part of God's character as those cited above. Names like Just, Judge, Mighty & Terrible, and Refiner give us pause because mankind is sinful and He is perfect. It is a scary thing to boast of God being a God of Justice when we are not without sin.

Today's name is one of those names. When I saw the meaning of the Hebrew word I could not find it in me to see my God as *Revenger*. The name comes from "negama", which means, "avengement." The root of this word means, "revenge." My Western mindset has a difficult time with God being both Forgiver and *Revenger*.

I posed this question to a good friend and frequent source of knowledge, Dale Moore, Cullman, Alabama, to get another perspective. He shared some real wisdom, reflecting basically what Paul said in Romans. First, here is what Dale said:

> God is a God of Vengeance. He will bring forth justice. The problem arises within us. When we seek vengeance it is from an impure heart. God's motivation for all things is from righteousness, holiness, with no evil intent. Do I understand it all? No. It is true, nonetheless. It's the same idea as when God "repents" of something. He changes His mind or direction. It is not that He was incorrect or in sin before, as we associate with ourselves.[xiv]

Here is the way Paul said very similar things.

> Romans 3:1-8 (ESV) Then what advantage has the Jew? Or what is the value of circumcision? Much in every way. To begin with, the Jews were entrusted with the oracles of God. What if some were unfaithful? Does their faithlessness nullify the faithfulness of God? By no means! Let God be true though every one were a liar, as it is written, "That you may be justified in your words, and prevail when you are judged." But if our unrighteousness serves to show the righteousness of God, what shall we say? That God is unrighteous to inflict wrath on us? (I speak in a human way.) By no means! For then how could God judge the world? But if through my lie God's truth abounds to his glory, why am I still being condemned as a sinner? And why not do evil that good may come?—as some

people slanderously charge us with saying. Their condemnation is just.

Specifically, look at verse 5. "But if our unrighteousness serves to show the righteousness of God, what shall we say? That God is unrighteous to inflict wrath on us? (I speak in a human way.) By no means!" The phrase "inflict wrath" has the same meaning as *Revenger*. God does not sin in seeking revenge.

So, as you can clearly see, God is *Revenger*. The main difference is the motivation. He never acts out of spite – the process of getting even. He is only bringing justice to avenge the wrongs done against His Children. Rest easy as a Child of God. He has already exacted His revenge for your sin when Jesus was slain on the cross. The price has been paid. Now live with your Father in peace.

Righteous

Psalm 5:8 (ESV) Lead me, O LORD, in your righteousness because of my enemies; make your way straight before me.

We first encountered this attribute of God when we looked at Jehovah-Tsidkenu (The Lord Our Righteousness). I encourage you to go read it if you have not already done so. That particular name, however, focuses more on God making us righteous. He is the Lord That Sanctifies.

Today's name speaks directly of God's character. He is *Righteous*. This comes from the Hebrew word "sedana", which means, "rightness, subjective, moral." The root word is "sadaq", which means, "to be right, cleanse, clear self, just."

Any time you think of humans, these are not the words that come to mind. After the fall of Adam man inherited a sin nature. It is impossible for man to be "right" again without Jesus. In order for us to have a fallen nature, there had to be a place from which to fall.

Adam received his nature from God Himself. Adam was created righteous. He was "right" from God's perspective. *Righteous* created one in His own image. When Adam chose to sin he "fell" from that place of righteousness.

The only hope we have now is for *Righteous* to change us, remake us as it were, so that we can once again be "right." This is called the new birth. God recreates our spirit so that we are once again able to have fellowship with *Righteous*.

> 2 Corinthians 5:17 (ESV) Therefore, if anyone is in Christ, he is a new creation. The old has passed away; behold, the new has come.

You see, salvation is when we are baptized, or immersed, into Christ by the Holy Spirit. This is not water baptism, but instead a rebirth of our spirit by the Holy Spirit. Jesus' blood overwhelms (baptizes) us, which washes away all unrighteousness.

> 2 Corinthians 5:18-19 (ESV) All this is from God, who through Christ reconciled us to himself and gave us the ministry of reconciliation; that is, in Christ God was reconciling the world to himself, not counting their trespasses against them, and entrusting to us the message of reconciliation.

We have an amazing God. He is *Righteous*. He created us to be righteous, just like Him, and has made a way for us to become righteous once more. Submit to the plan He has for you and live life as He intended for you to live.

Rock

2 Samuel 22:32 (ESV) "For who is God, but the LORD? And who is a rock, except our God?

This is one of my favorite images that God used to reveal Himself to man, and more specifically, Israel and the Church. I shared on this subject at communion last year. Here are those thoughts that sum up what scripture shares on this name: *Rock*.

Communion – 2014 06 01

The *Rock* – Jesus Christ

After leaving Egypt for the trip to the Promised Land, Canaan, the Israelites wandered in the wilderness for 40 years. During this time of wandering they came to a place of needing water two different times. They were thirsty, their animals were thirsty, and there was no water available. When they called on Moses to give them water, he turned to the Lord.

During the first episode the Lord gave Moses instruction to "strike the rock" to get water. He obeyed. Water came forth so that all of the people (estimates have them at 3-5 million people) AND their livestock received all the water they needed. All of this water came from a rock. The people rejoiced and went on with wilderness life.

During the second episode the Lord gave Moses instruction to "speak to the rock" to get water. Moses was upset with the people because of their constant complaining. Out of this anger he struck the rock a second time. Water still came forth, enough to water all of the people and their animals. The people rejoiced and went on with wilderness life.

Moses, however, received correction from the Lord. Because of the one, seemingly simple, act of disobedience the Lord did not allow Moses to enter into the Promised Land that he dreamed of for 40 years.

Moses learned some things from this encounter. Near the end of his life, Moses sang a song recorded in Deuteronomy 32 where he declares "He is the *Rock*, His work is perfect". In another place he said, "… of the *Rock* who begot you, you are unmindful, and have forgotten the God who fathered you." And again said "How could one chase a thousand, and two put ten thousand to flight, unless their *Rock* has caused them to surrender? For their rock (little 'r') is not like our *Rock* (capital 'R')."

Moses was introduced to The *Rock* when he asked to see God's glory. In Exodus 33 it tells us that God placed Moses on a *Rock*. Then when He passed by, He placed Moses in a cleft in the *Rock* and covered him with His hand. Then God removed His hand so Moses could see His back. Moses knew the *Rock*. He found safety, protection, and provision in the *Rock*.

When assuming leadership after Moses it was apparent Joshua knew The *Rock*. We can see this in Joshua 24:26-27. "Then Joshua wrote these words in the Book of the Law of God. And he took a large stone, and set it up there under the oak that was by the sanctuary of the LORD. And Joshua said to all the people, 'Behold, this stone shall be a witness to us, for it has heard all the words of the LORD which He spoke to us. It shall therefore be a witness to you, lest you deny your God.'" The Stone had heard all the words spoken, and would be a witness.

Gideon encountered the *Rock*. The Angel of the Lord asked Gideon to place meat and bread on a rock, and then pour broth over it. The Angel touched the *Rock* with the end of His staff and fire came out of it, and consumed the meat and bread. Gideon built an altar and named it Jehovah-Shalom: The Lord is Peace.

Hannah made a declaration when she took Samuel to the temple to dedicate him to the Lord. "No one is holy like the Lord, for there is none besides You, Nor is there any rock like our God."

In David's song, just before his death, said, "The Lord is my rock and my fortress and my deliverer." The last words David spoke were, "The Spirit of the Lord spake to me, and his word was in my tongue. The God in Israel said, the Rock of Israel spake to me."

In Psalm 18 David declares, "The LORD is my rock and my fortress and my deliverer; My God, my strength, in whom I will trust. For who is God, except the LORD? And who is a rock, except our God? The LORD lives! Blessed be my Rock! Let the God of my salvation be exalted."

Isaiah said, "Behold, I lay in Zion a stone for a foundation, A tried stone, a precious cornerstone, a sure foundation."

Matthew, Paul, and Peter all referred to Jesus as the "Chief Cornerstone."

Here is the best part. That Stone, Jesus, is still with us today. He is the very foundation of our faith. He was from the beginning, and will always be. One question came to mind as I looked at the story of Moses and the people of Israel as they journeyed. How was it that there was always a Rock around when they needed one?

The answer is found in 1 Corinthians: Moreover, brethren, I do not want you to be unaware that all our fathers were under the cloud, all passed through the sea, all were baptized into Moses in the cloud and in the sea, all ate the same spiritual food, and all drank the same spiritual drink. **For they drank of that spiritual Rock that followed them, and that Rock was Christ.**

Imagine the sight. God's people were led by a pillar of cloud by day, a pillar of fire by night. The cloud kept them moving in the right direction, provided shade from the intense heat. Then at night the pillar of fire gave them assurance of God's presence and provided warmth through the cold nights. That sounds just like the Holy Spirit; The Comforter, The Guide.

Then, behind them, The *Rock* was following them, being their rear guard, giving them support and strength.

This is modeled for us in the Old Testament, but we have a better covenant. These things are no longer pictures or examples of what God can do. Now it is reality! Now we have the Holy Spirit that dwells in us, to lead us and give comfort. Now we have The *Rock*, which is Christ, upon which we can build our lives and know we are anchored on a sure foundation that cannot be shaken or eroded in any way.

So, we choose this day to remember The Stone that has heard everything God has said, and now stands to bear witness to us of the Truth of God. That Stone the world rejected at the cross, buried in a hole in the ground, now lives as the Son of God, our Elder Brother, that sits at the right hand of God, praying for you and me. Eat the bread, drink the cup, and remember The *Rock*.

Jesus came as a Baby, died as a Lamb, but revealed Himself as the *Rock*. Come, let us adore Him!

Rock of My Refuge

Psalm 94:22 (ESV) But the LORD has become my stronghold, and my God the rock of my refuge.

When my wife was expecting our first child every development was met with excitement and wonder. The process of a single cell becoming a baby was more than we could fathom. As our baby grew inside his mother, what started out as a "cavernous dwelling" eventually became a tight, cramped space.

Toward the end of the pregnancy this child would try to free himself from his cramped quarters by pressing his feet on his mother's ribs and attempt to straighten his body. This caused by wife much discomfort; so much so that she would nearly drop to her knees. Delivery could not come soon enough.

How does this relate to the topic at hand? The name of God for today is *Rock of My Refuge*. The word "rock" comes from the Hebrew word "tsur" which means, "cliff, a rock or boulder." It comes from the Hebrew word "sur" which means, "cramp, confine." The other word "refuge" comes from the Hebrew word "mahseh" which means, "shelter, place of hope."

While in the womb our son felt cramped, confined, and wanted out. However, it was the very best place for him to continue to develop because he was not ready to come out.

The *Rock of My Refuge* can sometimes feel like a tight place. Our will wants to break out and do what we think is best. But God has knowledge of what is best for us.

He knows the "due date" for our deliverance into His plan and purpose for our life. Trust Him. He is not trying to imprison us. We are there by our own will. Unlike my son trying to escape the womb, *Rock of My Refuge* will let us free to pursue our own will.

If we can find it in us to allow *Rock of My Refuge* to complete His work in us during the time of restraint, we can come out of this ready to breathe fresh air into our lungs and experience the embrace of the One that loves us completely. As He feeds us the milk of His word, and we hear His voice whisper in our ear, we grow stronger; more capable of fulfilling our destiny.

I know this may seem to contradict some of the "freedom in Christ" message. But the truest form of freedom comes when I operate inside the boundaries that *Rock of My Refuge* has established for me.

Rock of My Salvation

> Psalm 89:26 (ESV) He shall cry to me, 'You are my Father, my God, and the Rock of my salvation.'

Today's name is *Rock of My Salvation*. Combining these two words is a bit of an oxymoron. As we saw last time, the Hebrew word interpreted "rock" means, "cliff, a rock or boulder, refuge." Its root word means, "to confine." In contrast to that is the Hebrew word "yeshua", which is interpreted as "salvation." It means, "something saved," and comes from a root word that means, "open, wide, free."

When you put these together you get an interesting view of the work of God in our life. When we accept the salvation provided for us through the sacrifice of Jesus, and become identified with Him in His death, burial, resurrection, ascension, and seating in heaven, we enter into a place of refuge; a tight, secure place in God. In that place, and only in that place, are we then free. We are able to plumb the depths of the freedom found in the love of Christ.

> Ephesians 3:14-19 (ESV) For this reason I bow my knees before the Father, from whom every family in heaven and on earth is named, that according to the riches of his glory he may grant you to be strengthened with power through his Spirit in your inner being, so that Christ may dwell in your hearts through faith—that you, being rooted and grounded in love, may have strength to comprehend with all the saints what is the breadth and length and height and depth, and to know the love of Christ that surpasses knowledge, that you may be filled with all the fullness of God.

Only in the constraint of God's love can we be free. Consequently, anything we can do from the position of God's love we can do with no condemnation! That is true liberty defined.

The Hebrew word for "salvation" is very similar to the word for Joshua, which is "yehoshua." Joshua is the Hebrew origin of name for Jesus. The *Rock of Our Salvation* is Jesus Christ, the Messiah, Whose birth we celebrate at Christmas. The Believer's destiny is to be conformed to His image. We are to allow everything that is not found in Jesus to fall away from us: both behavior and attitudes. We are then commanded to love as He loved; selfless, sacrificial, holy.

> Matthew 22:36-40 (ESV) "Teacher, which is the great commandment in the Law?" And he said to him, "You shall love the Lord your God with all your heart and with all your soul and with all your mind. This is the great and first commandment. And a second is like it: You shall love your neighbor as yourself. On these two commandments depend all the Law and the Prophets."

In Christ we are free; free from sin, and constrained to love. That is freedom indeed!

Rose of Sharon

> Song of Songs 2:1 (ESV) I am a rose of Sharon, a lily of the valleys.

This is another poetic name for God. It is used in the Song of Songs (or Song of Solomon) in reference to the Lover (Jesus) speaking of His Love (the Church). The reference is more than poetic. It is also prophetic: *Rose of Sharon*.

> Isaiah 35:1-2 (ESV) The wilderness and the dry land shall be glad; the desert shall rejoice and blossom like the crocus; it shall blossom abundantly and rejoice with joy and singing. The glory of Lebanon shall be given to it, the majesty of Carmel and Sharon. They shall see the glory of the LORD, the majesty of our God.

The ESV translation uses "crocus" in place of rose (KJV), even though it is the same word. The reason for this is because the *Rose of Sharon* is believed to be the saffron-crocus flower. It is a very common flower in the plain known as Sharon.

I could easily see why it would be used to describe our Lord. It is a perennial that has a beautiful purple color. Each saffron flower has three vivid crimson stigmas. Combine these two things, purple color for royalty, and three crimson stigmas, it becomes a very fitting prophetic image of Messiah, who is THE *Rose of Sharon*.

Additionally, you can grind the stigma from the saffron and make a spice. This spice is very rare because of the number of flowers needed to make just a pound of the substance, and it is made by hand. This spice is known to have medicinal qualities, healing or improving a number of physical ailments. This, too, reminds me of our Lord, the Healer.

The meaning of the word "Sharon" in Hebrew is "to be straight or even, to make right."

When you combine these two words the meaning is very clear. The *Rose of Sharon* is a picture of the Lord Jesus Christ, our Messiah, who came to "make right" the things that separated us from Father. He is in love with His Bride, the Church, and gave Himself for Her.

Do not make His sacrifice in vain. Receive Him as your Lord. Let Him be the *Rose of Sharon* in your life.

Ruler

Judges 8:23 (ESV) Gideon said to them, "I will not rule over you, and my son will not rule over you; the LORD will rule over you."

There is little argument among non-atheists that God is Ruler. There is much debate from that point on over what type of Ruler He is. This particular name for God gives us some insight into exactly how God Rules.

The word "ruler" comes from the Hebrew word "mashal," which means, "to have dominion, governor." These words do not speak of a dictator. It does not speak of someone that rules by fear or vicious violence inflicted on those being ruled. When one has dominion there is no need for this type of behavior. The Ruler and His subjects acknowledge the relationship in which they engage one another.

In a monarchy, there is a king and his subjects. A true king does what is best for those within his domain. He acts in ways to bring about good for the lives of his subjects and further the advance of the kingdom.

A king takes the throne in one of three ways: by birth, bestowal, or conquest. When one is born into the royal family he becomes heir to the throne. If there is no rightful heir within the royal linage the throne can be bestowed upon an individual chosen by the reigning king. The last way is to wage war against a kingdom and conquer it, and in doing so take the throne by conquest.

When considering this in light of God there are several ways to apply this. First of all, God created the heavens and the earth. In doing so, He has dominion over all of creation. He is Ruler. As such, He bestowed dominion to man. Man, through the scheme of satan, gave that dominion over to satan.

Secondly, after the fall of Adam, God had to enter into His creation as a man in order to redeem man through the laws that govern His creation. He did this by sending His Son, Jesus, to become a human, live a sinless life, and take back the dominion that man ceded to satan during the fall.

> John 1:14 (ESV) And the Word became flesh and dwelt among us, and we have seen his glory, glory as of the only Son from the Father, full of grace and truth.

Jesus came, first of all, as a King by birth; He was the Son of the Ruler, God. He became a man, born of a woman, laid aside His royal linage in order to save mankind.

Secondly, Jesus became King by bestowal. God bestowed upon Him a name that is above every name.

> Philippians 2:9-11 (ESV) Therefore God has highly exalted him and bestowed on him the name that is above every name, so that at the name of Jesus every knee should bow, in heaven and on earth and under the earth, and every tongue confess that Jesus Christ is Lord, to the glory of God the Father.

Lastly, Jesus became King by conquest.

> Ephesians 4:8-10 (ESV) Therefore it says, "When he ascended on high he led a host of captives, and

he gave gifts to men." (In saying, "He ascended," what does it mean but that he had also descended into the lower regions, the earth? He who descended is the one who also ascended far above all the heavens, that he might fill all things.)

By this we see that God the Father is Ruler; He created all things. Jesus is Ruler on three levels; birth, bestowal, conquest. As Believers, we are in a Kingdom, not of this world, that is ruled by King that loves us without reserved, that created us for the purpose of expanding His Kingdom by making disciples, helping them find their true identity as sons and daughters of the King (God) and joint heirs with the King (Jesus).

Salvation

> Psalm 91:16 (ESV) With long life I will satisfy him and show him my salvation."

There are 171 references to "salvation" in the King James Version of the Bible. It is a common word heard in churches. Every believer has most likely heard this word used in describing the experience of becoming a Christian.

However, *Salvation* is not an experience. It is a person, Jesus Christ. The word "salvation" is the Hebrew name from which Jesus is derived. It means, "something saved, deliverance, aid, victory, prosperity, health, help."

I have changed some of the words that I use to describe the Christian life. Instead of calling someone a "Christian," I prefer the word "Believer." The word Christian was actually used in scripture as derogatory comment toward those who were following the teachings of Jesus. It implied they were being "little Christs," simply imitating what Jesus came to show us. Someone who is born again is not imitating anything. They have received a new spirit on the inside that came from the Holy Spirit. That is genuine re-birth, not merely becoming a copycat.

Another word that I no longer use is "saved." Instead, I use the terminology that Paul gave us Ephesians 1 and 2. I refer to the experience as "identification with Christ," His death, burial, resurrection, ascension, and seating at the right hand of God.

You don't have to agree with me on any of this for us to walk in fellowship. These words just help me as I attempt to walk out the relationship that I have with God. He is *Salvation*.

Consider some other references to *Salvation* found in scripture.

> Luke 2:25-32 (ESV) Now there was a man in Jerusalem, whose name was Simeon, and this man was righteous and devout, waiting for the consolation of Israel, and the Holy Spirit was upon him. And it had been revealed to him by the Holy Spirit that he would not see death before he had seen the Lord's Christ. And he came in the Spirit into the temple, and when the parents brought in the child Jesus, to do for him according to the custom of the Law, he took him up in his arms and blessed God and said, "Lord, now you are letting your servant depart in peace, according to your word; for my eyes have **seen your salvation** (Jesus) that you have prepared in the presence of all peoples, a light for revelation to the Gentiles, and for glory to your people Israel."
>
> Acts 4:12 (ESV) And there is **salvation in no one else** (Jesus), for there is no other name under heaven given among men by which we must be saved."
>
> Revelation 12:10 (ESV) And I heard a loud voice in heaven, saying, "Now the **salvation and the power and the kingdom of our God and the authority of his Christ have come** (Jesus), for the accuser of our brothers has been thrown down, who accuses them day and night before our God.

When you encounter Jesus, you have found *Salvation*. When you allow the Holy Spirit to baptize you into Christ (new birth), identify yourself with Christ, His death, burial, resurrection, ascension, and seating at the right had of Father, you are a Believer. Let us embrace *Salvation*, Jesus Christ, and allow Him to live through us so others can come to know *Salvation* as well.

Satisfier of Desires

> Psalm 145:16 (ESV) You open your hand; you satisfy the desire of every living thing.

Today's name for God has been hotly debated for a long time. Some argue that the desire of man has been corrupted by sin with no hope of redemption. In other words, man could never have a "righteous" desire; it is simply not in him, even after being saved. Some even go to the extreme of isolating themselves from society and live in monasteries to remove any evil influence that would cause them to have a fleshly desire.

Another perspective is that the only desires that God will respond to are those that God Himself places in man. Most of these folks teach the sovereignty of God to the extent that nothing happens in the life of man that God did not orchestrate.

To me, the Believer still has a will and can have his own desires that are not evil. I believe that as our soul is being saved (renewing of the mind – Romans 12:2) our desires reflect the transformation being accomplished in us as we submit ourselves to the work of the Holy Spirit as He conforms us to the image of Jesus.

> Romans 8:29 (ESV) For those whom he foreknew he also predestined to be conformed to the image of his Son, in order that he might be the firstborn among many brothers.

This is God's desire for every person.

When you look at the Hebrew words used in Psalm 145:16, you see a clear picture of the nature of God as the *Satisfier of Desires*. The Hebrew word for "satisfy" is "saba," which means, "to sate." We do not use this word much today, but we are familiar with "saturate," which is based on this word. It means, "fill to satisfaction."

The Hebrew word for "desire" is "rason." It means, "delight." It comes from the root word "rasa," which means, "; to be pleased with; specifically to satisfy a debt." From this we see that the *Satisfier of Desires* wants to saturate us with delight. It is His heart for us to be filled with the "joy of our salvation." (Psalm 51:12)

Consider these verses that refer to the *Satisfier of Desires*.

> Psalm 37:4 (KJV) Delight thyself also in the LORD; and he shall give thee the desires of thine heart.

> Psalm 103:2-5 (ESV) Bless the LORD, O my soul, and forget not all his benefits, who forgives all your iniquity, who heals all your diseases, who redeems your life from the pit, who crowns you with steadfast love and mercy, who satisfies you with good so that your youth is renewed like the eagle's.

For the sake of being complete let me add this thought. The fact that God is the *Satisfier of Desires* does not mean that every Believer will wear designer clothes, live in a mansion, and drive a Mercedes. I have actually heard someone say, "Shopping at Wal-Mart is a sin, because God wants better things for you." Oh, how far we have missed the Gospel message.

As we pursue the Lord, and as He pursues us, the "stuff" really isn't the focus. Whatever we desire as we seek Him will all of heart, He said He would "satisfy us with delight." I'm o.k. with that.

Satisfier of the Longing Soul

Psalm 107:9 (ESV) For he satisfies the longing soul, and the hungry soul he fills with good things.

God has been pursuing man since the original sin in the Garden of Eden. If you remember the story, God is the one who called out, "Adam, where are you?" He is still pursuing us today. When He encounters someone who is also pursuing Him there is a divine connection that brings life and peace; satisfaction.

We are the creation of God whether we pursue Him or not. But when we realize we are not complete without Him, a longing develops is our heart; a longing that can only be filled by Him. The good news is that He is ready to respond to our longing, and will satisfy it completely.

The Hebrew word "saba" means, "to saturate, to fill completely." The *Satisfier of the Longing Heart* will totally meet your expectations, and exceed them.

The problem is not in His ability to satisfy. The problem is with the lack of longing in our heart.

The Hebrew word used for "longing" is "shaqaq", and means, "to seek greedily, have an appetite." From this we see that God is not moved by merely thinking about Him. Our thoughts must grow into a desire for relationship, to again be one with our Creator.

Consider these verses.

2 Chronicles 16:9 (ESV) For the eyes of the LORD run to and fro throughout the whole earth, to give

strong support to those **whose heart is blameless toward him.** You have done foolishly in this, for from now on you will have wars."

Matthew 7:7-8 (ESV) "**Ask**, and it will be given to you; **seek**, and you will find; **knock**, and it will be opened to you. For everyone who asks receives, and the one who seeks finds, and to the one who knocks it will be opened.

Deuteronomy 4:29 (ESV) But from there **you will seek the LORD** your God and **you will find him**, if you search after him with **all your heart** and with all your soul.

Deuteronomy 6:5 (ESV) You shall love the LORD your God with **all your heart** and with all your soul and with all your might.

Jeremiah 29:13 (ESV) You will **seek me and find me**, when you seek me with **all your heart.**

If we seek we will find. If we ask He will answer. If we knock He will open. He is already seeking for us for the purpose of intervening in our situation. He wants to come with His strength to change our circumstances if we will only turn our heart toward Him, the *Satisfier of the Longing Heart*.

The last step in our identification with Christ in salvation is being seated with Him at the right hand of Father God. This is what Paul meant when he said, "Set your mind on things above." (Colossians 3:2) We do this by changing our focus. It comes by changing the longings of our heart.

Colossians 3:1-2 (ESV) If then you have been raised with Christ, seek the things that are above, where Christ is, seated at the right hand of God. Set your minds on things that are above, not on things that are on earth.

This is not new age "mind over matter" jargon. This is our spirit calling out to the Spirit of God. When that divine connection is made, the *Satisfier of the Longing Heart* will move heaven and earth, if needed, to totally fill the longing of your heart. As a matter of fact, He already has moved heaven and earth by sending His Son, Jesus, so that we can be reconciled to our Creator, God.

Savior

> Luke 2:11 (ESV) For unto you is born this day in the city of David a Savior, who is Christ the Lord.

We all need a Savior. Without Jesus we would have no hope of ever knowing our Creator. Of course, the Creator knew this, and sent us a Savior; His own Son, Jesus Christ.

The word "savior" is derived from the Greek word "soter", which means, "deliverer." The root of "soter" is the Greek word "sozo," which means, "to save." Jesus came to save us. He did this by bringing us back into right standing with God. He delivered us from the grip of satan, the kingdom of darkness, and brought us back to the Kingdom of God.

> Colossians 2:13-15 (ESV) And you, who were dead in your trespasses and the uncircumcision of your flesh, God made alive together with him, having forgiven us all our trespasses, by canceling the record of debt that stood against us with its legal demands. This he set aside, nailing it to the cross. He disarmed the rulers and authorities and put them to open shame, by triumphing over them in him.

> Colossians 1:13-14 (ESV) He has delivered us from the domain of darkness and transferred us to the kingdom of his beloved Son, in whom we have redemption, the forgiveness of sins.

Many refer to the process of becoming a Believer as "being saved." President Jimmy Carter made popular the phrase "born again" to refer to becoming a Believer.

Whether you call it saved, born again, redeemed, washed in the blood, etc., it all comes back to Jesus. He is the Author and Finisher of our faith. (Hebrews 12:2) The end result is still the same. God has reconciled us back to Himself through the Savior-Deliverer-Sacrificial Lamb-King, Jesus.

If you have never known Jesus as Savior, find out what all He did for you. You might be surprised.

Shade on Your Right Hand

> Psalm 121:5 (ESV) The LORD is your keeper; the LORD is your shade on your right hand.

This name for God is one that is not very familiar to our Western-culture mindset. The "shade" part we understand fairly well, or at least we did before air conditioning. However, the significance of the "right hand" doesn't really ring a loud gong for us. Let's consider a few things as we learn to see God as the *Shade on Your Right Hand*.

First of all, it does not mean that only your right hand will be shaded. Right "side" might be a more appropriate term for our way of thinking. In the Eastern mindset geographical orientation was not positioned toward the North as we do today. It was oriented toward the East. This would make "right" toward the South. At the time of this writing most of the known world was north of the equator. Consequently, the intensity of the sun's rays came from the "right." Being a mostly desert climate, shade was crucial to the well-being of individuals that lived during this time.

Another insight into the significance of the "right hand" comes from battle. The warrior of the day carried a shield and a sword; the sword in his right hand, the shield in his left. This left his right side exposed. Having someone fighting with you on your right side would guard against attack from your unshielded right.

Some commentators on this passage believe the metaphor of shade and right hand are not connected. Instead, they feel the verse should read, "The Lord is your keeper, the Lord is your shade; He is on your right hand." This doesn't significantly change the meaning of the text. But thinking of it this way, it gives us even more reason to love and appreciate our God.

I love this name, *Shade on Your Right Hand*, because it speaks to the level at which the Lord involves Himself in our lives. It shows the tight relationship He was to forge with us. He wants to walks with us as He did with Adam in the Garden.

We love the names of God like Healer, Provider, All Mighty, etc., but realize that day in, day out, God is right beside us providing *Shade on Your Right Hand*.

Shadow from the Heat

Isaiah 25:4 (ESV) For you have been a stronghold to the poor, a stronghold to the needy in his distress, a shelter from the storm and a shade from the heat; for the breath of the ruthless is like a storm against a wall,

For those of us in the South we know what heat can be like. In the dog days of summer there is no escaping the heat. It seems to literally stick to you.

However, there is another way to look at this word. Heat is also used to describe intense trials or troubles. It can also refer to pressure being applied to a person or situation, as in "turn up the heat."

This name for God, *Shadow from the Heat*, is more closely aligned with the second application of heat. The Hebrew word for "shadow" is "sel" which means, "shade." It comes from the word "salal" which means, "to hover over." The second part of this name, "heat", comes from the Hebrew word "horeb" which means, "drought or desolation." It comes from another word, "hereb" which means, "drought, or also interpreted as a cutting instrument, such as knife, sword, etc."

From this we see that the *Shadow from the Heat* watches over us to keep us from being destroyed by intense heat, or dryness. It reminds me of Shadrach, Meshach, and Abednego. (Daniel 3) The king had the furnace turned up seven times hotter than normal before throwing the men into the fire. While there were in the furnace those witnessing the event counter four men in the flames. The

Shadow from the Heat was with them to keep them from destruction.

Another reference that comes to mind is the word spoken to Mary by the angel when he presented the invitation to become the mother of Jesus. Mary had some questions. She considered the "heat" that would come from others discovering she was pregnant, even through she knew she had never been with a man. The angel assured her by saying, "The Holy Spirit will come upon you, and the power of the Most High will overshadow you..." (Luke 1:35) She was promised that the *Shadow from the Heat* would be near to keep her through the trying times to come. This comforted her to the point of agreeing to be the mother of God's son.

When Jesus asked others to follow Him He promised that there would be trouble. He also said, "Be of good cheer because I have overcome the world." The *Shadow from the Heat* would watch over His beloved, the Church, to keep them in times of drought and intense pressure. Trust Him as Mary did, and say, "Be it unto me according to Your word."

Shepherd

Psalm 23:1-6 (ESV) The LORD is my shepherd; I shall not want. He makes me lie down in green pastures. He leads me beside still waters. He restores my soul. He leads me in paths of righteousness for his name's sake.

Even though I walk through the valley of the shadow of death, I will fear no evil, for you are with me; your rod and your staff, they comfort me.

You prepare a table before me in the presence of my enemies; you anoint my head with oil; my cup overflows. Surely goodness and mercy shall follow me all the days of my life, and I shall dwell in the house of the LORD forever.

The writer of this psalm knew the subject very well. David was raised by a shepherd, to be a shepherd. David not only lived the life of a shepherd, he had a revelation of The *Shepherd*. He knew it was in God's heart to care for His people as a shepherd cares for his sheep. Even after David became king he never lost his heart for the people.

The Hebrew word for "shepherd" is "raa," which means, "to tend a flock; literally, to pasture it (feed it)." The shepherd usually did not own the sheep in the herd he was tending. That added to the commitment of being shepherd. You were a steward over someone else's property.

This is a good picture of the modern-day shepherd (pastor, minister, overseer, etc.). They do not own the sheep (members of the congregation) that they lead. They are given charge to feed them; nothing more. Jesus is our example. He is the Good Shepherd.

In order for us to rightly relate to our God, it is important to know His character and understand His ways. Sheep follow the shepherd and trusts him explicitly, without reserve. We must come to our *Shepherd* the same way. True faith, or unfeigned as the KJV describes it in Timothy, leads us to trust The *Shepherd* with our lives, willing to follow wherever He leads us, knowing He always has our best interest in mind.

The Believer's goal is to know God as *Shepherd* the way David describes in Psalm 23. If we can do that our life will be blessed like the sheep blessed by the shepherd; every need supplied, every care handled by the shepherd, growing and reproducing the way we were intended.

Shield

> Psalm 3:3 (ESV) But you, O LORD, are a shield about me, my glory, and the lifter of my head.

This is one of my favorite verses of scripture. I love the image created when I think of God, Himself, lifting the head of one that is hanging down. However, we already covered *Lifter of My Head* in a previous post. Also included in this verse is today's name: *Shield*.

The Hebrew word used here is "magen", which means, "shield, or buckler (small shield)." It comes from another Hebrew word, "ganan", which means, "to hedge about." The shield's primary purpose is to protect one from the blows of the enemy. Our God is a Shield about the Believer.

This metaphor is also used in the New Testament. Consider these verses describing the Full Armor of God.

> Ephesians 6:13-18 (ESV) Therefore take up the whole armor of God, that you may be able to withstand in the evil day, and having done all, to stand firm. Stand therefore, having fastened on the belt of truth, and having put on the breastplate of righteousness, and, as shoes for your feet, having put on the readiness given by the gospel of peace. In all circumstances take up the shield of faith, with which you can extinguish all the flaming darts of the evil one; and take the helmet of salvation, and the sword of the Spirit, which is the word of God, praying at all times in the Spirit, with all prayer and supplication.

When our faith is placed in God, Who is THE Shield, then all of the flaming darts of the enemy miss their mark. They are extinguished by the Almighty before they are able to bring the harm and destruction they intended. It is clear that the enemy knows this. Look at Job.

> Job 1:10 (ESV) Have you not put a hedge around him and his house and all that he has, on every side? You have blessed the work of his hands, and his possessions have increased in the land.

If this was part of the covenant God had with Job, how much more is this true in the life of the Believer? We have a better covenant bought with the blood of Jesus, sealed by the Holy Spirit.

> Hebrews 8:6 (ESV) But as it is, Christ has obtained a ministry that is as much more excellent than the old as the covenant he mediates is better, since it is enacted on better promises.

Our God is our *Shield*. He protects us from the enemy. He keeps us safe by "hedging us in" where He is. For in His presence we have complete peace and safety.

Slow to Anger

Psalm 103:8 (ESV) The LORD is merciful and gracious, slow to anger and abounding in steadfast love.

It is very difficult for me to view God as *Avenger* or *Revenger*, but we have seen previously that scripture describes God in these ways. We are commanded to "be angry and sin not." (Ephesians 4:26) From this we understand that it is possible to be angry and not be opposed to God's ways, otherwise it would be sin.

God can be angry. Many passages in the Bible confirm this. Angry is the only way many people can relate to God. A very popular sermon by Jonathan Edwards from 1741 is titled, "Sinners in the Hands of an Angry God." Many evangelical preachers still use this approach in their preaching. It is not the heart of God.

As the psalmist shared, God is first and foremost "merciful and gracious." If He does get angry, it comes slowly. God is *Slow to Anger*.

The Hebrew words used here are very interesting. The word for "slow" is pretty straightforward. It's the Hebrew word "arek", which means, "long (as in longsuffering), patient, slow to anger."

The word for "anger" is the Hebrew word "ap" which means, "nose, or nostril." It comes from the word "anap", which means, "to breathe hard." The picture being painted here is of someone breathing hard, nostrils flared; in other words, angry.

Usually when someone finds themselves in this condition it is due to getting worked up over some circumstance. It usually starts with frustration and then escalates to full blown, red-faced, veins popping, anger. Again, I have a difficult time seeing our God in this way.

Could it be that we have misunderstood something regarding this? What could anger God to this degree? My belief is that God is *Slow to Anger*, to the point that He never gets to this level of anger. At the very least, God's anger is much different than the human emotion called anger.

Most of the instances attributing anger to our God contain conditional language. "If you do a certain thing it will kindle, or provoke, God's anger." I cannot find many explicit references that say that God was, or is, angry. The closest thing we have to this in the New Testament is when Jesus disrupted the sales in the temple. Even in this passage it does not say, "Jesus was angry."

I think, at best, we do not have a clear understanding of anger; at worst, we have tried to impose human emotion on the One that created all things. Let's spend more time seeking the heart of *Slow to Anger* in order to clearly understand His ways. Then, let's work at becoming a little slower to anger ourselves.

This much I do know: God is not angry at the lost. He loves them, and wants to see them reconciled back to Himself through the provisions made by Jesus; His death, burial, resurrection, ascension, and seating at the right hand of God. The Holy Spirit is drawing them to repentance. God is *Slow* (longsuffering) *to Anger* and wants to see ALL people come to repentance. Let's get on His side of the process. Let's work WITH Him to see people reconciled to

God. This is accomplished much more quickly through love and prayer than it is by anger and condemnation. Let's represent our Lord well.

Son of God

> Daniel 3:25 (NKJV) "Look!" he answered, "I see four men loose, walking in the midst of the fire; and they are not hurt, and the form of the fourth is like the Son of God."

It is interesting that the first mention of the *Son of God* comes from a king that had no regard for God. Yet, he recognized the extra man in fire as one that looked like the *Son of God*.

The next reference in scripture of someone using the name *Son of God* is when satan came to Jesus in the wilderness to tempt Him. Three times satan said, "If you are the Son of God …?" Each time Jesus responded with a verse found in the Old Testament.

> Luke 4:2-13 (ESV) for forty days, being tempted by the devil. And he ate nothing during those days. And when they were ended, he was hungry. The devil said to him, "If you are the Son of God, command this stone to become bread." And Jesus answered him, "It is written, 'Man shall not live by bread alone.'"

> And the devil took him up and showed him all the kingdoms of the world in a moment of time, and said to him, "To you I will give all this authority and their glory, for it has been delivered to me, and I give it to whom I will. If you, then, will worship me, it will all be yours." And Jesus answered him, "It is written, "'You shall worship the Lord your God, and him only shall you serve.'"

> And he took him to Jerusalem and set him on the pinnacle of the temple and said to him, "If you are the Son of God, throw yourself down from here, for it is written, "'He will command his angels concerning you, to guard you,' and "'On their hands they will bear you up, lest you strike your foot against a stone.'" And Jesus answered him, "It is said, 'You shall not put the Lord your God to the test.'" And when the devil had ended every temptation, he departed from him until an opportune time.

As a child, Jesus knew He was the *Son of God* when He was only twelve years old.

> Luke 2:48-50 (ESV) And when his parents saw him, they were astonished. And his mother said to him, "Son, why have you treated us so? Behold, your father and I have been searching for you in great distress." And he said to them, "Why were you looking for me? Did you not know that I must be in my Father's house?" And they did not understand the saying that he spoke to them.

In Luke's account of Jesus' life he gives the linage of Jesus. It ends with another reference to the other *Son of God*, Adam.

> Luke 3:23-38 (ESV) Jesus, when he began his ministry, was about thirty years of age, being the son (as was supposed) of Joseph, ... the son of Enos, the son of Seth, the son of Adam, the son of God.

Jesus was the second Adam. He came to undo what Adam brought to the human race through his sin in the

Garden of Eden. Jesus became the One whose heel would be bruised in the crushing of the serpent's head. Jesus succeeded in His mission. He was born of a virgin, conceived by the Holy Spirit, lived a sinless life as a man filled with the Spirit of God. He died as the perfect lamb whose blood washed away our sin. He was raised from the dead, defeating hell and the grave for us. He ascended to heaven and was seated at the right hand of God, "far above all rule, and power, and dominion, and every name that is named", so that we once again reign in life. Jesus then sent the Holy Spirit to abide in us forever.

That, my friend, is the Good News, the Gospel of Jesus, which provides us with a way back to our Creator. Thank you, Jesus, the *Son of God*, for paying the price for us!

Song

Exodus 15:1-2 (ESV) Then Moses and the people of Israel sang this song to the LORD, saying, "I will sing to the LORD, for he has triumphed gloriously; the horse and his rider he has thrown into the sea. The LORD is my strength and my song, and he has become my salvation; this is my God, and I will praise him, my father's God, and I will exalt him.

As a worshipper this is one of my favorite names for God. In my teenage years wearing buttons with slogans was the fad of the day. During a youth group trip to Gatlinburg I came across a button that said, "He is my *Song*." I wore it for years.

One of the first "modern" worship songs I learned was written to these verses. It was such fun singing the Word of God. He is our *Song*.

The Hebrew word for "song" is "zimrat" which means, "instrumental music; by implication, praise." It comes from the word "zamar" which means, "to strike with the fingers, as touching the strings of a musical instrument."

God is our *Song*! Think about that. If you apply the implication from this it means that we are the instruments; the fingers of God plucking, as it were, on our heartstrings to release His *Song* in the earth. That is why it is so important for us to stay "in tune" with God, our *Song*.

Here is something really enlightening. There is another Hebrew word from which "zamar" is derived. It means, "prune." When you hear of God "pruning" us it usually has bad implications. Let's think of it this way. The strings on a stringed instrument must be maintained. They need constant attention in order to make beautiful music.

If you've ever been to a symphony the 1st chair violinist is the concertmaster. He or she is responsible for tuning the orchestra before the conductor takes the stand. If you watch closely you will see a constant pre-occupation with their instrument. They want to keep it "pruned" so the orchestra will remain perfectly tuned.

This is a great picture of the Holy Spirit's work in the life of the Believer. Jesus is the conductor of the orchestra, The Church. We play our Song and in doing so we present our God to the world. God is our Song.

Consider this verse:

> Ephesians 5:19 (ESV) addressing one another in psalms and hymns and spiritual songs, singing and making melody to the Lord with your heart,

What if we lived our lives trying to play the same song with other Believers instead of constantly causing dissonance (discord) in the Body of Christ? Each instrument of the orchestra is drastically different. A wide variety of sounds are created by these instruments, generated by various means (bowing, plucking, blowing, beating, etc.). However, when each one releases its sound under the direction of the Conductor they make a glorious sound that resonates with the hearts of all that hear it. This is the Gospel of Jesus Christ; God's love expressed to all who will listen.

Soon Coming King

Revelation 3:11 (ESV) I am coming soon. Hold fast what you have, so that no one may seize your crown.

These are some of the words Jesus spoke to the Church at Philadelphia. The phrase "Soon Coming King" is not found in scripture, but because Jesus made this comment, and He is THE King, it is not a stretch to attribute this name to Him: *Soon Coming King*.

Since John wrote down The Revelation of Jesus Christ that he received while in exile on the Isle of Patmos, scholars have been trying to predict the date and followers of Christ have been awaiting His return. What I have come to learn is that "soon" is relative.

Peter said, "With the Lord one day is as a thousand years, and a thousand years as one day." (2 Peter 3:8) Every parent has experienced the "are we there yet" when travelling with young children. They have no concept of time. Our precious little dog, Bee, was the same way. When we left the house she was placed in a small pen in the kitchen. When we returned home she would dance around with such excitement, even if we were only gone ten minutes! We miss her greatly.

I do not believe Jesus gave us this promise to create anxiety on the part of the Believer. Nor did He utter these words to be used as some kind of threat for evangelism. Instead, if you look at the context of the passage cited, Jesus was assuring those in Philadelphia to continue doing what they were doing.

Revelation 3:10 (ESV) Because you have kept my word about patient endurance, I will keep you from the hour of trial that is coming on the whole world, ...

The Church of Philadelphia was being encouraged to keep the Word, patiently going about the work of making Disciples. "Hold fast what you have." It is clear they had a grasp on the revelation of who Jesus is, and were diligent about sharing the Truth with others.

Soon Coming King. How soon is soon? No one knows except the Father. (Matthew 24:36) If you consider what Peter said, it could be any "day" now! If we will take our eyes off the clouds and look around us, we will find that sharing the love of God we have with others will make the time pass much more quickly.

Strength to the Needy

Isaiah 25:4 (ESV) For you have been a stronghold to the poor, a stronghold (KJV uses strength) to the needy in his distress, a shelter from the storm and a shade from the heat; for the breath of the ruthless is like a storm against a wall,

The thing I love most about the Old Testament are the pictures the writers give us to view God. I think we have lost some of that in the modern church. You can hear the unfamiliar tone in our prayers. Any terms other than God, Lord, or Jesus are written off as "religious jargon." Ironically, we tend to use multiple monikers when referring to our spouse or close friends.

Imagine, for instance, your wife's name is Sue (or, for you ladies, your husband's name is Bob). If I spoke to her the same way some pray to God, our conversation might go something like this:

Sue, wife, what's for dinner, Sue? Spouse, when will dinner, wife, Sue, be ready, wife? And wife, Sue, spouse, let me know when to, wife, come and, spouse, eat, Sue.

I think you get the picture. That's the reason I embarked on this study of the Names of God. As a Believer and a worshipper I want to have a vocabulary to use to express my feelings to my Lord. If this is your first time to read one of these I encourage you to go back, as you have time, to re-read the previous 180 +- names.

Today's name is *Strength to the Needy*. A favorite verse-that's-not-in-the-Bible verse is, "The Lord helps those that help themselves." That could not be any farther from the truth. The Lord is looking for those who have utterly failed. Most of the time we cannot even approach God until we have come to the end of our ability to help ourselves.

The Hebrew words used here help us understand God in this role. Maoz, interpreted "strength", means, "a fortified place, a defense." It comes from the Hebrew word "azaz", and means, "stout." "Needy" come from the word "ebyon," and means, "want (including feelings), destitute." It is derived from the Hebrew word for "breathe." It speaks to basic human needs, even the breath we breathe.

God is *Strength to the Needy*. If we never view ourselves as being in need, it leaves God little room for Him to provide us with His strength. But, if we acknowledge the need for God in our life, He comes and provides a defense for us; one that is stout against any attack, in order to provide for our needs.

This is not a genie-in-a-bottle god. This is the Creator, that when we commit our life to Him, He takes it seriously. When you give up your rights He comes with His life, zoe life, and provides for our needs like no one else can.

Let's chose today to hand over the keys of our life to *Strength to the Needy* and let Him protect us. He is faithful!

Strength to the Poor

> Isaiah 25:4 (ESV) For you have been a stronghold (KJV says strength) to the poor, a stronghold to the needy in his distress, a shelter from the storm and a shade from the heat; for the breath of the ruthless is like a storm against a wall,

Today's name is very similar to the name we looked at last time. *Strength to the Poor* differs in an important way. "Poor" comes from the Hebrew word "dal" which means, "dangling, weak or thin." The basic difference in poor and needy is the way you arrive at the condition. God has promised to be strength to both.

Needy, as we saw last time, is when you are destitute. It may have been a change in circumstance that got you there, or perhaps an accident that incapacitated you for a season. God promises to help.

Poor, on the other hand, is a state of being. It is one not capable of managing by themselves. This speaks of the elderly, or chronically ill. God promises to help.

In both of these instances the New Testament Church should be a resource for these folks. Consider the words of our Lord.

> Matthew 25:32-40 (ESV) Before him will be gathered all the nations, and he will separate people one from another as a shepherd separates the sheep from the goats. And he will place the sheep on his right, but the goats on the left.

Then the King will say to those on his right, 'Come, you who are blessed by my Father, inherit the kingdom prepared for you from the foundation of the world. For I was hungry and you gave me food, I was thirsty and you gave me drink, I was a stranger and you welcomed me, I was naked and you clothed me, I was sick and you visited me, I was in prison and you came to me.'

Then the righteous will answer him, saying, 'Lord, when did we see you hungry and feed you, or thirsty and give you drink? And when did we see you a stranger and welcome you, or naked and clothe you? And when did we see you sick or in prison and visit you?' And the King will answer them, 'Truly, I say to you, as you did it to one of the least of these my brothers, you did it to me.'

Compassion is one of the strongest motivations we see in Jesus. It moved Him often to do things beyond reasonable so that those in need would be comforted. Let us make it our prayer that THE Church would find the compassion of Jesus and show the world the *Strength to the Poor* is still on the throne and compelling them to come back home to Him.

Strong

> Psalm 89:8 (KJV) O LORD God of hosts, who is a strong LORD like unto thee? or to thy faithfulness round about thee?

It is very easy to think of God as being *Strong*. After all, He did create everything! However, many times Jesus is portrayed as an effeminate male with pale skin and long curly hair, usually with a beam of sunlight illuminating His fair skin. Jesus was the Son of God. He, too, is *Strong*.

I'm not speaking of only physical strength, even though as a carpenter I'm sure Jesus was no weakling. Jesus is *Strong* in every aspect. He withstood the temptation of satan in the wilderness. He drove out those that desecrated the temple. He prayed in Gethsemane until His sweat became drops of blood. He led a group of men, including tax collectors and fisherman, by His strength. Kings feared Him. Religious people despised Him. Those are not the traits of a weak man.

The word "strong" comes from the Hebrew word "hasin" and means, "firm." It's root word means "compact." The Greek word interpreted "strong" is "energeia" and means, "efficiency."

Both of these meanings appropriately describe our God. *Strong* is founded on nothing greater than His own Word. (Hebrews 6:13) He is so steady that His shadow doesn't even move. (James 1:17) God did not rest on the seventh day of creation because of fatigue. He did so to model for us the need of finding our rest in Him.

He is our strength, but He is also our rest. That is one benefit to being "yoked" together with our Lord. When we are weak, He through our weakness, is made strong in our life.

> 2 Corinthians 12:9 (ESV) But he said to me, "My grace is sufficient for you, for my power is made perfect in weakness." Therefore I will boast all the more gladly of my weaknesses, so that the power of Christ may rest upon me.

Our God is Strong. Yet He has the ability to deal with us in our weakness.

> Matthew 12:20 (ESV) a bruised reed he will not break, and a smoldering wick he will not quench, until he brings justice to victory;

You can trust Him completely. You can rely on Him and never be disappointed. He is *Strong*.

Sustainer

> Psalm 3:5 (ESV) I lay down and slept; I woke again, for the LORD sustained me.

Even when we are not aware of the Lord's presence He is there. When we become a Believer, a Follower of Christ, He takes on the role of *Sustainer*. Infants, when learning to walk, do not realize they are not walking on their own, but the parent is always there to help them along.

When Jesus was about to leave earth and return to His Father's side in Heaven He told those with Him, "I am going to send another Comforter, the Holy Spirit, to be with you forever." The Holy Spirit is our *Sustainer*.

The meaning of the Hebrew word "samak" is "prop, lean, take hold of." That is exactly the role the Holy Spirit is in our life. He was sent to empower us to be witnesses. When we don't have the strength or courage to speak the truth about Jesus, the Holy Spirit "props us up" to the point that we can.

When we grow weary in pursuing the will of God, the Holy Spirit is there for us to lean on and make it through the valley. The writer of Jude, the other disciple named Judas (the brother of James, not the one that betrayed Jesus) let us in on a way to tap into the power of the Holy Spirit.

> Jude 1:20 (ESV) But you, beloved, building yourselves up in your most holy faith and praying in the Holy Spirit,

If there is a need "build ourselves up" then apparently we can get to that place. It is good news to know that our Lord made provision for those needing-to-be-built-up moments by sending us the Holy Spirit. He is available for us to "take hold of" when we need Him.

> Hebrews 12:1-3 (ESV) Therefore, since we are surrounded by so great a cloud of witnesses, let us also lay aside every weight, and sin which clings so closely, and let us run with endurance the race that is set before us, looking to Jesus, the founder and perfecter of our faith, who for the joy that was set before him endured the cross, despising the shame, and is seated at the right hand of the throne of God.
>
> Consider him who endured from sinners such hostility against himself, so that you may not grow weary or fainthearted.

Our *Sustainer* keeps us in the race. Years ago I used to listen to a teacher named Marilyn Hickey. She always had such an interesting way of describing things. She commented once, "the game is not over until we win." I like that with our Lord before us as the prize, and the Holy Spirit in us to help us run the race, we will experience His "perfecting" in us until we see Him face to face. Selah!

Teacher

> Psalm 119:12 (ESV) Blessed are you, O LORD; teach me your statutes!
> Psalm 119:26 (ESV) When I told of my ways, you answered me; teach me your statutes!
> Psalm 119:33 (ESV) Teach me, O LORD, the way of your statutes; and I will keep it to the end.
> Psalm 119:64 (ESV) The earth, O LORD, is full of your steadfast love; teach me your statutes!
> Psalm 119:68 (ESV) You are good and do good; teach me your statutes.
> Psalm 119:108 (ESV) Accept my freewill offerings of praise, O LORD, and teach me your rules.
> Psalm 119:124 (ESV) Deal with your servant according to your steadfast love, and teach me your statutes.
> Psalm 119:135 (ESV) Make your face shine upon your servant, and teach me your statutes.

All of these verses are from one psalm. Psalm 119 is the longest psalm with 176 verses. There is mention of God's teachings in 171 verses. It is divided into 22 sections, one for each letter of the Hebrew alphabet. It clearly shows the desire on behalf of our God to be our *Teacher*. It matters that we know the will of God. How better to know His will than to learn His precepts.

Jesus was known as the Good *Teacher*. Obviously, He was so much more, but He did teach. He taught with words and He taught with actions. His teaching was never meant to elevate Himself, but to bring others up to where He was.

When Jesus promised to send the Holy Spirit, one of the roles He would fill in our lives is that of *Teacher*.

> 1 Corinthians 2:9-10 (ESV) But, as it is written, "What no eye has seen, nor ear heard, nor the heart of man imagined, what God has prepared for those who love him"— these things God has revealed to us through the Spirit. For the Spirit searches everything, even the depths of God.

Jesus came to show us the Father. The Holy Spirit is given to teach us His ways, even the deep things of God. Allow the *Teacher* to instruct you in how to live and love. He will reveal the Father's heart so that we can know Him fully.

The Amen

Revelation 3:14 (ESV) "And to the angel of the church in Laodicea write: 'The words of the Amen, the faithful and true witness, the beginning of God's creation.

There is a word that is used in just about every church but most do not know what it means. They say it because of tradition. Their father said so they say it. Some preachers even request you to say it. There are sections of the church titled by this word. It is "amen."

Jesus referred to Himself as *The Amen* when speaking with John regarding the letter to the Church at Laodicea. It is a Greek word which means, "firm, trustworthy, surely." It is derived from the Hebrew word "amen" which means, "sure, faithfulness, truly."

The Greek word "amen" appears 152 times in the New Testament. It is primarily interpreted as "verily" in the KJV, or "truly" in more recent translations. I'm about to tread some dangerous waters in the next paragraph or so, but please be assured of this: I believe in the divine inspiration of scripture. However, I do not believe in the divine transcription or translation of scripture.

The Holy Spirit breathed on men and they wrote the texts. Men then transcribed those original texts many times over several centuries. Then an attempt was made to create an English version of those transcripts. The most famous of which is the Authorized King James Version of the Bible. There has been numerous other translations completed since then that I believe to be more credible than the KJV. Here's why.

The KJV was written using the most credible manuscripts available to them at the time. Since that time there has been numerous other transcripts discovered that pre-date those used by the KJV translators. There were some discrepancies noted where some of the more recent manuscripts contained words that were not in the older ones. These differences do not alter the original meaning. For the most part they are superfluous, such as adding the word "amen" to the end of just about every book in the New Testament.

Paul actually did write the word "amen" at the end of some of his epistles. He also used the word quite often for emphasis. Here is one example.

> Romans 1:24-25 (ESV) Therefore God gave them up in the lusts of their hearts to impurity, to the dishonoring of their bodies among themselves, because they exchanged the truth about God for a lie and worshiped and served the creature rather than the Creator, who is blessed forever! Amen.

I think it is intended to have the same effect as the word "selah" found in the Old Testament. The KJV translators decided it would make a fitting end to all of the books.

Paul gave an example of where people in a gathering would say "amen" to things that were being spoken by those in the meeting. It indicated their agreement. And thus, a tradition was born.

> 1 Corinthians 14:16 (ESV) Otherwise, if you give thanks with your spirit, how can anyone in the position of an outsider say "Amen" to your

thanksgiving when he does not know what you are saying?

In essence, what was happening here is that someone would make a comment, or as Paul said, "Give thanks," and then others would echo with "amen." Or as we might say today, "That's the truth," or "So be it."

There's much more that could be said here but it's not the forum for a long dissertation. I just wanted to give some background behind "amen." Let's return to the subject at hand. Because the use of "amen" has become so commonplace in the Church we lose some of the significance to what Jesus meant when He made the reference to Him being *The Amen*.

What Jesus was saying to John is this: Tell the Church at Laodicea that I saw the creation. I was there. I can say the "amen" to all God did in the beginning. And I also know your works.

That brings an authority to the message John was to deliver that could not be repeated by anyone else but Jesus. He is *The Amen*, or "the Truth." He still has the authoritative voice in our lives today. The Word of God, communicated by the Holy Spirit, is compelling us as He did the Laodiceans to consider our ways. See if what we have is the real thing. Let us be a little more cautious in giving the "amen" to what is spoken until we can prove it to be true.

The Christ

> Matthew 16:16 (ESV) Simon Peter replied, "You are the Christ, the Son of the living God."

When we see the name "Christ" we think of it as part of the official name for Jesus: Jesus Christ. However, the gospel writers referred to Jesus differently. They used *"The Christ."* There is a difference.

For centuries the people of Israel had been waiting on someone to come and deliver them from the oppression they experienced from various conquerors. They called him Messiah. He was the Promised one from God that would finally bring them peace.

Messiah and Christ are synonymous. Messiah is Hebrew; Christ is Greek. Both words mean, "anointed one." So when the New Testament writers referred to Jesus as *The Christ*, they meant that He was The One, The Messiah, who would come and redeem Israel by conquering her foes. He would assume the throne of David as King.

> John 1:40-41 (ESV) One of the two who heard John speak and followed Jesus was Andrew, Simon Peter's brother. He first found his own brother Simon and said to him, "We have found the Messiah" (which means Christ).

While none of these things were accurate in a physical sense, they were every bit true in the spiritual sense. Jesus was *The Christ*, but He came to redeem mankind back to a right relationship with their Creator. He would reign from the throne of David, but it would a spiritual Kingdom.

Another way to look at the name Jesus Christ, and a way to remember what His role would be, is to say, "Jesus, The Anointed One." Here is why it is important to see it this way. When Jesus left the earth to go to Heaven and be seated at the right hand of The Father, He told those present He would send Another Comforter, One like Himself. That, of course, was the Holy Spirit.

As New Testament Believers and followers of Jesus, we also have been anointed with the same Holy Spirit that anointed Jesus. If we fail to see this aspect of our salvation we will never live up our potential. That is why I stress repeatedly that the process of salvation is not just forgiveness of sins and a ticket to Heaven. We must identify with Christ in every aspect: His death, burial, resurrection, ascension, and seating at the right hand of God.

It is in being seated with Jesus that we access our authority. It is through the indwelling of the Holy Spirit that we access the anointing to live the Christian life. We need Jesus Christ: Jesus, the Son of Man, and Christ, The Anointed One. Jesus became the sacrifice required for our redemption. Christ empowers us to live for Him.

Let us worship *The Christ*, The Son of The Living God! He is worthy.

The Door

This Name for God is exclusively given to Jesus. It is a name that He used for Himself: *The Door*.

> John 10:1-7 (ESV) "Truly, truly, I say to you, he who does not enter the sheepfold by the door but climbs in by another way, that man is a thief and a robber. But he who enters by the door is the shepherd of the sheep. To him the gatekeeper opens. The sheep hear his voice, and he calls his own sheep by name and leads them out. When he has brought out all his own, he goes before them, and the sheep follow him, for they know his voice. A stranger they will not follow, but they will flee from him, for they do not know the voice of strangers."
>
> This figure of speech Jesus used with them, but they did not understand what he was saying to them. So Jesus again said to them, "Truly, truly, I say to you, I am the door of the sheep.

The Greek word for "door" is "thyra" which means, "portal or entrance." He was the way the sheep (The Church) would gain entrance into God's Kingdom. There is only one door! He is the only way into God's presence.

The Old Testament alluded to this by using symbols.

> Exodus 12:7 (ESV) "Then they shall take some of the blood and put it on the two doorposts and the lintel of the houses in which they eat it.
>
> This is part of the instructions given to Moses prior to the first Passover. Every house that had blood on the

doorposts would be spared from the death of the first born of the household. Jesus came and fulfilled the Passover by being crucified as *The Door*, applying blood "once for all."

There's one other image that I had never correlated to Jesus until now.

> Isaiah 6:4 (NKJV) And the posts of the door were shaken by the voice of him who cried out, and the house was filled with smoke.

I love this scene in Heaven. As the angels worshipped the Lord by crying, "Holy, holy, holy is the Lord of Hosts. The whole heart is full of His glory!" (Isaiah 6:3), it says, "The posts of The Door" was shaken. The Hebrew word for "door" is "sap" which means, "a vestibule (entrance way); also a dish (for holding blood or wine).

The Door described in Heaven is both an access (The Door) into heaven AND the provision (The Blood) required for the forgiveness of sin, the payment for entrance into Heaven. Jesus fulfilled both of these. *The Door* was sent from Heaven as the man, Jesus, to live a sinless life and become the Perfect Lamb that would be sacrificed for us as payment for sin. In doing so, He opened the portal of Heaven so men could be reconciled back to God.

I love the Word of God. There are no wasted words in it! You can find God on every page, in every picture, and in every word.

The Head of the Body

Ephesians 5:23 (ESV) For the husband is the head of the wife even as Christ is the head of the church, his body, and is himself its Savior.

One of the clearest metaphors used in scripture to describe how the Believer interacts with our Savior, Jesus Christ, is through the image of the human body. We know that the head (brain) controls everything that goes on in the body. In the same way, Jesus, *The Head of the Body* (Church), is to control everything that goes on in the Church.

The meaning of the original language is very interesting. The Greek word "kephale" which is interpreted as "head" means, "to captivate, seizing; literally – to take hold of." "Body" is derived from the Greek word "some" which means, "body, whole." It comes from the Greek root "sozo" which means, "to save, deliver, protect."

When you consider these meanings you can see the correlation very clearly. The job of the husband in marriage, according to scripture, is to captivate his bride; to lover her unconditionally. Conversely, the greatest need in a woman is to be secure. The Bridegroom (Jesus) has come to captivate His Bride (Church) to bring wholeness, deliverance, protection, and salvation.

If you are male this picture may be difficult for you to picture. This stems from the overwhelming fascination our minds have with sex. It is difficult to picture having a wife without the sexual component. The relationship between Jesus and the Church is in no way sexual. I believe that is why Paul exhorted us men in his letter to the Church in Ephesus to picture this from the perspective of the husband toward his wife.

Our purpose in the marriage is to love our wife as Jesus loves the Church, by giving Himself for Her. It is important, however, for us to also remember the word Paul gave us concerning "submitting ourselves one to another in the fear of God." (Ephesians 5:21) And men, yes, this does include our wife. As fellow Believers we are to submit one to another. When this is evidenced in both the husband and wife there is never an issue of "Who is in charge" in the marriage.

The Church is no exception. If we will get the spiritual "hierarchy" out of the New Testament Church we will have way less issues. Everyone in the Body of Christ is to submit to the other Members, and all of us are to submit to *The Head of the Body*, Jesus. Instead of trying to find ways to be "more in charge," let's look for ways we can serve one another more effectively.

Allow *The Head of the Body* to rule over you in every aspect of your life. You will be more complete as you live for Him.

The Life

> John 14:6 (ESV) Jesus said to him, "I am the way, and the truth, and the life. No one comes to the Father except through me.

John is the only gospel writer that records this statement from Jesus. Jesus explained to His disciples that His main purpose was to show them the Father. The following verse says this.

> John 14:7 (ESV) If you had known me, you would have known my Father also. From now on you do know him and have seen him."

So when He says, "I am *The Life*," He is declaring to them that the Father is *Life*. John had understood this revelation from Jesus. When John decided to write his account of the gospel story, he used "life" as a common thread.

> John 1:4 (ESV) In him was *life*, and the *life* was the light of men.

> John 5:26 (ESV) For as the **Father has life in himself**, so he has granted the Son also to have *life* in himself.

It is clear that this aspect of Jesus' teaching impacted John in a profound way. We need to get this revelation into our spirit, because it is truly a game-changer. Look at the meaning of this word. The Greek word for "life" is "zoe" which means, "life." It comes from a root word that means, "live." That looks rather simplistic, but this is the life given to us by God.

In our Western mind we think of life as the series of events that occur between birth and death. The real meaning of this term is the difference between dead and alive. In other verses the word "quicken" is used.

> Romans 8:11 (ESV) If the Spirit of him who raised Jesus from the dead dwells in you, he who raised Christ Jesus from the dead will also give life to your mortal bodies through his Spirit who dwells in you.

When you are born, your body is alive but your spirit is dead toward God. Our spirit is the real life of the human. It is what separates us from all other creatures on the planet. The only way for our spirit to live is to receive *The Life* given by God, through the Holy Spirit. This is the life Jesus came to bring to us. It is *The Life* that comes from the Father. Consider this verse.

> John 11:25-26 (ESV) Jesus said to her, "I am the resurrection and the life. Whoever believes in me, though he die, yet shall he live, and everyone who lives and believes in me shall never die. Do you believe this?"

The reason we needed a resurrection is because we were born spiritually dead. When we believe in *The Life*, Jesus Christ, and identify with His death, burial, resurrection, ascension, and seating at the right hand of the Father, and then receive the Holy Spirit sent to us by Jesus, we experience true LIFE. This "zoe" life!

John summarizes this revelation in the first epistle bearing his name. These three verses give a clear understanding that Jesus, *The Life*, came to lead us back to the Father, the Giver of Life, so that we could be reconciled to Him.

> 1 John 1:1-3 (ESV) That which was from the beginning, which we have heard, which we have seen with our eyes, which we looked upon and have touched with our hands, concerning the word of life— the life was made manifest, and we have seen it, and testify to it and proclaim to you the eternal life, which was with the Father and was made manifest to us— that which we have seen and heard we proclaim also to you, so that you too may have fellowship with us; and indeed our fellowship is with the Father and with his Son Jesus Christ.

Think on these things. Begin to realize all that this means to the Believer. If you are in Christ then you have *The Life* of God in you. That is transformational! Think about it.

The Resurrection

John 11:24-26 (ESV) Jesus said to her, "I am the resurrection and the life. Whoever believes in me, though he die, yet shall he live, and everyone who lives and believes in me shall never die. Do you believe this?"

One of the people Jesus was close to died. Jesus visited the home of Martha, Mary, and Lazarus on several occasions. When Lazarus was sick they sent word for Jesus to come. Lazarus died before He arrived.

The exchange between Jesus and Martha is representative of how many feel about Jesus. They believe, but they don't REALLY believe. Look at the dialog.

John 11:23-27

Jesus: "Your brother will rise again."

Martha: "I know that he will rise again in the resurrection on the last day."

Jesus: "I am the resurrection and the life. Whoever believes in me, though he die, yet shall he live, and everyone who lives and believes in me shall never die. Do you believe this?"

Martha: "Yes, Lord; I believe that you are the Christ, the Son of God, who is coming into the world."

Jesus was trying to tell Martha that Lazarus would live, but Martha put it off to the end of time when everyone would rise. So many in the church do not believe Jesus is active in their life right now! The Holy Spirit was sent to bring all that Jesus came to give us, and to give it to us NOW! We just have to believe.

Jesus knew before He arrived at Martha and Mary's house that Lazarus was dead because He planned to raise him from the dead.

> John 11:11-15 (ESV) After saying these things, he said to them, "Our friend Lazarus has fallen asleep, but I go to awaken him." The disciples said to him, "Lord, if he has fallen asleep, he will recover." Now Jesus had spoken of his death, but they thought that he meant taking rest in sleep. Then Jesus told them plainly, "Lazarus has died, and for your sake I am glad that I was not there, so that you may believe. But let us go to him."

Jesus would use this experience to teach His disciples an important truth. After demonstrating the resurrection of the dead Jesus then declared, "I am *The Resurrection.*" Notice He did not say, "I have the ability to raise the dead." Instead, Jesus wanted to impart a deeper truth; something that would change them if they could only believe.

We saw last time that Jesus is *The Life*. Here He is emphasizing that not only can He give life, but He can restore life to dead things. He is *The Resurrection*. That is good news to us because we were born dead, spiritually speaking. Jesus, *The Resurrection*, can bring us back to life and restore His life in us as God created in the beginning.

I'm so glad that when our Father put together a plan to bring mankind back into relationship with Him that He thought of everything. God's plan was executed to perfection by Jesus. If you have never met *The Resurrection* call on Him today. He is ready to bring you back to life!

The Risen Lord

> Luke 24:33-34 (ESV) And they rose that same hour and returned to Jerusalem. And they found the eleven and those who were with them gathered together, saying, "The Lord has risen indeed, and has appeared to Simon!"

This is the essence of the Gospel. Without a *Risen Lord* our faith is meaningless. Every major religion has a savior. Each of them has a messiah. But none of them have a *Risen Lord*! Our Savior, sent from God, lived as the Son of Man, all the while being the Son of God, so that through His sacrifice on the cross redemption was made available to every person.

But it did not end there. He was resurrected from the dead, defeating death, hell, and the grave in the process. He now lives to see to it that everything He purchased through His death is made available to you and me. That is good news!

> 1 Corinthians 15:3-8 (ESV) For I delivered to you as of first importance what I also received: that Christ died for our sins in accordance with the Scriptures, that he was buried, that he was raised on the third day in accordance with the Scriptures, and that he appeared to Cephas, then to the twelve. Then he appeared to more than five hundred brothers at one time, most of whom are still alive, though some have fallen asleep. Then he appeared to James, then to all the apostles. Last of all, as to one untimely born, he appeared also to me.

If the only proof of Jesus being raised from the dead is an empty tomb there would still be room for doubt. Paul nails that argument to the wall. Over five hundred people saw *The Risen Lord.*

Jesus demonstrated the most important aspect of our faith when He came back from the dead. Living our lives modeled after the example of Jesus, loving our fellow man, doing good deeds to all we meet, is a great way to live. However, if this life is all there is, we are still doomed to a futile existence. Without the Blessed Hope of eternity with our Maker, Christianity is just like every other religion.

But, we have the Blessed Hope of seeing our Risen Lord, just as the five hundred plus did.

> 1 John 3:2 (ESV) Beloved, we are God's children now, and what we will be has not yet appeared; but we know that when he appears we shall be like him, because we shall see him as he is.

Our journey will be completed on that day. We are destined to be like Jesus. That is the work of the Holy Spirit being carried out in the life of every Believer. But on that day, we will be like Him! That is the Blessed Hope that carries us forward in our Christian walk.

The True Vine

> John 15:1 (ESV) "I am the true vine, and my Father is the vinedresser.

Every living thing draws its life from something or someone else. A seed must have nutrients from the soil and water in order to live. A newborn must have a mother to nurse. Even the manliest survivalist needs the nutrients found in nature to sustain his life. This is especially true when it comes to being alive spiritually.

Many times in scripture a vineyard is used to explain the relationship we have with our Creator.

> John 15:4 (ESV) Abide in me, and I in you. As the branch cannot bear fruit by itself, unless it abides in the vine, neither can you, unless you abide in me.

> Matthew 20:1 (ESV) "For the kingdom of heaven is like a master of a house who went out early in the morning to hire laborers for his vineyard.

> Matthew 21:28 (ESV) "What do you think? A man had two sons. And he went to the first and said, 'Son, go and work in the vineyard today.'

There are many others. It is certainly a fitting analogy. A vineyard requires painstaking details in order to thrive. First there is the challenge of finding the strain of grapes you want to grow. Rich soil is also needed to assure a good yield of fruit. The vinedresser works tirelessly pruning the vines and keeping pests away from the vineyard so that the harvest will be plenteous.

This is an excellent picture of the Church. Jesus is the pure seed of the Word of God. He is *The True Vine*. The Holy Spirit prepares the soil of men's hearts to receive the seed sown. The Father is the Vinedresser and never sleeps or slumbers in His care for the vineyard so that the harvest will be great.

Our purpose, once we are grafted into The True Vine through salvation, is to grow and produce fruit. The Father will do His part to keep us productive. We simply have to allow the life-giving nutrients from The True Vine to flow through us, allowing His Holy Spirit to transform us into productive parts of the Vineyard, His Church. Let us learn to work with Him to assure the greatest harvest possible.

The Truth

> John 14:6 (ESV) Jesus said to him, "I am the way, and the truth, and the life. No one comes to the Father except through me.

Our society has devolved, in my opinion, to the point that "the truth" is very difficult to obtain. I'm reminded of a comment made by Susan McDougal, an accused co-conspirator in the Clintons "Whitewater" scandal, as she is being taken to jail for contempt of court for not answering questions on the matter. She said, "They don't want to hear my truth."

That comment speaks volumes of where we are as a society. If we can each have a version of "the truth" then there can never be absolutes. That is why there are so many conspiracy theorists. They are convinced everyone has something to hide.

The sad reality is that man can never declare something to be absolute. In science, we proclaim to have discovered "absolute zero", but yet things can still get colder than absolute zero. In mathematics, we have defined the ratio of the radius to the circumference of a circle and call it π but its true value is not computable because it is an irrational number (a never ending decimal). The most common form of Geometry was developed by Euclid. We use it every day to build buildings, and for the most part it works. However, it is based on things existing in a plane (perfectly flat space) yet our world is not flat.

There are many more examples but this is not the forum for that discussion. I simply want to emphasize the need humans have for "the truth" but will never find it in ourselves. We must look outside of our knowledge and understanding. That is when we find *The Truth*, Jesus Christ. Everything we have need of is found in Him.

We get the English word "truth" from the Greek word "aletheia" and simply means "truth". It is derived from another Greek word "alethes" which means "true", but it gets its meaning from two other Greek words which mean "not concealed." In other words, "truth" means not hiding anything. When our courts swear in witnesses, they command them to tell the whole truth, and nothing but the truth. They even ask us to swear that we will.

Jesus came and showed us the Father. Until that time, God had been somewhat of a mystery to man. Jesus "unconcealed" God for us. He demonstrated the character of God, taught us the love of the Father, and became flesh so we could behold God's glory.

> John 1:14 (ESV) And the Word became flesh and dwelt among us, and we have seen his glory, glory as of the only Son from the Father, full of grace and truth.

Once we become a Christian, our sole purpose is to be found in sharing *The Truth* with others. That is what will change hearts. That is the only hope for our world. Let us put aside "our truth" and take up Jesus, *The Truth*. How do we do that? Easy. Just follow the Lord's teachings.

> John 8:31-32 (ESV) So Jesus said to the Jews who had believed him, "If you abide in my word, you are truly my disciples, and you will know the truth, and the truth will set you free."

As we allow the words of Jesus to dictate our behavior it will transform us to the point that we experience true freedom in every aspect of our life. When we have nothing to hide there is no longer any cause for shame. If we speak the truth we don't have to keep track of what we have said. Allowing *The Truth* to shine through us will have an impact on our world.

The Way

> John 14:6 (ESV) Jesus said to him, "I am the way, and the truth, and the life. No one comes to the Father except through me.

Most of us have never had the experience, or the need for that matter, of carving a new path through a forest or field of brush. Most have never explored the mountain range for a more convenient pass. We have, however, all benefitted from those that have. Travelling the highways in Tennessee it is very easy to see that someone forged a path for us. It is evident from all of the exposed rock that was cut through to make the road straight and smooth.

We have a Forerunner. His name is Jesus, *The Way*. He came to earth to show us how to get back home to our Father, Jehovah God; Creator of all things. In this instance He did more than carve a path through the dark, sinful world. He also became our mode of transport through the process. Look at the meaning of *The Way*.

The Greek word used here is "hodos" which means, "a road, a progress (the route, act, or distance), a mode or means." *The Way* is not just a road map, some mental understanding of direction. He is also the means by which we make it home. *The Way* is not a tool or an app that we follow to get to Heaven. He is a person with Whom we develop a relationship and walk the path together.

> Hebrews 10:19-22 (ESV) Therefore, brothers, since we have confidence to enter the holy places by the blood of Jesus, by the new and living way that he opened for us through the curtain, that is, through his flesh, and since we have a great priest over the

house of God, let us draw near with a true heart in full assurance of faith, with our hearts sprinkled clean from an evil conscience and our bodies washed with pure water.

Jesus gave His life in order to open the "portal" (as we saw in the post on *The Door*) but then sent us the Holy Spirit to guide us as we walk back to Father's house.

Ephesians 2:18 (ESV) For through him we both have access in one Spirit to the Father.

We benefit by the Forerunner's trailblazing. We also get to rest along the way knowing that He is with us to lead us, comfort us, empower us, heal us, forgive us, whatever-is-needed-in-the-moment us, until we reach Home. He is such a great Savior. Let's walk in *The Way* today and experience His perfect peace.

Through All

Ephesians 4:4-6 (ESV) There is one body and one Spirit—just as you were called to the one hope that belongs to your call— one Lord, one faith, one baptism, one God and Father of all, who is over all and through all and in all.

Today's name is more of an attribute, or truth, about God. He is *Through All*. We previously looked at the names Omnipresent (God is everywhere) and Omniscient (God knows all things). We have also looked at God as Omnipotent (all powerful). *Through All* speaks more to how God enables all things to happen.

Look at the language used here. This name is a combination of two Greek words, "dia" (through) and "pas" (all). "Dia" means, "the channel of an act." "Pas" means, "all." There aren't many ways to express "all," but in this case it truly means "all." You can then derive the meaning of the phrase Through All to mean, "the channel by which all things occur."

There is a theology concerning God known as Predestination. I believe in a form of predestination, but not to the extent of most. The theology of Predestination in the purest form says that everything we experience, good or bad, is directly because of God. When it comes to bad things, some use the language of "God allowed it to happen" because they cannot bring themselves to say that God would actually inflict bad things on us. (I know this is way simplified, but there is not room here for a complete treatise on the subject.)

Here is my simple response to this theology. God has predestinated each of us to be conformed to Jesus. That is His desire (destiny) for every person born to earth.

> Romans 8:29 (ESV) For those whom he foreknew he also predestined to be conformed to the image of his Son, in order that he might be the firstborn among many brothers.

Blessings come because of the covenant we have when we become Christians. Bad things occur as a result of sin in the earth; not because of "a sin" committed by the Believer, but as a result of the fall of man in the Garden. Christ came to redeem us from the curse, but also promised that as long as we were in the world we would have tribulation.

My preferred way to view today's name, *Through All*, is not to apply it in a universal way. Instead, I see the context of the verse in Ephesians as clearly speaking to, and about, Christians. Therefore, I see it as God being able, and willing, to help us, the Believers, *Through All*. Consider these verses.

> Philippians 4:10-13 (ESV) I rejoiced in the Lord greatly that now at length you have revived your concern for me. You were indeed concerned for me, but you had no opportunity. Not that I am speaking of being in need, for I have learned in whatever situation I am to be content. I know how to be brought low, and I know how to abound. In any and every circumstance, I have learned the secret of facing plenty and hunger, abundance and need. **I can do all things through him who strengthens me**.

This is where I have landed as far as my faith is concerned. I know some will think I'm not trusting God enough, or that I don't have enough faith. If so, my hope is that I'm still growing and learning how to trust more fully. Until then, I believe *Through All* will be with me every step of the way as I journey toward "being transformed into the image of Jesus."

Trust

> Psalm 71:5 (ESV) For you, O Lord, are my hope, my trust, O LORD, from my youth.

Today's name is similar to one we looked at earlier. The meaning of *Trust* comes from the Hebrew word "mibtah" which means, "a refuge, security, or assurance." This differs slightly from the Hebrew word "mahseh" where we get the English word *Refuge*. It means, "a shelter."

The basic difference in these two is the attitude of the one inhabiting the place. When one goes to a "mahseh" (refuge) it might be to get out of the rain, or intense heat; a place of convenience. However, when one seeks out a "mibtah" (trust), the emphasis is on safety; perhaps getting out of severe weather, or hiding from an eminent threat to their wellbeing. The root word used for "mibtah" is the Hebrew word "batah" which means, "to hide for refuge; be bold (confident, secure, sure), careless, put confidence, hope, trust."

Our Lord is both of these things in the life of the Believer. He is a *Refuge*, a place to rest and recharge. But, He is also our *Trust*. We can run to Him when we need to be sheltered from danger or peril. He is also our *Trust* that we can worship with abandonment without fear of being rejected.

> Hebrews 4:16 (ESV) Let us then with confidence draw near to the throne of grace, that we may receive mercy and find grace to help in time of need.

We can see both of these, *Refuge* and *Trust*, clearly demonstrated by Mary, the sister of Martha. There are three encounters that Mary had with Jesus recorded in the gospels. Each one shows us that Mary knew Jesus was a place of rest and comfort, and One to be worshipped.

> Luke 10:38-42 (ESV) Now as they went on their way, Jesus entered a village. And a woman named Martha welcomed him into her house. And she had a sister called Mary, who sat at the Lord's feet and listened to his teaching. But Martha was distracted with much serving. And she went up to him and said, "Lord, do you not care that my sister has left me to serve alone? Tell her then to help me." But the Lord answered her, "Martha, Martha, you are anxious and troubled about many things, but one thing is necessary. Mary has chosen the good portion, which will not be taken away from her."

Mary knew that *Refuge* was in their house. She rested at His feet and enjoyed His presence.

> Luke 7:37-38 (ESV) And behold, a woman of the city, who was a sinner, when she learned that he was reclining at table in the Pharisee's house, brought an alabaster flask of ointment, and standing behind him at his feet, weeping, she began to wet his feet with her tears and wiped them with the hair of her head and kissed his feet and anointed them with the ointment. (John later identifies the woman as Mary, Martha's sister.)

In this incident we see Mary approaching Jesus as a place of *Trust*. She came boldly and worshipped the One who took away her sin and shame.

John 11:32-35 (ESV) Now when Mary came to where Jesus was and saw him, she fell at his feet, saying to him, "Lord, if you had been here, my brother would not have died." When Jesus saw her weeping, and the Jews who had come with her also weeping, he was deeply moved in his spirit and greatly troubled. And he said, "Where have you laid him?" They said to him, "Lord, come and see." Jesus wept.

Mary's brother, Lazarus, had died. Jesus came to Bethany where Mary, Martha, and Lazarus lived. When Mary encountered Jesus she went to the familiar place – the feet of Jesus. She found *Refuge* and *Trust* in the same place. Jesus was moved to tears when He saw the brokenness of Mary. Jesus knew the love she had for Him, and that compassion led Him to bring Lazarus back from the dead.

The challenge for some Christians is this: when trouble comes they have only looked at Him as a place of *Trust* (safety from trouble), and have never known Jesus as *Refuge* (a place of rest). The more time we spend in *Refuge* (resting and being refreshed) the more comfortable we will be seeking Him as *Trust* (approaching with assurance, knowing He will protect us).

Just remember, He loves us and welcomes us to know Him as both.

Truthful

> 1 Samuel 15:29 (ESV) And also the Glory of Israel will not lie (truthful) or have regret, for he is not a man, that he should have regret."

We recently looked at the name, *The Truth*, which is similar to this one. I believe there is something more we can learn by examining God as being *Truthful*. Even though this name is not used explicitly you can see in the above verse that is a valid expression: "He cannot lie."

We discovered that the root meaning of *The Truth* is "nothing hidden." It means that God holds nothing back from us. He reveals His complete character to those who are in relationship with Him. Additionally, God cannot lie. He is *Truthful*. The Hebrew word is "shaqar" which means, "be untrue." When you add the "not" in front of this it means, "cannot be untrue;" in other words, always true.

Very few things in our world are "always true." It has been said that the only things certain in life are death and taxes. I know this was not given as a real absolute, but my friend and I took this saying to task when we were in high school. Here's our conclusion.

First of all, death is not certain. If you are alive when the Lord returns you will not experience physical death. Regarding taxes, you don't actually have to pay them. You can opt to have your possessions seized and go to jail. So, in fact, death and taxes are not certain at all.

We then set out to determine which two things are certain. In our estimation this is the list: conception and judgment. The only way to be considered a human being is for an egg and sperm to unite to conceive a child. Without being conceived then you never exist. The Bible tells us that every man will be judged.

Of course, all of this is humanly speaking. When it comes to God, all He is capable of is "Yes and amen."

> 2 Corinthians 1:20 (ESV) For all the promises of God find their Yes in him. That is why it is through him that we utter our Amen to God for his glory.

He does not have the capacity to lie. He IS Truthful! He is pure, righteous, and just. He made us in His image, and His purpose for us when we are saved to become like Him again; that includes being truthful. The only way this can occur is for us to allow the Holy Spirit to help us control our thoughts and words.

> 2 Corinthians 10:5-6 (ESV) We destroy arguments and every lofty opinion raised against the knowledge of God, and take every thought captive to obey Christ, being ready to punish every disobedience, when your obedience is complete.

This is only done by the Holy Spirit's work in our life. Allow the *Spirit of Truthful* to overwhelm you, and bring you back into a place of speaking only words that are true.

The words to a song came to mind and I'll share them here. A great way to start becoming more like *Truthful* is to worship Him. These lyrics were written by Gloria Gaither. Consider this, especially the lines in bold.

"I Will Praise Him"
by Gloria Gaither and John W. Thompson

Verse:
Lofty words pious repetitions
Phrases great and small are not what He demands
Open hands are more than just a gesture
I bring all of me and He brings all of Him
Sweet communion I hardly know
Where He stops and I begin
Sweet freedom there's no price too high
It's been worth it all to know I'm clean within

Chorus:
I will praise Him
Knowing that my praise
Will cost me ev'rything
I will praise Him
Praise Him with a joy
That comes from knowing that I have held back nothing
And He is Lord
He is Lord[xv]

Selah! (Think about these things.)

Upright

Psalm 25:8 (ESV) Good and upright is the LORD; therefore he instructs sinners in the way.

I have never flown an airplane but I have heard pilots speak of the phenomena of losing their sense of orientation. They cannot tell which way is up. That is the reason airplanes are equipped with a gyroscope. It uses Earth's gravity to help determine orientation. Without the constant of gravity, orientation is impossible.

God is our spiritual gravity. He is *Upright*. The word "upright" comes from the Hebrew word "yāshār" which means, "straight." The root word is "yāshar" which means, "to be straight or even; figurative to be, or to make, right." He is not found to be right. He defines right. Anything that is not Him is off center or unbalanced; uneven. He alone is the standard by which everything else is measured.

Regardless of what occurs in our world, *Upright* is always the same. He cannot be moved or changed. He is not relative, but instead relevant. He sent His Son, Jesus, into a world that had fallen from its perfect creation and allowed sin to skew the definition of "standard." We cannot know if we are right-side-up without the gyroscope of *Upright*. One of my favorite songs from the group Truth speaks to this topic. Look at the chorus highlighted in bold print.

Living Life Upside Down
by Gary Driskell and Karla Worley

John has a new way of lookin' at life
He's tired of his job, of his kids and his wife
He says the secret to his success
Was in leavin' and finding himself
Now he's someone to somebody else
You say we've risen to a new age of truth
You're callin' it a spiritual godly pursuit
But I say, I say

What if we've fallen to the bottom of a well
Thinkin' we've risen to the top of a mountain
What if we're knockin' at the gates of hell
Thinkin' we're heaven bound
What if we spend our lives thinkin' of ourselves
When we should have been thinkin' of each other
What if we reach up and touch the ground
To find we're living life upside down

We've got a program for savin' the earth
While unborn children are denied their right to birth
One baby's blessed, another cursed
Have we made this world better or worse
Now that the life of a tree comes first
You say we've risen to a new age of light
You're tellin' me what used to be wrong is now right
But I say, I say[xvi]

    Without the gyroscope to indicate the orientation of the plane, a pilot could think he's turning upward toward the sky only to find out he has nosedived into the ground. I believe this is one of the reasons Christians struggle. They lose track of where they are, spiritually speaking, because they have allowed the voice of the Holy Spirit, *Upright*, to become unfamiliar. One of the prayers that I pray on a regular basis is to confess the words of Jesus. "My Sheep hear My voice, and a strangers voice they will not follow."

Let's keep our eye on the spiritual gyroscope, the Holy Spirit and the Word of God, so that we will never lose our sense of orientation to our Lord and His Kingdom.

Walks on Wings of the Wind

> Psalm 104:1-4 (NKJV) Bless the LORD, O my soul! O LORD my God, You are very great: You are clothed with honor and majesty, Who cover Yourself with light as with a garment, Who stretch out the heavens like a curtain. He lays the beams of His upper chambers in the waters, Who makes the clouds His chariot, Who walks on the wings of the wind, Who makes His angels spirits, His ministers a flame of fire.

This psalm is a poetic look at creation. These first four verses describe what things were like before Genesis 1:1. Our human minds cannot comprehend such a spectacular sight. The poet here is using imagery to describe what he is seeing as his mind is allowed to plumb the depths of God's awesomeness.

The phrase where we get today's name for God is not easily quantified, nor is it intended to be. It's much like the drawing made by a three year old. It is something that only they understand in their unskilled artwork. However, we still can try to glean some things from the psalmist because it is included in the cannon of scripture.

Let's look at the original language. The first word, "walk", is from the Hebrew word "halak" and means "generally to move about." The next word in the phrase is "wings" which comes from the Hebrew word "kanao" and means "an edge or extremity; a wing (of a bird or army), or a flap (of a garment or bed-clothing)." The last word in the phrase is "wind" which comes from the Hebrew word "ruah" and means "wind, breath, exhalation, life."

When you put them all together it says that God fills the expanse of all creation, like the air of the wind or the breath in our lungs; He is in all and through all.

> Genesis 1:1-2 (ESV) In the beginning, God created the heavens and the earth. The earth was without form and void, and darkness was over the face of the deep. And the Spirit of God was hovering over the face of the waters.

I believe this is what the psalmist had in mind. The vast expanse of an "earth without form and void" was abstract and as far as the human mind could understand stretched to the edge of existence, or "wings". The only way the Holy Spirit could be "hovering over the waters" is if He were in flight, or "on the wings".

> Genesis 1:3 (ESV) And God said, "Let there be light," and there was light.

The Spirit then "breathed" out into the vast nothingness and creation came to order. The amazing part of all of this is the same God that brought an entire universe into existence wants to do the same thing in you and me. Before our spirit is recreated when we are saved, our life resembled the "vast nothingness" before creation. But God was "hovering" near, waiting on our cry for help. When we reached out from our lost darkness we found Him, the one who *Walks on the Wings of Wind*. He breathed into us His life and we came into order.

Wisdom

> Daniel 2:20 (ESV) Daniel answered and said: "Blessed be the name of God forever and ever, to whom belong wisdom and might.

The definition of wisdom is "the quality of having experience, knowledge, and good judgment; the quality of being wise." This certainly describes our God. Every experience we have is because of Him; He created us, and the world in which we live. All knowledge comes from Him. He is the Righteous Judge. It makes sense, then, that He is *Wisdom*.

Proverbs is often described as the book of wisdom. Here's what it has to say about *Wisdom*.

> Proverbs 4:7 (ESV) The beginning of wisdom is this: Get wisdom, and whatever you get, get insight.

Solomon wrote the book of Proverbs. Read his story of how he became so wise.

> 2 Chronicles 1:7-12 (ESV) In that night God appeared to Solomon, and said to him, "Ask what I shall give you." And Solomon said to God, "You have shown great and steadfast love to David my father, and have made me king in his place. O LORD God, let your word to David my father be now fulfilled, for you have made me king over a people as numerous as the dust of the earth. Give me now wisdom and knowledge to go out and come in before this people, for who can govern this people of yours, which is so great?" God answered Solomon, "Because this was in your heart, and you

have not asked for possessions, wealth, honor, or the life of those who hate you, and have not even asked for long life, but have asked for wisdom and knowledge for yourself that you may govern my people over whom I have made you king, wisdom and knowledge are granted to you. I will also give you riches, possessions, and honor, such as none of the kings had who were before you, and none after you shall have the like."

Out of all the things Solomon could have chosen, he knew that gaining *Wisdom* would get him everything else.

It is the same with Jesus. Some seek Jesus to get peace. Some seek Him out of guilt from doing wrong. Some want the blessings that come from knowing Jesus. While all of these are benefits from knowing Jesus, it is not the reason we should desire Him. We seek Jesus because He is the very source of life. He is the way back to our Father, God.

In the Garden of Eden mankind lost its relational access to God. Sin became a barrier between God and man. Jesus came to restore right relations with God by paying the price to remove sin and its consequences. Now, knowing Jesus is the beginning of wisdom because He then leads us to the true Wisdom, our Creator God.

Then Jesus did one more thing. After He ascended to heaven and was seated at the right hand of Father, He sent us the Holy Spirit, another Comforter, Who would lead us into all truth.

> John 16:13 (ESV) When the Spirit of truth comes, he will guide you into all the truth, for he will not speak on his own authority, but whatever he hears

he will speak, and he will declare to you the things that are to come.

In light of this, Proverbs 4:7 could be rewritten like this: The beginning of Wisdom is this: Get Jesus, and the Holy Spirit will give you insight. When we identify ourselves with Jesus, His death, burial, resurrection, ascension, seating, and then receive the Holy Spirit, we are fully restored to right relationship with *Wisdom*. In this sense, *Wisdom* is the principle thing.

Worthy

Revelation 4:9-11 (ESV) And whenever the living creatures give glory and honor and thanks to him who is seated on the throne, who lives forever and ever, the twenty-four elders fall down before him who is seated on the throne and worship him who lives forever and ever. They cast their crowns before the throne, saying, "Worthy are you, our Lord and God, to receive glory and honor and power, for you created all things, and by your will they existed and were created."

I have heard many people say things like, "When I get to Heaven, the first thing I'm going to do is find my family." Or, "When I get to Heaven, the first thing I'm going to do is ask Paul what he meant about …" The truth is, when we get to Heaven nothing else will matter except God.

John painted a picture for us of what is going on in Heaven. Everyone in Heaven is worshiping our Creator Who sits on the throne, and His Son with Him, our Savior.

The word "worship, or worth-ship" comes from the word "worthy". The Greek word for "worthy" is "axios" and means "deserving, comparable or suitable." There truly is only one deserving: Jehovah God. There is no one comparable to Jesus. No one is more suitable than the Holy Spirit. The Godhead, Three-In-One, is the only One deserving of our admiration and praise. He is *Worthy*.

Luke 3:15-16 (ESV) As the people were in expectation, and all were questioning in their hearts concerning John, whether he might be the Christ,

John answered them all, saying, "I baptize you with water, but he who is mightier than I is coming, the strap of whose sandals I am not worthy to untie. He will baptize you with the Holy Spirit and fire.

John the Baptizer knew where he stood in the grand scheme of things. Even though his birth was miraculous, and even though he was chosen to be the forerunner of the Messiah, he knew there was no comparison to Jesus. My friend, Ed Chinn, recently posted on his FaceBook page the following observation.

> "The meaning of awe is to realize that life takes place under wide horizons, horizons that range beyond the span of an individual life or even the life of a nation, a generation, or an era."
> - Abraham Joshua Heschel

I really love this view from Rabbi Heschel. And this is why I've grown to dislike the word "awesome." The way it is used in American culture is the savage murder of language.[xvii]

John knew there was only one that deserved awe. He knew his place in the worthy ratings. This is not false humility. John knew his place. He declared it boldly to those who asked. "I am the voice of one crying in the wilderness. Prepare the way of the Lord. Make His paths straight."

When we are rightly related to *Worthy* we can have the same boldness we see in John. This is my definition of true humility; knowing who we are in Christ, and knowing that He alone is *Worthy*.

Let us go about our day declaring the One *Worthy* of all praise. He is awesome!

Yahweh

This last name is the most common name given to God that never appears in scripture. There is a simple explanation. The Hebrew word "yhwh" is the transliteration of the name Israel used to refer to God. It appears in scripture over 6500 times. They had so much respect and awe for God that they would never speak the name, and when written, only the consonants were used. When this word was translated into English the translators chose to use LORD (all caps) to represent "yhwh". There are six exceptions to this in the KJV as listed below.

Genesis 6:5	GOD
Exodus 6:3	JEHOVAH
2 Samuel 12:22	GOD
Psalm 83:18	JEHOVAH
Isaiah 12:2	JEHOVAH
Isaiah 26:4	JEHOVAH

All of these appear in all caps like LORD. The "yhwh" was pronounced "Yahweh" in English, but the Hebrew pronunciation is "yeh-ho-vaw'", hence the name "JEHOVAH."

Regardless of the representation used, the Hebrew word "yhwh" means, "the self-Existent or Eternal." Our God is supreme. He is the only true God.

Self-existent means He was not created; His is eternal, from everlasting to everlasting. He has need of nothing; all-sufficient. No one or nothing is greater than Him; omnipotent, omniscient. This is why Israel had a difficult time even writing down or speaking His name.

The third of the Ten Commandments says:

> Exodus 20:7 (ESV) "You shall not take the name of the LORD your God in vain, for the LORD will not hold him guiltless who takes his name in vain."

This is where the belief that certain phrases were "curse words," because using them would bring the Lord's judgment. I do not believe that is what is meant by "vain" in this instance. The Hebrew word "shav," translated "vain," means "in the sense of desolating; evil (as destructive), literal (ruin) or moral (especially guile)."

I had to look up the meaning of "desolating", and what I found is very eye-opening. It means, "make (a place) bleakly and depressingly empty or bare; make (someone) feel utterly wretched and unhappy."

What God said to Moses on Mt. Sinai is this: "Do not represent Me to others in a way that makes Me seem bleak, empty, or bare." When we speak of God as being anything other than the self-existent One that He is, we are taking His name in vain.

Paul said it like this:

> 1 Timothy 1:6-7 (ESV) Certain persons, by swerving from these, have wandered away into vain discussion, desiring to be teachers of the law, without understanding either what they are saying or the things about which they make confident assertions.

The KJV uses the phrase "vain janglings". The Greek word for this is "mataiologia" which means, "random talk, i.e. babble." It comes from a root that means, "idle talker." Much of our religious jargon that has developed over the centuries falls into this category. Some cannot even speak of God without drawing on this vast array of god-speak that makes us sound spiritual. Paul is imploring Timothy to keep it real. Speak the truth about our God and not make Him out to be bleak, empty, or bare, but instead tell the Good News that there is life and hope, peace and joy, to be found in Him!

My wife is a counselor. She talks with people from many different religious traditions. She never attempts to correct theology where they may differ. However, she will never allow them to speak wrongly of God. Most of our problems stem from a wrong image of our Creator. When that is wrong, it is difficult to get anything right.

I hope this study has been helpful in getting us to see the truth about God, and all the names by which He is known. I hope it helps you give voice to what you feel toward Him in your times of worship and prayer. I hope you continue to dig into the subject because as the subtitle of this book states, "It's a non-exhaustive look at an inexhaustible subject."

Thanks for reading!

About the Author

Dudley lives in Florence, Alabama, with his wife, Martha. Their three children are grown.

Dudley developed a love for language during his senior year in high school from a very unlikely source; an assistant football coach teaching English for the first time. Since then words, and language in general, has been a hobby.

He is a graduate of the University of North Alabama.

After pursuing a successful career in computer science, Dudley entered full-time ministry in 1998. Since then he has taught lessons on worship, traveled to Mexico, Kenya, Ireland, and the UK teaching on worship, and using worship as a means of communing with our Creator God.

Other books by Kurios Publishing:

    Event vs. Process

End Notes

[i] Copyright: <a href='http://www.123rf.com/profile_allexxandar/#44222287'>allexxandar / 123RF Stock Photo</a>
Copyright: <a href='http://www.123rf.com/profile_vivilweb'>vivilweb / 123RF Stock Photo</a>
[ii] Above All © 1999 Integrity's Hosanna! Music (Admin. by Capitol CMG Publishing (IMI))
LenSongs Publishing (Admin. by LenSongs Publishing, Inc.)
[iii] Ibid.
[iv] The Church Triumphant. © 1973 William J. Gaither, Inc. (Admin. by Gaither Copyright Management)
[v] What Sins Are You Talkin' About. © 1978 Ben Speer Music (Controlled by Ben Speer Music/SESAC)
[vi] http://www.amazon.com/God-Mundane-Reflections-Ordinary-People/dp/1937063968/
[vii] In Christ Alone © 2001 Thankyou Music (Admin. by Capitol CMG Publishing)
[viii] More (Than You'll Ever Know) © 1973 Universal Music - Brentwood Benson Tunes (Admin. by Brentwood-Benson Music Publishing, Inc.)
[ix] http://www.creationtips.com/bitter_sweet_water.html
[x] Jesus, Lover of My Soul. Written by Charles Wesley circa 1740. Public Domain.
[xi] from http://www.bible-researcher.com/chesed.html
[xii] (http://www.collective-evolution.com/2015/05/03/quantum-entanglement-verified-why-space-is-just-the-construct-that-gives-the-illusion-of-separate-objects/)
[xiii] "The Mental Universe" ; Nature 436:29,2005) (source) (http://henry.pha.jhu.edu/The.mental.Universe.pdf)

[xiv] From Dale Moore. 2015 12 16. via FaceBook chat session.
[xv] © 1978, 1979 New Spring (Admin. by Brentwood-Benson Music Publishing, Inc.)
William J. Gaither, Inc. (Admin. by Gaither Copyright Management)

[xvi] © 1991 Word Music, LLC (a div. of Word Music Group, Inc.)
[xvii] from Ed Chinn FaceBook post on 2016-02-08.

Made in the USA
Columbia, SC
24 June 2019